A LOW LIFE IN HIGH HEELS

I ♡ Holly

The **H**olly **W**oodlawn Story

A LOW LIFE

Holly Woodlawn with Jeffrey Copeland

St. Martin's Press   New York

IN
HIGH
HEELS

A LOW LIFE IN HIGH HEELS: The Holly Woodlawn Story.
Copyright © 1991 by Holly Woodlawn and Jeff
Copeland. All rights reserved. Printed in the United
States of America. No part of this book may be used
or reproduced in any manner whatsoever without
written permission except in the case of brief
quotations embodied in critical articles or reviews. For
information, address St. Martin's Press, 175 Fifth
Avenue, New York, N.Y. 10010.

Design by Maura Fadden Rosenthal

Library of Congress Cataloging-in-Publication

Woodlawn, Holly.
    A low life in high heels : the Holly Woodlawn
story / Holly Woodlawn with Jeff Copeland.
        p.   cm.
    ISBN 0-312-06429-2
    1. Woodlawn, Holly.   2. Motion picture actors
and actresses—United States—Biography.
3. Transvestites—United States—Biography.
I. Copeland, Jeff.   II. Title.
PN2287.W64A3   1991
791.43'028'092—dc20
[B]   91-21817
                                                  CIP

First Edition: November 1991
10 9 8 7 6 5 4 3 2 1

*T*his book is dedicated to my parents, who have loved me, cried for me, and supported me when I was up, down, and sideways! It is also dedicated to those who have known the struggle of being different, endured the fear of rejection, and mustered the courage to survive.

Dear Dorothy,

There's no place like home!

CONTENTS

INTRODUCTION

When I cast Holly in the film *Trash*, I had never met him. Someone had brought to my attention an article in some throwaway underground newspaper that discussed in great detail Holly's success as a major star of Andy Warhol productions. Since Holly had never been in any of the films and I had never even met him, this brazen lie must have appealed to my comic sense. I simply had a hunch that here was some kind of "character" or personality. Although Andy pointed out that Holly was someone who had tried to rob him by charging an expensive camera to his account, the combination of lying and larceny only increased my curiosity. When I asked Holly on the phone to show up at the location of the film I was starting that weekend, I purposely decided to forego any meeting or interview beforehand, something unusual even for me. While I have always cast people very quickly depending on personality, I had never cast anyone before or since without having met them first. But without mentioning it to Holly, his interview in the paper had given me the idea for a major part of the film I wanted to make. It was to be a picaresque account of the life of a drug addict in a general sense, but specifically I thought: What if this poor negative character was involved with someone quite the opposite, someone who was hellbent on survival instead of destruction, someone who lied and stole and cheated to get something out of life, as opposed to someone drifting inexorably down the gutter to death?

It is still astonishing to me today that just such a person showed up at my house on the Lower East Side that Saturday afternoon. How could I have guessed that Holly would turn out to be this volcano-like mountain of energy and positivism, a powerful but always good-natured life force that just shrugged off every kind of horror and adversity with an expression or a gesture that clearly showed he was indomitable, that today's troubles would all soon be over, and that tomorrow's disaster would be met with a similar reaction?

That afternoon, I photographed for only about one hour, but I knew within minutes of filming that my hunch was right and my instinct had paid off. I knew that I had my two basic characters and I would then have a movie. On that first day I saw only a glimmer of what Holly was capable of later on in filming but Holly struck me then as now as a basically very shy and unassuming person, unfailingly polite and instantaneously likeable. That so much determination and energy lurked beneath this facade was still, that first afternoon, only another hunch.

When the film was released, it was a great success with both audiences and critics. It played all over the U.S. and Europe. Everywhere the reviewers praised Holly's bravura performance, many comparing it to the work of Anna Magnani, which is high praise indeed. Holly generously gave me that performance; I didn't trick it out of him. Although he had never acted before on film, what I think I did was somehow suggest that I knew he could do it. I hope I contributed a sense of confidence to him that produced the results that appear on the screen.

Since we really only filmed Holly's scenes on a few afternoons, I can't say I ever really got to know very much about Holly's actual life. Following the success of *Trash*, I very much wanted to star Holly in another film and thought of *Women in Revolt* as a vehicle. Once again he appeared at the location we were to film for the opening scene, this time a fancy Upper East Side apartment instead of a Lower East Side basement. I told Holly on the set that the character was to be a well-to-do kept woman who decides to reject the man who provides for her as a result of her commitment to the women's liberation movement. I recall Holly turning up a little late, about four or five o'clock, but that was no problem. Perhaps he'd had a few drinks. The scene was very good, very funny, but from the things Holly was saying during the scene, I had to ask him when it was finished if he knew very much about the women's liberation movement. Always positive, plunging in where angels fear to tread, Holly answered, "Oh, yeah, sure. They think that women should have the right to vote, isn't that it?" That was about the sum total of Holly's knowledge of that subject.

Unfortunately, when additional scenes were staged that included Candy Darling and Jackie Curtis, Holly strangely enough failed to respond to those occasions. Instead, he remained subdued, allowing Candy and Jackie to dominate the scenes. Having read Holly's book, I now know why.

Actually, most of the book is to me a great revelation of an extraordinary life—a real-life version of Patrick Dennis's Belle Poitrine and Gore Vidal's Myra Breckinridge. But the book's tone of voice did not surprise me at all. Throughout the retelling of this life, the constant humor, the resilient good nature, and the generous spirit of this uniquely talented individual, this was the same Holly Woodlawn I had known, someone not very much different than the person he presented to the camera. It was my great good luck to have met Holly and to have had him in two films. Now I feel I know another side of him, a more serious and fuller side of a difficult life with roller-coaster ups and downs that would daunt the strongest personality. But not Holly. He makes this unusual life read as entertainingly and engagingly as if it were one more of his impersonations—something that was there only to be made fun of, a life that only existed to be laughed at. In both the good and the bad, there was always something to be enjoyed. To have survived such a life with such fundamental good nature intact can only be regarded as another of Holly's extraordinary performances.

Paul Morrissey

"Holly came from Miami, F-L-A,
hitchhiked her way across the U.S.A.
Plucked her eyebrows on the way,
shaved her legs and then he was a she—
she says, 'Hey, babe, take a walk on the
wild side.' "

—Lou Reed
Walk on the Wild Side

CHAPTER 1

Trash Star Found
in Trash Can

*H*ollywood, California.

Well, here I am, lounging by my sumptuous *piscine* listening to the oldies on my newfangled boom box while nibbling a macaroon and sipping a Diet Coke ... its cool taste heightened with a dollop of rum, of course. And as I gaze dreamily at the horizon, I see the Hollywood sign peeking at me through the dense Los Angeles smog. It's hard to believe I finally made it to the glamour capital of the world. It's even harder to believe that it's choking on this brown muck that permeates the air. And to think people have the nerve to cast me the evil eye whenever I light up a cigarette! My pack-a-day habit couldn't possibly compare to the amount of pollution produced from one of those foreign tin cans congesting the freeways. So, to save the planet's air quality, I gave up driving and kept on smoking. One does have to compromise for the sake of others.

Smoking was a very fashionable thing to do at one point in our lives, but like Hollywood, its glamour is long gone. But then, glamour is cheap in this town. Like everything else in Hollywood, it's a facade, an image founded on hype. It's very Warholesque, if you don't mind my saying so. Andy was big on facades, but then so was I. Like my cohorts Candy Darling and Jackie Curtis, I went all out to put up a front and hide my true self from the world.

Candy, Jackie and I were the last pack of Superstars churned out by the Warhol Factory in the early 1970s. In our minds, being a Superstar was like being a piece of art, and I wanted that status. I needed that stamp of approval. Without it, I was nothing. Not that this so-called status ever paid the bills. I've been photographed by Scavullo and Avedon, and I've partied with the rich and famous. I was fawned over by Hollywood royalty and I was invited to meet the Queen Mother. Still, I was living on welfare and feeding off friends. Friends who saturated my ego with praise and told me I was fabulous. I couldn't help but believe this Superstar bullshit was for real, and that I was indeed above the other welfare low-lifes on Avenue D. After all, I was a movie star, and the inspiration for Lou Reed's hit "Walk on the Wild Side," a song about lives so reckless and so bizarre that I find them hard to believe myself.

"Walk on the Wild Side" was Lou Reed's biggest hit, and it was based on the truth. Controversial truth, that is, spilling the beans on us all. I always wondered why I couldn't have been one of those colored girls do-do-doing in the background. I was a scarlet woman—how colored can one get? Like Nathaniel Hawthorne's Hester Prynne, I was indeed a woman of scandal, having scorched the New York underground with my blazing libido, driven by an insatiable quest for a roll in the hay, a tumble in the weeds, or, for lack of a better analogy, a good time. But unlike the traditional run-of-the-mill heroine seen in our classic novellas, I was also a man.

Shocking, but true! It's a wonder I wasn't tarred and feathered for my antics, but I wasn't—hail Dorothy! Thank God! And hallelujah!

It's a wonder I even survived this walk on the wild side, although to say I walked makes it sound so pleasant. Honey, I trudged! I crawled! I groveled! And then there were the times when I waltzed.

This roller coaster ride of a life wasn't all that sordid, however. There were times when it was quite rich. But for the most part, once I had gotten past the candy-coated glamour, I was usually left with sticky fingers. I was blinded by the fame and couldn't see past my latest clipping in *Interview* or *Vogue*.

It's funny, really. I never thought I could be famous when I was a kid. I mean, Liz Taylor was famous. Lana Turner was famous. Howdy Doody was famous! But me? I was Harold Ajzenberg, a shy, skinny kid with buck teeth who happened to have a passion for tight pants, mohair sweaters, and mascara. Which was unheard of in the Sixties . . . for a boy! Little did I know that years later, while flitting around in the infamous backroom of Max's Kansas City (home of the bad, beautiful, and voracious New York underground), I would be discovered. By that time, though, I had dumped the Harold Ajzenberg persona and had upped myself to the ranks of a high-spirited goddess with a bottle in one hand and a pill in the other. Like Athena, I burst upon the scene in full regalia as Holly Woodlawn.

The name "Holly" was inspired by the Holly Golightly character in *Breakfast at Tiffany's*, because we shared the same ear-piercing whistle for hailing cabs; "Woodlawn" was derived from another source. You see, up until the late Sixties, a majority of Warhol's female Superstars were young heiresses to family fortunes. Baby Jane Holzer, Ultra Violet, Edie Sedgewick, and Susan Bottomly were among the spoiled little principessas just itching to pounce upon their waiting thrones. And there I was, itching for food stamps and pouncing on men! Hell, the only fortune I could claim was in a cookie, and even that was usually stolen. So, to groom myself for stardom, I knew I needed an image. Something grand, statuesque, and fabulous! I wanted to be the next Venus de Warhol, and with that thought in mind, it was decided that I, a former housewife, go-go dancer, and Miss Donut of Amsterdam, New York, was to become the heiress to the Woodlawn Cemetery. Hell, it sounded good; I figured anyone with all that granite and marble had to be worth something. And so, with this merger of a Truman Capote character and a New York City graveyard, Holly Woodlawn was born.

The difference between Holly and Harold was immense. It was like comparing a brown moth to a psychedelic butterfly. Harold was lifeless and insecure. Holly, on the other hand, was loud and outrageous, a psychedelic darling of the underground. A voluptuous vixen! A pop tart! A saucy sexpot unleashed to wreak havoc among the bewildered.

"Free pussy!" I would scream, flailing my arms into the air while grinding my way through the steamy back-room crowd, hoping to reap (or at least grope!) some booty. And you can bet that I was a sight to behold in my white vinyl go-go boots, backless minidress, untamed hair, and a face boasting more paint than the goddamned Mona Lisa!

"Hello, dahling, you devine creature you!" I wailed Tallulah-like as I sailed through the sea of crazed booze hounds, speed freaks, wanna-be's and never-will-be's. Sliding up to the bar, I was about to slug down a double when I heard those magic words:

"Where's the twenty bucks ya owe me?"

It was my faithful friend, Jackie Curtis, still wearing the same filthy rag of a dress she had worn for the past five years! That despicable dimestore floozy was no doubt desperate to cash in on my welfare check which, ESP-like, she somehow divined had arrived early in the muggy New York afternoon.

Of the three Warhol "girlettes," Miss Curtis was by far the least convincing and the most conniving. That tramp was to womanhood what snags are to nylons. Her entire flimsy persona relied on safety pins to hold it together, and still she was hobbling around on a broken shoe. By this time, however, Miss Curtis had just appeared with Candy Darling in Andy Warhol's cinematic extravaganza *Flesh*. It didn't matter how shitty she looked—she was a star. And a Warhol Superstar at that.

"You look fabulous!" I beamed, grabbing her by the head and straightening that hideous yak hairdo she called her Barbra wig. But before she could respond, Curtis was pushed aside as the crazed sea of debauched revelers parted and Andy exclaimed from his *table de celebrité*:

"That face!"

"That hair!" I screamed. "Where'd you get it, from a goat in Tibet?"

The crowd gasped. Obviously enthralled by my star-like magnetism, Warhol rushed to my side, fell to his knees and pleaded for me to star in his next film.

"Ooooooh," I vamped. "Plead a little lower!"

Well, so much for glorified memories. The rotten truth be known, Andy Warhol never begged me to be in one of his movies. He didn't even ask me. He didn't know who I was. The real creative force behind Andy's films, Paul Morrissey, had never seen me at Max's and he didn't know my name or have any idea where I came from; he just thought I might be interesting. What really got me noticed by these movie moguls of the underground were two highly illegal and unethical acts:

Act One: While passing myself off as the Warhol Superstar Viva, I walked into a camera store with a so-called friend and attempted to charge a two-thousand-dollar camera to Andy's account. When the store clerk called the Factory to approve the sale, my friend fled for his life and left me standing at the counter. Luckily, I had the sense to run after him and so escaped with my life. But no camera.

Act Two: During the run of Jackie Curtis's off-Broadway play *Heaven Grand in Amber Orbit*, where I was featured as a chorus girl, I gained media attention upon professing to a newspaper reporter that I was an Andy Warhol Superstar. And if that wasn't enough, I pulled out all the punches and agreed to be interviewed for a feature story! You can imagine the Factory's surprise when they got hold of the paper and saw this story on a Superstar they had never met.

According to Morrissey, he was intrigued by my boldness. Andy had a pretty good idea I was the one who tried to pull off the camera heist, but after reading the newspaper article, Paul—having recalled seeing me at Max's—had a hunch I might be good on film.

By this time, Morrissey wasn't hanging with the Max's crowd. He had drifted away, and instead of contacting me directly, he had a friend give me his number at home. When I called the next day, Paul asked if I'd be interested in being in his next film, some Warhol epic being filmed on the Lower East Side.

Stardom! But I had never been in a movie before. I hadn't even taken an acting lesson. Where was all the pain one must endure? An elegantly manicured hand fluttered about my fevered brow. It was too soon! I couldn't memorize lines—only phone numbers. Thank God Paul chose that timely moment to explain that there would be no lines to memorize.

"No lines!" I retorted. "What the hell kinda movie is this?"

"I'll give you the lines," he said.

"I don't do drugs!" I immediately announced, prompting Paul to explain that before filming he would give me the *outline* of the scene, and once the cameras rolled, it would be up to me to make up the dialogue as we went along. This seemed like a good deal. I was paid twenty-five bucks to let him film whatever jibberish happened to fly out of my mouth. And as the story goes, Holly Woodlawn was given the part of a down-and-out trash collector/connoisseur whose big motivation is to get laid by her impotent junkie boyfriend and obtain welfare. What perfect typecasting! The film, appropriately titled *Trash*, became a cult hit and my life hasn't been the same since.

Max's Kansas City was to the New York underground what Schwab's Drugstore was to Hollywood. All you had to do was hang out, look fabulous, and with the bat of a false eyelash, you were a star. I felt just like Lana Turner! Now, as I said earlier, I had never taken an acting lesson. Who had the time for vocal coaches, dance lessons, or rehearsals? Who had the money? We didn't go to school to be fabulous; we *were* fabulous! Hell, as far as method acting was concerned, a stiff vodka martini seemed the best method of all. No discipline. No struggle. No nothing. And yet there I was, wallowing in the bliss of having landed my first film role, a role that guaranteed an unforgettable ride on the Warhol gravy train. And I was on board for the run!

Overnight, I became a curious phenomenon. A celebrity. A media star. But not your typical Hollywood star, mind you. I was a Warhol

Superstar; a vixen of the underground. Finally, little Harold Ajzenberg was somebody.

Visions of the film's premiere filled my mind even before shooting commenced. It would be spectacular, to say the least. Just think, my name, "Holly Woodlawn," stretched across the marquee in all those lights. Limousines would be lined up for blocks while Andy, Paul, and a slew of Factory players, enveloped by paparazzi, played to every available camera angle gorging their insatiable egos. Yes, this would be a true gala event. One of the most glamorous moments of my life. And the biggest question on everyone's lips was——?

"Where is Holly?" asked Sylvia Miles.

"Anybody seen Holly?" screeched Andrea Whips Feldman.

"Where the hell's Holly?" belched Brenda DeBanzi.

Brenda DeBanzi? Who the fuck is Brenda DeBanzi? Anyway, where was I? Oh yes, WHERE WAS I? On this, possibly my grandest moment, I, Holly Woodlawn, star of stage, screen, and Max's Kansas City, was not in the flashes of paparazzi as I deserved, but stuck in the goddamned clink with a sixty-seven-year-old black man who kept screaming for poontang! I hadn't the foggiest idea what he was whining about and politely asked that he remove his greasy paw from my thigh.

"C'mon, give me some of dat good stuff," he grumbled, leaning forward to grope my chest, only to double over into a fit of grisly coughs.

"Get away from me, you beast!" I hollered in my heavily Bronxed accept. "Je suis no do dat shit!"

His name was Willie, a two-time murderer whose only desire was *moi*. His face was like that of a pug and his body wasn't much better. He was always chewing something, like a cow savoring a wad of cud. This, however, was fine, just so long as the bastard wasn't savoring me! What did I look like, a cheap tramp?! I was a well-bred, Southern-raised, Puerto Rican Jew! I had my pride! I had my dignity!

"I have my period!" I shrieked, hoping this would excuse my participation in his lustful whims. But Willie didn't care. He knew what he wanted and he was going for it, cornering me in the cell. His large black hands reached for my body. His eyes were bulging. His chest was wheezing. I screamed for help, but my pleas only seemed to excite him. He moved in on me, grinning and drooling, licking his chops. I screamed again, but no one came. This was it. My final moment. God, of all things, why this oversized prune? He unzipped his pants and pulled it out. It finally dawned on me how he murdered his victims.

"Oh, no! Not the hose! Please . . . not the hose!" I cried, throwing myself against the cell bars in despair.

What was he going to do, bludgeon me to death with that thing? Or simply plow me into oblivion? His mammoth shadow fell over me. My eyes grew wide with fear. Suddenly, he grabbed me by the throat, forcing my mouth to open. Thoughts raced through my pounding little head. What could I do? What would I do? Slap it? Beat it? Wrestle it? NO! I did what any red-blooded American Beauty rose would do: I zipped up his zipper!

Ol' Willie let out a shriek heard from here to Tobago! And while he was struggling to unsnag himself, I began to scream hysterically for help.

Then, out of nowhere, it hit me: a bucketful of ice water thrown by a guard accusing me (Holly Woodlawn, star of stage! Screen! And Max's Kansas City!) of sexual harrassment!

"How dare you! Don't you know who I am? I'm Holly Woodlawn! I'm a movie star!"

"Hollywood who?" he growled, pressing his fat jowls into the bars for a closer look.

"Holly Woodlawn!" I stomped with vengeance.

"Shud up or I'm haulin' yer ass off to isolation!" he yelled.

This was uncalled for! There I was about to be impaled by King Dong and the guard threatens to drag me (Holly Woodlawn, star of stage! Screen! And Max's Kansas City!) off to isolation.

"I'm a Superstar!" I screamed back in defense, dripping with water as I heard him walk down the hall. "I'm a Superstar! A Superstar . . ." I blithered to myself as I sank to the cold, hard floor in tears. I hadn't even signed my first autograph and already I was a fallen star, spending my big premiere in jail looking no more glamorous than a drowned rat.

Life in the slammer wasn't so bad once I got used to the decor. It wasn't the Waldorf, but then it wasn't the gutter either. The cells were tastelessly decorated with gray bunk beds, an auto-flush toilet, olive drab blankets, and a basin with a small mirror that had the reflective quality of aluminum foil. Our regimented lives became as gray as the walls between which we were confined. Lights on at five A.M., followed by the wails of dawn: "Oh, Miss Thing! It's morning, girl," yawned the queens, followed by the hard sound of steel scraping against steel as the opening of cells echoed throughout the royal tombs.

The queens were, for those of you who do not know, the effeminate boys in the block of cells who were always carrying on about fashion, the latest gossip, and their "husbands" on the outside. Naturally, I led the parade and twirled the baton!

With our T-shirts tied into halters and our hair tied in rags, we'd flip through magazines and rip out the most colorful pages. Then we'd spit on the page and rub its color onto our cheeks, eyes, and lips. It wasn't easy being beautiful behind bars, but I was determined. I was not about to let the slammer inhibit my glamour!

The most colorful queens who come to mind were Morgana, Francesco, Chico, and Shasta.

Morgana (his real name: Morgan) was a tall, lanky black nineteen-year-old with a high voice and an expressive face who idolized the Supremes and fancied himself as the next Diana Ross, always screeching "Ain't No Mountain High Enough" with Chico and Shasta acting as Flo and Mary on backup. Morgana was in for robbing the panty department at Sears.

Chico was a Puerto Rican and Shasta was black, and they were in for dealing dope on the Lower East Side. They were locked in neighboring cells and were constantly bickering over who could sing higher, each trying to outdo the other while singing backup for Morgana.

"Ain't no mountain high enough—ooh, ooh! Ain't no mountain low enough! Oh, no! Ain't no river wide enough, to keep me from you—ooh!"

And then they started in, wailing at the top of their lungs, "Aaahhhh, ah—oh, oh! Whew, hew! Ahhhhhhh, ah, ah, ah!"

These jailbirds thought they were songbirds, and there was no shutting them up—unless, of course, one was outwailing the other, which ultimately started a fight.

"Hey, motherfucker, don't ju go singing over me or I cut ju bad, bitch!" screamed Chico, shaking the bars of his cell in a fit of rage.

"Don't fuckin' fuck with me, motherfucker, or I'll cut out yo' gizzard and shove it up yo' ass!"

"I break ju fuckin' arm, faggot!"

"Listen, here, scaintch. Don't be callin' me faggot, you cocksucker!"

Well, this ranting and raving usually went on for about ten minutes, with each queen hurling insults back and forth until one of them— usually Shasta—spit out the most earth-shattering slur ever uttered in the history of low-life slander.

"Yo' momma eats dog shit and takes it up the ass!"

Oh, dear. The whole cell block stood still and not a peep could be heard. We were all overwhelmed with shock, I'm sure. Shasta was a bit taken aback himself, as Chico exploded into a tirade of heated Spanish babble until the guard waddled in with a bucket of ice water and cooled him down:

"Shud up or I'm haulin' you off to isolation!"

After our morning showers, our tasteful little breakfasts were served on a tacky metal tray that was slid under the cell gate. It was quite Continental, dishing the cell block dirt with the "girls" over dry toast, boxed cereal, and black coffee that tasted like it was brewed in the paddy wagon's radiator.

The big question around the joint was, "So, what're you in for?" Surrounded by the same boring prostitutes, drug dealers, and panty snatchers, I admit I was a classic case. I had committed a crime with style: grand larceny while impersonating a French diplomat's wife. *Quel dommage!* Hard to believe I went to such an extreme, but I needed the money. I needed the drugs.

In the late Sixties, the "in" thing to do was drugs, and I was very familiar with the trend. Seconals, Tuinals, urinals, and Methedrine were among my favorites, and I indulged often. Drugs made me feel good about myself. After a couple of Seconals, I became relaxed, and with a shot of speed I became fabulous. Drugs were an everyday occurrence for many of us, and became as common as breakfast.

It seemed like the more drugs one did, the more popular he or she became. For me, a misguided runaway caught between a pair of high-heeled pumps and hi-top sneakers, drugs meant acceptance, security, and a good time.

Max's Kansas City was a hub of drug-induced revelry, and one night around three in the morning after another debauched night in the backroom, my friends Chumley, Silver George (a Factory assistant), and I (along with some other nameless low-lifes) grabbed a taxi and sped off to Chumley's lavish Park Avenue address, an apartment she had sublet from Mme. Chardonet, a wealthy French diplomat's wife. It was party time again as we tore through the place like drug-crazed savages, shooting speed, popping downs, and guzzling booze while blasting *Color Me Barbra*, my favorite Streisand album.

It was during one of Babs's high notes when George (the little snake!) found Mme. Chardonet's bank book, passport, and credentials. George struck a high note himself, and it rang of cash. He was a clever little weasel, his beady eyes glistening and his smile slimy with greed as he slithered my way. The gutless little runt—he had the plots but he didn't have the *chutzpah* to stage them. And who would he turn to in this time of deceit? Yes, the persuasive little fox offered me the role of a lifetime: the challenging part of a French diplomat's wife who goes mad and decides to withdraw her entire life savings!

The plot sounded good. Simple. A challenge I couldn't resist. Rehearsals began with Chardonet's signature, which I mastered by copying it from a canceled check onto carbon paper, repeating it until I could scrawl it with ease. Then, to further embellish my characterization, George carefully pasted a reduced photo of myself over Mme. Chardonet's in her passport. The fact that the photo was taken while I was being swallowed alive by ostrich feathers with my mouth open and my arms in the air didn't seem to matter. All we could see was green. Now all I had to do was sashay into the U.N. dressed in a tasteful black Chanel dress with a pink scarf tied in my hair and a French accent to boot.

"*Bonjour, Monsieurs,*" I crooned as I breezed through security, making my way to the bank teller's window.

Well, to my disappointment, Chardonet only had six thousand dollars in her account, the cheap broad! And here I had thought we would've at least gotten enough to last a week. I became frugal, however, and only withdrew two thousand. So far, so good. The teller handed over the dough and I graciously accepted, glamorously sailing past security and into the cab where George patiently awaited. Yes, we were on our way to indulge in yet another irresistible smorgasbord of drugs, booze, and sex at Max's.

Unfortunately, I hadn't even nabbed the chance to dry-clean that damn Chanel dress when the gravy train derailed. We were broke again, with only a few empty syringes and a hangover to show for the money. Being an underground film star ain't cheap, honey. The price was often costly, exceeding the expectations of many. Some paid with cash. Others paid with their lives. But whatever the cost, it was a highly sought existence of oblivion and delirium, touched only by reality when your head was in the toilet. For me, however, it was just another dance on Warhol's tightrope of fame. All that mattered was being fabulous and looking glamorous.

My hands trembled as I tied the pink scarf in my hair, staring at myself in the mirror. I smoothed the black linen fabric over my waist, taking a deep breath. I needed a drink: a vodka martini, straight up with four olives, thank you. The first time everything went great. But now I was going back and I hadn't told Chumley. This gig was between George and me. We were going for the entire account. The rest of the haul. This time, we were going to suck it dry. It was straight down the line for the both of us—and that rat bastard wasn't even around!

"Be calm," I told myself, placing the passport in the wicker cat basket I tried to pass off as a purse. "You'll be fine."

The doorbell rang. It was my dear friend Estelle (his real name was Douglas, but we called him Estelle because he liked it). He had arrived to accompany me to the jackpot and before I knew it, we were in a cab heading for a bar. All I could think was, "Vodka!" and upon downing my sixth martini, the French accent came naturally.

"*Bonjour, Monsieurs*," I announced, staggering through security. "*Viva la France!*"

My arms flew into the air as I blew kisses to them all. I approached the teller and handed her the withdraw slip.

"Clean it out, sister!" I burped, slapping my hand on the counter.

I knew the jig was up when I immediately found two massive thugs on both sides of my svelte hips. They were escorts all right, but not to the cotillion, and my mind panicked as they walked me down the long, barren corridor, me jibbering and jabbering along the way, trying to convince them it was a mistake.

"But monsieurs, I beg your pardonz, you have got ze wrong person. I am not a criminal. I am a famous international woman."

"Yeah, right, lady," snickered one of the heavies.

"*Fermez la bouche!*" I snapped back, shaking my finger. "Katherine De Nerve and Charles De Gall are my best friends. How dare you insult me like thiz. *Viva la France*, you American doof. *Viva la France!*"

"Hey, lady—it's Viva Las Vegas. Now pipe down, will ya?"

They led me into a small, gray room with one curtainless window looking out onto the East River. A woman wearing a starched face with her hair wound tightly in a bun on the back of her head sat back behind a desk. She began to talk, but all I could hear were my temples pounding. My thoughts throbbed in my aching head as I searched for a solution. Maybe I could jump out of the window and swim to freedom. Or drown! Anything, God! Just let me erase this from my life.

No dice.

I was held for what seemed like an eternity inside those lifeless walls. How could I be so stupid? Sure, I stole some bubble gum as a kid. And maybe I did forget to return those clothes I borrowed from Saks. And Macy's. And Bloomies. And who could forget the time I tried to charge that camera to Andy's account? But grand larceny? It sounded so . . . so grand! But of course it was grand! After all, I AM the heiress to the Woodlawn Cemetery. I had a reputation to uphold.

Well, my temple toppled to the ground when Chumley was called in to identify me. I had left my own identification at home and that dear son-of-a-bitch friend of mine Estelle had fled like a bat out of hell when they carted me off. Chumley, the friend I had betrayed, was the only person who could identify me for the authorities. I contorted my face in every possible way, thinking she wouldn't recognize me, but it was to no avail.

Chumley had no idea what I had done, but she knew it was serious and when our eyes met, I saw the disappointment in her face. My heart plummeted into my stomach and for the first time in my life, I felt ashamed of who I was. Tears filled my eyes as I reached for her.

"I'm—I'm sorry, hon. I—"

But Chumley didn't reach back. She just stood there, staring at me in disbelief, and before I could explain the insanity, I felt the cold steel bracelets clasp around my right wrist. The police officer reached around and grabbed my left hand and cuffed it as well, and I was brusquely hauled off to the Women's House of Detention.

"Book her," were the kindest words anyone had said to me all day. This was the big house and I was in the big time, see. No more sequined heels for me, see. It was the ball and chain all the way. Luckily, I didn't get the chair, so there seemed to be somewhat of a future left in my tainted little life, although I wasn't quite certain where this future lay. At the moment, it seemed the only hope I had was to change my name to Mumbles and join the mob.

I was fingerprinted, photographed, and then taken off to the routine strip search. I had no idea what a strip search was, and became quite upset since the only experience I had was dancing topless as a go-go girl.

"Ah, it's nuthin', hon," said a skinny, bleached-out bimbo with sleepy eyes barely dressed in a leather miniskirt, halter top, and platform shoes. "They's just checkin' for drugs," she continued as we made our way to the stripping compound. Then her eyes lit up with hope. "You don't got none, do ya honey?"

If I had them, I wouldn't have been in this mess! All I had to do was shimmy out of my dress. No sweat, I thought, till I remembered that I was concealing something much more incriminating. Thoughts sprang about my head as I tried to resolve how I was going to explain being a man. Suicide was easier and Andy would surely get a kick out of it. He just loved screaming headlines, especially the juicy ones. Imagine Middle America's shock after reading, "Drag Queen Commits Hari Kiri with Teasing Comb in Slammer!"

But Middle America would have to wait for its grisly tabloid sensationalism, because the only thing that screamed that day was the matron after she told me to bend over and spread my cheeks.

"Get him outta here!"

By the end of the day, I was staggering through the Men's House of Detention (affectionately known as "the Tombs") in heels, ripped nylons, a now-disheveled dress, and mascara-stained eyes. What a horror it was to be thrown in a cell with forty straight men. Mean men. Men who loathed faggots. Some were old and scraggly. Others were young and rough. They were hard people who had led hard lives. And there I was, a young tender lamb cutlet amidst this pack of hungry wolves. I was definitely out of place, out of booze, and scared shitless.

"She's mine!" seethed one fat, wrinkled geezer with dirty teeth.

"No, she's mine," proclaimed another.

And then another, "Get away, she's mine!"

They started to approach. My eyes grew and my stomach shrank. So many men, so little time, and I was too petrified to enjoy it. Luckily, from the mass of lurching heathens bellowed a thunderous voice:

"Leave her the fuck alone!"

I looked up and there he was: a strapping, tall Latin with a bright gold tooth and shiny muscles that swelled beneath his ripped T-shirt.

"She's mine!" His voice roared like a lion staking out his territory.

"That's right," I told the rest of 'em, shaking my finger. "I'm his!"

"You gonna be okay," he reassured me, placing his hand on the small of my back.

I grew weak with desire as he walked me to his corner of the cell. He sat with me and, lighting two cigarettes at once, offered me one. I accepted, gazing into his heavily browed romantic eyes. He leaned forward, touching his lips to my cheek. I felt his massive chest strain as he pulled me into a hungry kiss. My loins erupted into flames of passion as he devoured my body, working his mouth into the side of my neck and down to my voluptuous titties. I threw my head back and resisted, but his force was immense.

"No! No!" I cried, beating onto his sweaty back. He pressed his heaving body against mine, causing my hormones to break into a chorus of "Babaloo!" My heart was a yo-yo, he held the string, and I didn't even know his name! Oh, what difference did it make? We had a quick Vegas-like wedding that night: he said "I do." I said, "I do, too!" And so we did. Zing! Went the strings of my vulva!

We were together not twenty-four hours when the guards entered the cell and hauled me off again.

"I love you, Raul," I wailed, clinging to his torso.

"My name's Ramone," he scowled. "Get this cheap broad outta my fucking sight."

"Cheap?! You goddamned son of a bitch! You can't talk to me like that, I'm a movie star! Guard, I want a divorce!"

So much for love behind bars. I was arraigned for two thousand dollars' grand larceny, with bail set at a thousand buckaroos. In the month that I was locked up, I had lost all hope of contact with the Warhol crowd, as well as most of the outside world. Vietnam was at its peak. Both Janis Joplin and Jimi Hendrix had died. Jackie Curtis was busily writing her next stage play. Candy Darling was busy being a blonde. Edie Sedgewick was living in a swimming pool. And Paul Morrissey was probably tossing around ideas for a new film.

I tried to call Andy for help, but the Factory chose to ignore my calls and letters. I can't say I blame them. A thousand big ones is a big favor to ask, especially from people I hardly knew and had tried to steal from before! Calling home was worse, as my mother accused me of disgracing the family name.

"My name is Holly Woodlawn!" I cried into the phone. "How could anyone connect that with Harold Ajzenberg?"

It seemed that everyone was content to forget me . . . at least until the release of *Trash* on October 5, 1970. Just when those sons-a-bitches thought they could leave me to collect dust in the dungeon, I had emerged upon the movie screen as the star of the show. The film

catapulted me into the media's eye, and I became a favorite among the critics. The fact that I was in prison heightened the sensational angle, which *Daily Variety* took full advantage of by blasting: "Trash Star Found In Trash Can" for all my neighbors to see. The attention certainly thrilled Andy, prompting him to see me in a different light. Sure, I was still a poverty-stricken low-life, but now I was a *famous* low-life, bathed in adulation. I had proven that I could be truly fabulous.

Yet even after the publicity, the praise, and the glory, the Factory still chose to leave me imprisoned. When a reporter called to inquire about my arraignment, a Factory spokesperson replied, "Holly only worked for us eight days. We're sorry she's in jail, but we're not responsible. . . ."

Nobody cared. Who could? Who was I? What was I? A runaway? A thief? A transvestite? A Diane Arbus bonanza?! I was playing gin rummy with half a deck and an empty bottle. I was not only confused, I was hurt as well.

Then one brisk October morning while dining on hard toast, a hardly boiled egg, and that hideous coffee, I heard those blessed words escape the guard's mouth:

"Holly Woodlawn, pack your panties. You're out on bail."

I was surprised, ecstatic, shocked; how'd he know I was wearing panties? But an even bigger mystery was: Who had posted my bail? It wasn't Jackie Curtis; she couldn't afford a new pair of nylons. And it wasn't Candy Darling; she was pinching her pennies for bleach. Who was this mysterious saviour?

I was taken downstairs to retrieve my clothing, where I received a note instructing me to take a cab to Larry Rivers's studio. THE Larry Rivers? That divine darling I had hobnobbed with so many times, the great artist whom even Andy regarded with awe? Yes, it was THE Larry Rivers, my Prince Charming, who (with a nudge or two from Miss Curtis, so I'm told) hauled out one thousand smackers to spring me from the clutches of doom.

Finally, to the bleats of trumpets blaring, the gates to freedom opened and I ascended from the Tombs like Lazarus, waving to the poor pagan suckers left behind. I would've belted out, "Forget your

troubles, come on get happy," but I wasn't wearing tap shoes or a fedora, and I hate to sing a cappella. Besides, I had a date with destiny. So I clicked the heels of my combat boots and screamed:

"Fuck yahs all!"

And on that happy yet raucous note, the black cloud shrouding my desperate skies began to part and, as I felt the light spill upon my ravaged breast, the bells rang! The cherubs danced! And my lungs sang:

"Free pussy!"

So there we were, clinking our champagne glasses and carrying on when someone—probably myself—started talking about *Trash.*

"Oh, Holly, you're wonderful in it," said Larry.

"It's true," giggled Pinky.

"You were a riot," interjected Jackie, shoving a press clipping under my nose. "By the way, did you see this write-up on me in the *Voice?*"

"Let's go see the movie," said Larry, setting down his glass.

"Oh, that sounds like fun," giggled Pinky, the champagne tickling her nose.

"Hey, you didn't miss this clip on me in the *Post,* did ya?" (Miss Curtis was forever carrying on about her clips.)

"Oh, Jackie, you spread so nicely across the page," I smiled politely. "Now what should I wear? I can't show up in this rumpled old thing," I said, pulling the Chanel dress out of my cat basket and shaking it out.

"Oh, it's not that bad," said Pinky, smoothing the dress out against my body.

"It looks horrible," added Jackie, striking a match to light her cigarette. "It's all wadded, wrinkled, ripped, and torn."

"I don't see any rips," I said, looking over the fabric. Suddenly, Jackie grabbed hold of the neckline and tore it down the middle. "You do now."

Curtis turned to Larry, cigarette still hanging from her crimson lips, and jabbered on. "Larry, Holly can't go to the movie looking like this. She's a star. We gotta take her shopping."

Curtis was a brazen broad who could finagle the silver lining out of a cloud if she wanted it badly enough.

Larry was a very generous man, with a heart of gold and a wallet full of credit cards. He turned one over to Pinky and told her to take Jackie and me to Bergdorfs and get the works. Jackie, Pinky, and I terrorized that store from top to bottom. I felt just like Barbra Streisand in her first TV special when she ran amok in the fur salon doing a tarantella on a sable coat while singing "Nobody Knows Ya When You're Down and Out."

After a hard day in every department including the *boite de beauté,* we threw back a couple of cocktails, hailed a taxi, and flew back to the loft, where we unpacked the haul and got ready for my coming out!

We had a load of shopping bags filled with dresses, shoes, stockings, purses—even a girdle for Curtis. We ripped our way through tissue, boxes, and plastic bags to each of our ensembles. Pinky's was a silver lamé backless minidress. Come to think of it, the dress didn't have much up front, either. But there was so much of her, she filled it out quite nicely, and it looked marvelous! A big, thick, white ostrich boa with silver tinsel was wrapped around her arms, so she could fling it from side to side while she strutted across the room in her silver mesh stockings and silver high heels—the pointy ones, with two big silver rhinestone bows on the toes. She was cute as a button and looked just like Little Annie Fanny from the *Playboy* cartoons.

Curtis had bought a tasteful chartreuse, blue, and orange floral-print number that looked like a housedress. I think the only difference was that this one didn't come from a thrift shop and cost five hundred dollars! It had little sleeves and a big blue cabbage rose sewed right on the hip. Well, Curtis—believing in herself as an *artiste de haute couture*—decided the dress needed some revamping and proceeded to do so. First, she ripped the flower off of the hip and pinned it in her hair. Then she decided that the length was too long. It didn't show enough leg, she thought, so she ran into the kitchen and came back with a pair of scissors and proceeded to make it shorter.

Satisfied with the length, she decided that the neckline was all wrong, but with a snip, snip here and a rip, rip there, she had gotten herself a lower decolletté. Needless to say, we were all in shock after witnessing this spasm of creativity.

"Oh, maybe a little slit in the back, so I can walk easier!" thought Jackie aloud as we heard the fabric rip.

Soon there was no resemblance between the dress she got at the store and the thing that was on her back, which was usually the case with Curtis. Her black pumps were too tight in the ankles, so Curtis took the scissors to them, too. And the fishnet stockings she had purchased were too small, but Curtis—determined as she was—

groaned and moaned while she forced them over her manly legs. And as far as the rose in her hair was concerned, Curtis couldn't leave well enough alone. She scrounged around in the bottom of her bag, found some glitter and dumped it on that poor flower! Then she sprinkled some on her eyelids and sprinkled more on her lips.

Well, at least the panty girdle fit.

Then Miss Curtis reached into her prized shopping bag and pulled out her little black book and started to call everyone we knew to let them know that I was making my big debut that very eve. She called Paul Morrissey, the Factory, Andy, the press, the theater, and even a few phone numbers she had found on a filthy old bar napkin. Even John Springer, publicist to such luminaries as Liz Taylor and Joan Crawford, was coming. Oh, it was going to be a true gala after all!

I wore a red sequin dress. And while dressing for the night's extravaganza, it dawned on me just how chivalrous Larry's gesture had been. You see, Larry didn't know me that well. Oh, sure, I had been to his place several times for dinner with Curtis, but Larry and I weren't the best of friends. I liked him, I respected him, but I never dreamed he would bail me out of prison. After all, what had I done to deserve such kindness?

I was later told by Curtis that he was appalled by the Factory's blind eye to my plight, leaving me in jail. Larry was just a nice guy who was compelled to come to my rescue. It was a gesture I'll never forget.

As far as Andy and the Factory are concerned, I don't harbor any resentment toward those motherfuckers at all. Truthfully, I was not offended by their reaction to my imprisonment because they didn't owe me anything. I admit, I felt completely abandoned at the time, but it was my fault. I stole the money, I had to pay the piper, and I was willing to do so.

The same goes with feeling exploited. Everyone—the "Superstars," mostly—felt cheated and exploited. Valerie Solanas got so pissed off she stomped over to the Factory and shot Andy! And every now and then, I do get a bit irritated by the fact that Trash did make zillions of dollars and that I was left in the gutter, but I can't hold that against

Andy or the Factory. If I'm angry with anybody, it's with myself for having been so careless in my youth. After all, who knew then that what we were doing (which just seemed absurd at the time) would amount to zillions of dollars in film revenues?

So, yes, maybe I was exploited. *C'est la vie!* Andy didn't owe me anything. It was a trade-off. He gave many of us fame and we gave him something to talk about. True, he made a lot of money and many of us—myself included—did not. Obviously, darling, he got the better end of the stick, but that's the breaks, you know? The fact that he was a talented artist and a commercial genius had nothing to do with my financial state. That was my responsibility.

Every now and then I'd drop by the Factory on Union Square and Andy would help me out with some loot. I only asked for so much, either to pay the rent or straighten out a bill at Max's, but I never took advantage. Hell, how could I, living from hand to mouth, take advantage of a millionaire? Well, I can think of a dozen ways now, but it just didn't enter my mind then, oddly enough. What was I thinking?

But I digress. Where was I?

Oh! So Larry, Jackie, Pinky, and I (looking fabulous by this point) piled into Larry's waiting limo, where we knocked off two bottles of Dom Perignon and dashed off to the Cinema II, where *Trash* was playing. "TRASH" was spelled out in huge black letters on the marquee and, to my amazement, there was a crowd lined up around the block waiting to get inside! Actually, there were 378 people, to be exact. I know because we had to go around the block several times before we could pull up to the theater's entrance. My heart was pounding like a jackhammer, I was so nervous.

The people were thrilled to see us. Berserk was more like it. I was freaked! When they realized who I was, they started charging at me like I was the only girdle left at the semiannual Macy's sale! To tell you that I was terrified is putting it mildly. I was flabbergasted, frightened, excited, and loaded to boot! The thoughts that entered my mind! Why, one would've thought that I was about to be tossed to the bottom of a seething volcano, the way these savages carried on. Only then did I realize that these hoodlums attacking me were actually my fans, screaming and chanting at the top of their lungs in a slow rhythmic beat, "Holly . . . Holly . . . Holly!"

"Can I have your autograph?" asked one, having pushed a pen and a piece of paper in my face.

I was astounded by the request. Someone actually wanted my autograph? It felt so strange as I scribbled my name across the blank piece of paper, but it was a moment I shall never forget. Right there on Lexington Avenue and Sixty-second Street in front of the divine Cinema II artsy fartsy theater, I, Holly Woodlawn, the effervescent populuxe Warhol Superstar diva supreme, signed my very first autograph.

After twenty-eight minutes of signing, waving, and working my way toward the entrance, I finally blew my last kiss, thanked them all for coming, and scurried inside, where I was met by the film's director, Paul Morrissey, and the cinema's proprietor, Don Rugoff. Rugoff kissed my trembling hand, and since I was still a little shaken from all the commotion outside, I asked if it was possible for me to calm my frayed little nerves with a teensy glass of the complimentary bubbly that was flowing in honor of my arrival.

Well, half a bottle later, after a few more thank you's, waving and kissing the air, I was ready to sit down. Actually, by this time, I was ready to fall down! I wasn't feeling very well balanced. There were butterflies bouncing off my stomach walls, not to mention a few wreaking havoc in my head! Oh, the terror of it all! Going into a crowded theater to see oneself on the big screen for the first time is quite unnerving, even though I had seen the reviews and knew I had been well received by the critics.

"Holly Woodlawn, especially, is something to behold," wrote Vincent Canby of *The New York Times*. "[She is] a comic-book Mother Courage who fancies herself as Marlene Dietrich, but sounds more like Phil Silvers."

"*Trash* . . . is a witty, poignant situation comedy about some utter degenerates . . . it seems hardly necessary to point out that Holly Woodlawn is a female impersonator. His part is scripted for a girl, and he plays it with the energetic girlishness of a top-flight romantic comedienne," wrote Peter Schjeldahl of *The New York Times*.

I sat, gripping the edges of my seat as I heard the opening music play. It sounded like it had been composed for a 1930s Hal Roach comedy. Then the credits began to roll across the screen. I couldn't believe I was seeing *my* movie. Was I dreaming this, or had I really achieved something worthwhile? I was not just a movie star—I was a Warhol "Superstar." I was going to be primped and pampered by the emperors of fashion, photographed and featured in *Vogue* and *Bazaare*, live the high life among the rich and famous, swathe myself in furs, feed on caviar, dine on wine, and live off unabashed glamour. All this and welfare, too. Some girls have all the luck.

My mind gorged on dreams of what lay ahead as I waited with baited breath to see my name, praying to God that it was going to show up. Where was it? I had seen Andy's, Paul's, Joe's, Andrea's—Oh, my God, had they forgotten my name? I tensed and began to bite my lip. Maybe I was still in the slammer and this was all a dream. Maybe I wasn't even in this movie. And then, suddenly, my eyes lit up as the very last credit danced across the screen.

". . . and introducing . . . Holly Woodlawn."

I was fit to be tied.

CHAPTER 3

Born to Be a Beauty Queen

I was with my Uncle Virgilio (who was only six years older than I) when I saw a movie for the first time, at the Plaza Theater in Puerto Rico. God, how we worshipped the movies and their stars. Maria Felix (the Spanish version of Elizabeth Taylor), Libertad Lamarque (Evita had thrown her out of the country because she was jealous of her popularity with Peron), and Cantinflas (a Latin blend of Charlie Chaplin and Harpo Marx) were among the stars we idolized, but Lola Flores was our all-time favorite. She was a famous flamenco dancer who wore a red polka-dotted ruffled dress with a long train and a rose in her hair, held by a big Spanish comb. She scorched the silver screen with her dark, gypsy good looks, and boy, could she raise hell with castanets! Every weekend we'd rush out to a matinee to catch one of her pictures and then run home as soon as it was over to imitate her scenes in the bedroom mirror. My most vivid memory is of her wearing a red flamenco dress in all that Spanish drag while singing "Pena Penita Pena." It was riveting! Why, she danced right off the screen and into my little Puerto Rican heart . . . and all for the price of a peseta!

My uncle was a flamboyant kid and a fabulous dancer. He imitated Lola's every move with such grace as he glided across the polished wood floor, snapping his castanets while I stood behind and imitated his every move. Everyone thought we were so cute! He also sang very well, and whenever he started to belt out a note, you can bet your bottom dollar I was right behind him, singing along. He was full of talent and I admired him so much, I couldn't help but follow him everywhere he went. And since I was only three years old, you can imagine that I was quite a pain in the ass!

My childhood in Puerto Rico was a lively one, to say the least. Having been raised in a household of eight aunts, one uncle, five cousins, two grandparents, six chickens, three pigs, and other assorted "family members," I don't recall a moment's peace. Every time I turned around, we were celebrating someone or something's birthday!

My favorite holiday was Three Kings Day, also known as The Epiphany. It is the Puerto Rican equivalent to Christmas and it is celebrated on January 6, the day when the three wise men arrived in Bethlehem and lavished the baby Jesus with gifts of frankincense, myrrh, and gold. It's the most glorious holiday of them all! Every year the entire village dressed up like shepherds and made a procession to the church.

My grandmother would spend hours hovering over her black antiquated Singer sewing machine, rhythmically pumping the foot pedal as she fed yards of brilliantly colored material under the darting needle, creating little costumes for Uncle Virgilio, my cousins, and me. You should have seen the fabrics that passed under that needle! Shimmering red, yellow, and purple satins sparkling with glitter and sequins. We were all clad in little ruffled bolero jackets (similar to the ones worn by Xavier Cugat's band) and carried brightly colored staffs of crepe-paper flowers. I suppose you could say that Three Kings Day was my first real taste of glamour. To look at us, you'd think we were off to star in a Carmen Miranda musical!

I loved to dress up in all that regalia. Early in the morning we would get all decked out (although the adults were also dressed as shepherds, their costumes weren't as flamboyant) and make a Technicolor procession to the church for the Epiphany pageant, followed by the high mass. Afterward, all the villagers gathered in the town square for the great celebration, led by the town band. My grandfather played the trumpet. I was so proud of him, I'd run through the crowd, tug on ladies' dresses, and point, "That's my Poppy! That's my Poppy!"

Later in the morning, we would go back home to exchange gifts, drink rum (I always finagled a nip), and then roast the pig. We'd eat the *"lechon asado"*—which means roast pig—drink some more, and open our gifts. It was like having Christmas and Thanksgiving all rolled into one. All the families would get together, cook all day, get loaded, and have a ball!

Living in Puerto Rico was like living in a fairy tale. I was born in that lush tropical paradise on October 26, 1946, to a Puerto Rican mother and an American soldier of German descent. He had traveled to the country on leave, met my mother at a dance, and the two fell head over heels in love. My mother became pregnant and so they wed, but the marriage was brief. They were both very young and the soldier, homesick for his native land, got cold feet and fled.

For some reason, all of my aunts had shiftless husbands, too, probably because they rebelled against my grandfather's strict upbringing. Instead of landing decent, hard-working men, they always wound up with the drunks, women beaters, and other useless derelicts. Not long after they had left home to get married, my aunts were knocked up, knocked about, and came wandering home one right after the other, knowing that Mommy and Poppy would take them back into the nest. We had quite a houseful, to say the least!

I'll never forget the night my Aunt Tete's husband Ramone walked out. He and Tete were next door in the bodega hanging out at the bar when, in a drunken rage, he started to beat her. Poppy heard

Tete's screams and charged out of our house, mad as a bull, with all of my aunts, Mommy, and us kids parading behind. He burst into the bodega and pushed Ramone against the bar. Ramone fought back and before we knew it, he was on top of Poppy trying to kill him! He had his hands around Poppy's throat, strangling him. Mommy and my aunts were screaming, and I was so frightened! It was the most horrible sight I'd ever seen. I grabbed the first thing I saw—a two-by-four barricade—and started to hit Ramone across the back. By this time, I was so overcome with fear I was crying and screaming, beating him as hard as I could. Suddenly, the men in the bodega tore Ramone from Poppy and my grandmother rushed to my side, embracing me with her warmth, trying to calm my sobs.

Ramone was hauled off to jail and never heard from again. I guess you could say the same happened to all my aunts' husbands! Not one of 'em were worth his salt, the shiftless sons-a-bitches.

My mother tried to take care of me as best as she could. For a while, we had lived with one of my aunts in San Juan, the capital of Puerto Rico, but it was really rough for my mother. She was working several jobs simultaneously. One of these was in a little shop that sold handmade Spanish linen and silk, where she would sit all day rolling edges on silk handkerchiefs.

In 1948, when I was two, my mother decided it was impossible for her to support both of us from the meager pay she was getting from rolling hankies. She felt there was no other choice but to head for the land of opportunity—Neuva York—or Nueva Jork, as we pronounced it. She was sure the sidewalks were paved with gold! (Why is it that everybody from an underdeveloped country thinks like that? Don't they look at pictures? I mean, New York is the world's tallest concrete latrine—besides Pittsburg. Of course, we didn't know that then, and all we could see was pie in the sky.)

I was two years old, barely able to talk, when Poppy—who was sensitive to my mother's dreadful dilemma—thought it better that she go to New York alone, get herself situated, and then send for me. With this goal in mind, my mother packed her bags (including a few assorted lace hankies) and headed for "La Manzana Grande!" She was determined to take a bite out of the Big Apple.

I don't remember much about my mother during these early years because she was always working and then moved away. It was my grandmother who raised me as a toddler and, because I formed such a strong maternal bond to her, it was natural that I called her "Mommy." Mommy nurtured my love for my real mother and often told me beautiful stories about how my mother lived in a faraway land that a person could get to only by plane. "One day you'll go there to live with her," she promised. It sounded so magical to me then. And every week, I would get letters in the mail from that faraway land. Mommy would read them to me while showing me pictures of my mother, keeping a vivid picture of her painted in my mind. I remember being enamored with my mother's beauty. I can still remember one of the snapshots. She was very glamourous, wearing a wide-brim hat, high heels, and the prettiest smile. She looked just like Ava Gardner.

About a year later, when I was three, my mother had met and become engaged to a wonderful Polish Jew named Joseph Ajzenberg. They had a lot in common. They had both left their families behind in other countries when they immigrated to New York. But while my mother's move to New York was fueled by ambition, Joe's was fueled by survival—he had fled Poland for his life. As a teenager, he escaped the Nazi invasion only because his parents had used their entire life savings to ensure their son's freedom. He came to New York penniless and started at the bottom. Eventually he became a waiter at a summer resort in upstate New York, where my mother was working as a waitress. Since he had no family of his own, he was thrilled to learn that she had a three-year-old son, and he promised that once they were married, they would send for me.

I loved living with my grandparents. After all, I was the favorite grandchild. My grandfather had his own bedroom and I was the only one allowed to nap with him. Not even Mommy slept in his bed, so you can see I felt quite honored. But then, I was different from all of my cousins as well as the other children in town. Due to my German heritage, I was born a natural blond, and with my mother's piercing green eyes, I was a beauty. Everywhere we went, all the ladies fussed over me.

"Oh, isn't he cute? Such beautiful hair," they'd say. My grandparents would smile with pride and give me a big hug. How I loved the attention—that little thrill I would get deep down inside when I knew I was a rare, one-of-a-kind original. Boy, if they only knew just how rare I was to become!

We lived in a little yellow ramshackle house just outside of Ponce. Probably my fondest memory of the house is lying in bed with my grandmother, surrounded by lots of mosquito netting under tons of covers, snuggled against her back like a lion cub while the summer rain beat down upon the corrugated tin roof. The rain was so soothing. I can still hear it, tapping against the metal like a chorus line trying to find its rhythm. To me, the sound of the summer rain and the warmth of Mommy were home.

Every morning at the crack of dawn, the old rooster out back crowed up a storm and started a chain reaction that was heard clear into the next village. Moments later the floorboards squeaked as Mommy got out of bed and slipped into one of her pale floral-print housedresses. And as I rubbed the sleep from my eyes, I'd squint to see her slowly brushing her long black hair. She had such pretty hair. It shimmered like long strands of black silk in the morning light. It wasn't long before I heard her houseshoes smacking across the wooden floor, down the hall, and into the kitchen, where she started her morning chores. Another day had begun.

I pushed the sheets away and jumped from the bed, my bare feet scampering across the floor, to find her in the kitchen tying a white apron around her waist. Then she crossed to the windows, pushed open the wooden flaps, and secured them in place with a wooden pole. We didn't have glass in our windows. There was no need in those days. One didn't have to worry about being robbed in the middle of the night, because nobody had anything!

Mommy was a devout Christian and a helluva cook! The most important things in her life, it seemed, were cooking, taking care of her family, and reading the Bible. I can recall myself perched on the kitchen table, watching as she bustled around the small kitchen, grabbing a pot here, putting a skillet there. Cracking eggs, pouring milk. Frying this, boiling that. Oh, the wonderful smells of breakfast! In no time at all, the aroma of coffee and bacon filled the morning air. Mmmm, now *those* were the smells that I called home. And this was real coffee, made from steamed milk and freshly ground beans, with the rich taste of cappuccino—and boy, was it good with tons of sugar!

Within minutes the entire kitchen was a hub of activity. Everyone was up and gathered around the table, chittering and chattering like a bunch of chipmunks at a nut rally. We kids were jabbering with our mouths full of food, the aunts were all giggling and gossiping, with Mommy—who had twenty thousand mouths to feed—slaving over the hot wood-burning stove while Poppy tried to make sense of it all. It was as crazy as a Ma and Pa Kettle movie, but it was wonderful.

One by one, the family would disperse from the table into the real world. My aunts were off to work in the plaza's City Hall, while the kids, all dressed up like little drones in those matching blue-and-brown plaid uniforms, were shooed off to Catholic school. I, of course, was much too young to attend (thank you, Mary, Mother of God!). Besides, I was far too content to romp in the rich tropical greenery of my own backyard. Imagine the bluest sky you've ever seen set behind tall green palms swaying in a cool morning breeze. The yard was a vibrant kalei-doscope of color, with a large crepe-myrtle tree looking like a giant bouquet of crinkly red flowers. The far end of the yard was surrounded by exotic flowering bougainvilleas, and cute little green frogs no bigger than a thumb nail hopped all over the place, calling out "Cokie, cokie."

Everything was so lush and wondrous. By the porch stood a big old guava tree not far from a large cluster of crimson-and-orange rose bushes—their colors so vibrant even the grandest fireworks display couldn't compare to their brilliance. There was also a huge hammock, fashioned from burlap sacks strung between two palm trees, that I'd swing on forever. And if I wasn't swinging, I was shaking the mango tree and biting into the fallen fruits. I rooted for grubs, ate nuts, and swung on vines. Honey, Cheetah couldn't have been happier!

I used to pick hibiscus flowers, pull out the centers, and suck out the nectar. And, on occasion, when I felt rambunctious, I chased the chickens and wrestled with the pigs.

At noon, Poppy would return home with loaves of freshly baked bread and fresh vegetables for Mommy to use in making that evening's dinner.

I loved Poppy so much. He was a good man, but he ruled his family with an iron fist. He held a tight rein on his children, and he would threaten to beat them with his belt should one of them step out of line. Poppy was very strict with my Uncle Virgilio, too. He wanted his son to amount to something more than a common laborer, and he strongly enforced education.

The day I left for New York was a sad one. Try hugging eight emotional aunts, six other kids, five chickens, three pigs, and one grandfather good-bye in one sitting! It's not easy, especially at the crack of dawn. Our rooster hadn't even crowed yet, it was so early!

Mommy and I boarded a hired car—there were no taxis in Puerto Rico at this time—and drove for hours on the winding roads through the jungles and mountains to the airport. I had no idea where I was going, and all this talk of the United States and New York simply confused me. Furthermore, I couldn't speak a dime's worth of English.

Finally, when we arrived at the airport, Mommy and I climbed the steps leading to the biggest thing I'd ever seen—an airplane! And it had only four propellers to keep it up!

My nose was pressed against the porthole glass when the plane began to shimmy down the runway. Oh, boy—now I was really scared! I buried my face into Mommy's side as the plane began to rumble and shake. Oh, God! This was it. We wouldn't get three feet off the ground before the thing would fall apart! This time I was sure it was curtains. I wrapped my arms tightly around Mommy, clinging to her for dear life as we took off like a rocket to the moon. Why in God's name couldn't we have taken a bus?

New York City was different from anything I had ever seen. Mommy held my hand as we walked down the pavement, my ears choking on the sounds of the screeching tires and blaring horns while my eyes filled with the sight of enormous concrete structures, unfamiliar streets, and strange people. Mobs and mobs of strange-looking people were heading in all directions; so many of them that their faces melted together with no more clarity than a blurred, distorted photograph!

I didn't see a palm or a guava tree anywhere. For that matter, I didn't see any trees at all! Wherever I turned, I had to look up, and if I wasn't careful, I'd bend my head so far back I'd topple over backward and fall to the ground! After all, I was just a little thing, six inches taller than a fire hydrant. I was lucky to see the top of a mail box.

It was strange seeing my mother for the first time in all those years, and at first I was a little shy, but she showered me with such love and affection, I couldn't help but love her back. When I met my new father, I was too young to understand the details of why he was not my biological father, so it was never explained. I was told that he was my father and that was that. Besides, what did it matter? I was happy.

Mommy stayed for about a month in our new home, something called an apartment in a strange village called the Bronx. The apartment was an enormous place, with high ceilings and a long hallway that cut right down the center between the living room and the two bedrooms. Green stenciling adorned the walls (stencils were very popular then) and I was awed by the vastness of it all. I felt as if I'd moved into a mansion!

The apartment's hallway was so long that whenever someone rang the front doorbell, it took a while for my mother to travel from the back of the apartment. Usually the doorbell would ring more than once, and then my mother always hollered at the top of her voice, "Take it easy!" I heard the words so often that they became the first phrase I ever said in English.

Eventually, the time came when Mommy had to go back home to look after Poppy and the gang. Tears filled her eyes as she hugged me before boarding the plane, and she made my mother promise I could return once a year to spend the summers with her in Puerto Rico.

"Take it easy!" I waved as she disappeared into the plane.

* * *

I was a bright little thing—so smart, in fact, that my mother lied about my age and enrolled me in kindergarten at the age of four. In the first grade I was excelling so rapidly that the school advanced me to the second grade. By this time, I had completely lost my Spanish accent and had become a full-blown Americano.

We stayed in New York for about two years, and I did visit Puerto Rico every summer. This was back when they had those clipper flights and it took eight hours to fly to the Caribbean. I had finally gotten used to flying, and was now a veteran of the skies. I would go by myself with a big picture of a plane with my name on it pinned to my jacket, and I was always taken into the cockpit to meet the captain and the crew.

When I was with my grandparents in Puerto Rico, my parents would work the Borscht Belt in upstate New York. One summer my father learned that a very high-class hotel, the Fountainbleu, was opening in Miami Beach, Florida. It was plush and sophisticated: "A hotel to end all hotels," he said. And they were hiring waiters and waitresses.

After I came back to New York, we packed our bags, hopped a plane, and made the big move to sunny, gaudy Miami Beach. Now, this was the mid-1950s, when Miami Beach was in its heyday. This was before Castro had taken over Cuba, so Havana was right next door—and it was in full swing! There were fabulous nightclubs everywhere! The beaches were filled with the richest people from all over the world. It was so ostentatious, in fact, that women would wear their minks to the beach! There were expensive, posh, Vegas-type nightclubs and casinos along Collins Avenue, and the strip pulsed to the bump, grind, and beat of highfalutin burlesque joints touting the likes of Belle Barth, Gypsy Rose Lee, and Sophie Tucker on their dazzling marquees.

When we first arrived, we settled in a little apartment in the Art Deco district of South Beach on Tenth Street. Practically all of it is torn down now, though they're trying to revive it, but at that time Art Deco was quite the rage. Along the ocean drive there was a row of pastel-colored motels as far as the eye could see, with palm trees swaying to the Cuban beat from nearby radios. Just across the street from the motels was the beach, with its paved sidewalks and white sands leading all the way into the beautiful blue ocean streching right up to the end of the earth. It was like stepping into a picture postcard. The only place I've ever known to come close is Rio.

Did I mention that Miami Beach attracted the most exquisitely beautiful people in the world? Yachts and sailboats were parked in the marina, shiny black Lincolns and Cadillacs lined the boulevards (this was long before the pimps could afford them), and bejeweled dames basked in the sun, nursing their cool Piña Coladas and Daiquiris. Miami Beach had become the Mecca of Jewish resorts.

Right in the heart of the strip-joint district, near Twenty-first Street and Collins Avenue, was a secluded little beach. It was located directly across the street from the Miami Beach Public Library, and one Saturday morning when I was about fourteen years old, while I was waiting for the library's doors to open, I decided to take a light stroll across the street and catch some sun. Not only did I catch some sun, I caught the moon as well. A rotund man tossed his cocktail to the wind, stripped out of his bikini, and screamed, "All right, girls, last one in's a rotten egg!" And off he bounced through the sands, running straight into the ocean with everyone laughing and carrying on behind him. The funny thing was, I had looked everywhere but there were no girls anywhere—just men!

Well, darling, I was shocked to learn that I had stumbled upon the only gay beach in all of Florida. And to think it was right across the street from my now *favorite* public library!

Loud Cuban salsa music blared from a nearby radio as all these men yukked it up, having the time of their lives. I had never before seen a real-life, honest-to-God homosexual—ever! Here were actual "queers," "fairies," "pansies," "Nancies," and "fags." And with that kind of terminology floating around in my head, how could I have helped but assume that all homosexuals were nellie little darlings with poofy hair coiffed to perfection, their shoulders caressed by feather boas, wearing a rock on every finger, and talking with a dead-giveaway lisp!? Boy, was I ever in for a surprise.

There they were, a smorgasbord of every type of man imaginable:

exotic, outrageous, fabulous, decadent! Big, little, hunky, chunky. Oh, so many men, so little time! And all in bikinis, to boot! Roasting in the sun like beef waiting to be marinated. I was fit to be tied! It was divine. But while I sat watching them cavort from afar, my fantasies of cavorting with them were shattered. A siren blared and voices screamed, "It's a raid!" It sure was—cops and helicopters were descending from every direction! Picture it: dozens of drunk, screaming queens scampering to gather their towels and picnic baskets to avoid being hauled away in shackles. I was nearly scared out of my skin. I ran away as fast as I could, terrified that I'd be nabbed, have my hands slapped into cuffs, and be tossed in the can forever.

That day really opened my eyes. Having been born into a Catholic family, I grew up believing in all the religious values instilled in me. I had never really formed any opinions of my own—particularly regarding sexuality or alternative lifestyles. But that day at the beach—seeing those men the way they were in reality, and not the way society depicts them—made me realize that there was more to being homosexual than the contrived stereotypical image. It also made me realize that perhaps these weird feelings I harbored deep inside me weren't as horrible as I had thought. After all, I had finally learned I wasn't the only one.

I always knew I wasn't like the other kids at school. In junior high, after class, when all the other boys were outside playing ball, *I* was home with a towel over my head playing Connie Francis! I would sing along with her records for hours, flipping the towel from one shoulder to the other as if it were some long, glorious ponytail.

At home the living room had an adjoining dining room and the two were separated by curtains. I found it very theatrical and decided it was my very own stage.

"Who's sorry now?" My face would cringe with dramatic pain as I mouthed the words into the imaginary hand-held microphone. "Who's sorry now?"

I'm sure my mother, who was sitting in the living room playing bridge with the girls, wondered when WHISH! the curtains would fly apart and there I'd be with a towel on my head and Connie Francis wailing in the background. Why, you should have seen their faces!

Their eyes were wide as saucers! My mother, of course, was speechless. And I could tell by their reactions that she and her friends were indeed awed by my talent.

My love for living-room shows flourished, and soon I had extended my repertoire to Broadway, performing the songs from *South Pacific*. Oh, how I wanted to erect a marquee on the roof. I can still see the vision: "Harold Ajzenberg . . . LIVE!" All the kids from school would be lined up around the block—even the ones who made fun of me. They'd all be ushered into the living room, now revamped into a theater, with my parents sitting in the front row. My mother would wear her best dress with an orchid pinned to the collar. And my father would shake hands with everyone, he would be so proud.

The curtains would rise and the spotlight would hit me as I sat behind a polished black baby-grand piano. I looked gorgeous, dressed in a blue tuxedo with a towel on my head! Oh, the crowd went wild in my mind—yelling, screaming, and trying to tear at my clothing. Oh, my God! It's true, I thought. I am the new Elvis!

"Harold! Harold!" Girls screamed my name and fainted. So did the boys! But as I began to sing along with Connie, I heard an unwelcome voice.

"Harold? Harold!" barked the old lady with a twisted face, standing in the back of the room. Wait a minute. What the hell is this old bag doing in my theater?

"Harold!" She clapped her hands, grabbed my shoulders, and shook me in my seat. All the kids laughed as I jumped, startled by this rude awakening. Oh, God. Reality had set in. I wasn't the new Elvis, and I wasn't on stage. I was in Mrs. Norman's eighth-grade math class and I was *bored*!

"What's the square root of four?" she snapped her paper-thin lips knotted up under her nose.

How the hell did I know? I didn't even care, but my mind pondered the problem anyway.

"Well, if you had four roots and put them in a square . . ."

Mrs. Norman crossed her arms, tapped her foot, and leaned into me, flashing the evil eye.

"What kind of root—sassafrass or ginger?" I replied earnestly, but when the kids laughed and her nostrils flared, I knew I was in trouble. Her eyes were overshadowed with a maniacal glaze, her mouth began to foam, and her entire body began to quake. I just knew she was going to combust. And she did.

Needless to say, I didn't show much interest when it came to school. But I was in heaven when I was having a living-room show. And when I entered the eighth grade, I hooked up with a girl who shared my enthusiam. We were the next Mickey and Judy, bound for Broadway with our own neighborhood musical revue. Every day after school we would meet either at her house or mine to design sets, rehearse our numbers, and plan our scripts.

Her name was Hooch. Nancy Hooch. She was a burly kind of gal who ate prune pits and dreamed of driving a dump truck. Oh, Nancy Hooch! My dear beloved Nancy Hooch, with her thick, bushy brown hair and her smooth, athletic body. At the ripe age of thirteen, she was four feet, seven inches of gum-chomping, chain-smoking vixen, able to hurl a spit ball farther than anyone in class and sporting a self-inflicted tattoo of a skull on her left shoulder. She was more woman than I could handle, and more man than I'd ever be!

One day during one of our rehearsals, she gave me the eye. The big one. (She had two, you know.) And she chomped her Bazooka, popped a bubble, and, peeling it from her nose, she snarled, "Hey! You wanna play strip poker?"

Strip poker? Yikes!

"What's that?" I asked sheepishly.

We played round after round, but not too many rounds went by until we just chucked the cards completely. We simply stripped, and I poked her!

After that, we'd rehearse every day after school. Of course, what we were rehearsing was no longer suitable for the stage. There we were, two voracious thirteen-year-olds, awkwardly bumping, grinding, and panting ourselves into a heated tizzy. Mickey and Judy never had it so good!

Norland Senior High was where I landed after eighth-grade graduation. I really wanted to go to Miami Beach High, since that's where all the upper-class kids went, but something happened and the school district was split in half. Some of us were hauled off to Miami Beach while the rest of us poor suckers wound up at Norland. Whatta dump!

School really began to get on my nerves and I began to cut class to go hang out at the gay beach. Usually, I called the school myself and pretended to be my mother, telling them how horribly sick I was and asking if I could please be excused from class. Well, during one of these calls, the school nurse had the audacity to put me on hold and called my mother on the other line! Oh, I was flabbergasted! I mean, the nerve of her, raining on my parade.

The real clincher came later, in my sophomore year. I had just turned sixteen and I wanted a car desperately! But my parents said I couldn't have one. I was a little miffed. You see, by this time, I had pretty much alienated myself from my peers at school and was spending most of my free time with the boys at the beach. And since they were older, they could drive and go to parties in the Coral Gables, which for the boys was the hoity-toity place to be. They seemed so grown up, and I felt like such a baby. I wanted to grow up, too. I didn't want to be stuck at home watching "The Lucy Show" with my mom! So, I got an idea.

By now, my father had been promoted to maître d' at the Fountainbleu. He arrived for work at four in the afternoon, parked the car in his reserved space, and would get off at one the following morning. The car was sitting there for nine whole hours—entirely wasted! My eyes brightened as I began to plot. It was easy as pie. I'd sneak my mother's set of car keys to the hardware store, make a duplicate set for myself, and "borrow" the car while my father was working! This was too good to be true.

"He's So Fine" blared from the radio as the boys and I cruised downtown Miami Beach with the top down in my father's new blue '62 convertible Chevy. And there I was at the wheel! Unfortunately, my curfew was at eleven and if I wasn't home, I'd catch hell up until the next day. So we'd replenish the gas tank and the boys would drop me off at my house around ten-thirty, drive the car back to the hotel, and park it in my father's space so no one would know the difference. Well, this routine went on for several weeks until the dreaded possibility came true: My father got off work early.

Dad assumed the car had been stolen and called the police. The police arrived, and as they went through the process of filling out the report, suddenly the "stolen" car arrives, filled with mad, raving, lunatic queens screaming, "He's so fine, do-lang, do-lang, do-lang!" Darling, my do-lang was done in for sure!

When the boys were asked how they got the car, they handed over my duplicate set of keys and spilled the beans. My father was furious. He called my mother immediately to see if I was home. I had already gone to bed, but she came into my room shortly after and woke me.

"Your father's coming home. He wants to talk to you," she said with a nervous voice. I don't think she really knew what was going on, but I sure did. Oh, God. This was going to be The Night of Hell! Feel the terror! Hear the screams! See the shock as two suburban parents realize that the boys their son has chosen to run with not only painted the town—they painted their faces!

I wish it was that campy. I wish I could make it sound funny. But it wasn't. It was the most devastating, traumatic event I had ever endured. It was also the turning point of my life.

When my father came home, all hell broke loose. I sat on the sofa in the living room, listening to the floorboards creak as my father paced back and forth. My mother sat in her overstuffed chair, staring at me with concern. I felt so ashamed. I wanted them to drag out the noose and get it over with already.

"Are they your friends?" my father asked sharply.

"No."

"But they know your name. If they're not your friends, how did they get the keys to the car?"

Where the hell was Perry Mason when I needed him? I didn't know what to say.

"I don't know," I responded.

My father looked down upon me and his eyes smoldered. His voice was adamant.

"Yes, you do." He leaned into me. I was so frightened. So angry. What did he want me to say?

The large wall clock ticked the seconds away. Seconds before my life would be changed forever. I stared back at my father.

"Yes, they're my friends."

"Do you know what they are?"

"No."

"But they're your friends. Didn't you know that they were queer?"

My mother began to cry. Queer. The ultimate disgrace. A real man would rather die than be branded with such a stigma. The floorboards creaked as my father walked toward me again. The clock ticked. My heart refused to give out. Why couldn't I just drop dead and get this over with before he asked the dreaded question?

"Are you queer?"

Too late now. I watched his jaw muscles tense. I dared not say it. I couldn't.

"No."

Why couldn't he just leave it at that? No, I'm not queer. Yes, I have queer friends. Maybe I didn't know they were queer. Maybe I was too naive. I was young. Maybe they just used me for the car. But he wasn't buying it. And he grilled me repeatedly. Over and over. Finally, I couldn't take it any longer. I was so confused. I didn't know what to do. I didn't know what else to say. I had to come clean, and with one quick, emotional outburst, I let it all out:

"Yes, I'm queer! I'm queer!"

Tears were streaming from my eyes. There, it was over. The horrible truth of it all spilled out before them. I was so full of hate and contempt that I admitted it in defiance. Just to hurt him. At that moment, I had become everything my father hated. And what made it even more devastating was that he had legally adopted me only days before.

I was so upset, I broke an ashtray and slashed my wrists! Well, it was more like a scratch, but I was so caught up in the drama of it all, I didn't know the difference. And after all, it's the thought that counts, right? Suicide seemed the only dignified way out of this mess.

Well, it didn't take long for the little men in white coats to come along and cart me off to a correctional facility known as Youth Hall. Luckily, Georgette, another queen from the beach, had gone off the deep end himself just days before and his parents gave him the same treatment. So we shared the same cell and the same sorrows. There we were: two distraught, angry teenagers with nowhere to run, nowhere to hide; parents who didn't understand, and Connie Francis on our minds. Who's sorry now?

Youth Hall didn't help; it just made matters worse. I was angry and ashamed while my parents were distraught and confused. We were all so confused. No one knew exactly how to deal with what had transpired. All I wanted to do was protect them. I didn't want to hurt them with the answers to where I was going, what I was doing, and those with whom I had been doing it! But the truth did hurt them, and our lives together became muddled with fear, guilt, and misconceptions.

There was so much I had to learn, and it wasn't anything I could pick up from public education. All throughout a young adult's life, he or she is taught, "Be yourself." Be an individual! But the truth is, my dear friends, when one is too much of an individual, then he or she is condemned. And I was not about to put up with that hypocritical bullshit. I needed to hear answers, not crap. Just who was I? And what were these feelings I didn't understand? What do I do? Where do I go? And most of all, Why me? Questions like these haunted me throughout my stay at Youth Hall, and when it came time to leave, I didn't have any answers. But I did realize one thing: There was more to life than self-denial. And most importantly, there was more to me.

Russell, one of the friends caught in my father's car, had also become rather discontented with his home life. He was always talking about leaving Miami and running off to New York. Eventually, he became obsessed with the idea, and he wouldn't shut up about it for a minute! He'd rattle on for days about Greenwich Village and Times Square and how fabulous they were, and then he'd berate Miami as being a glitsy little facade with nothing to hold it up but a bunch of Southern rednecks! "But if we went to New York, it would be different," he'd say with a gleam in his eye. "There'd be no school, no parents, and we could do what we want. For once and for all, we could be free."

That's all I had wanted these last couple of weeks: to be free. Free of the guilt from hurting the two people I loved the most because of something I couldn't help or change. And since my home life had become strained and uncomfortable, there seemed to be only one true solution. I was going to run away.

CHAPTER 4

New York or Bustier

*T*wenty-three perfectly cut aquamarines sparkled brilliantly in the palm of the store clerk's hand. The crow's feet tightened around his dark eyes as he squinted, holding the bracelet into the light for a better look.

"Hmmmm," he frowned, raising his furrowed brow. "I'll give you twenty-seven dollars for it. Take it for leave it." He laid the bracelet on the glass counter. Take it or leave it? This was an expensive piece of jewelry that I had stolen from my own mother, for Christ's sake! Twenty-seven dollars didn't even come close to its true value. It was worth at least seventy-five!

Hell, twenty-seven dollars wouldn't even buy me a ticket to New

York. Besides, I didn't dare think to betray my own mother over such a petty amount. Why, I just couldn't! I wouldn't!

I did.

It was the only way I could think of getting fast money for New York. I really felt horrible about it and still, up until this writing, whenever a reporter asks how I got the money for the trip, I simply tell them that I had earned it from a newspaper route. I guess you could say I still feel a twinge of guilt.

I didn't leave Miami immediately. Russell began to have doubts and we sought refuge with a friend of his, an older man who had his own place. His name escapes me, but he was a nice guy and he let us hang out until we got our plans nailed down. One thing was sure—there was no going back home. Especially after I had pulled the braces off my teeth one afternoon at a bus stop with a pair of tweezers! Boy, that was painful, but not half as bad as my parents' reaction would have been. They would've lynched me for sure.

Russell eventually came around, and we set our departure date for June 25. He was still short of cash, so he stole some money from his grandmother and, between the two of us, we were able to afford two one-way tickets to New Brunswick, Georgia.

When we finally boarded the bus that morning at a depot in downtown Miami, we were greeted by fanfare from all the boys. They had met us there to send us off with a sha-boom! They were all so exicted, waving, crying, and carrying on like mothers sending their boys off to the war. Well, I tried to share in the enthusiasm, but the truth of it was I felt rotten. My stomach was doing back flips like a cheap poodle act in a one-ring circus.

My heart ached as the last traces of Miami slipped past my view while I stared out of the grimy bus window. We were on our way, and no matter how many times I closed my eyes, I couldn't block out the guilt. The fear that my parents wouldn't forgive me for what I had done haunted me like a ghost as we drove along.

As the day dragged into night, Russell jabbered on like a mindless twit about how exciting it was, running away for adventure in the big city. Finally, our dreams were going to come true, he reassured me.

Dreams. I didn't have any dreams. I had nerve. Plain, gutsy, risk-taking nerve. Oh, sure, I dreamed of not having to go to summer school, not having to abide by my parent's rules, and not having to be responsible. I had no ambition, and I didn't want any. I didn't need it because I was spoiled. I had never gone without, so how could I have possibly known what I wanted out of life? I had no idea what life was about. And there I was: off to New York, with no money in my pocket but plenty of nonsense in my head. My dream was that I wouldn't have to wake up and face reality. Well, I was in for a surprise.

The sun didn't shine the next morning as we pulled into the New Brunswick depot. The sky was black and the air smelled of rain. We got off the bus and made our way to the U.S. Interstate highway and began to hitchhike, but without much success. As luck would have it, a roar of thunder echoed in the distance, stirring up a frightful wind that spun us in circles and tossed us along the road like two driftless tumbleweeds.

Torrents of rain began to pour as we ventured down the road with our thumbs extended. The cars passed, one after another, and the farther we walked, the longer the road seemed. By now, the rain was beating down upon us like steel pellets, stinging our faces and soaking our skin.

Lightning bolted across the tumultuous sky and burst into a thunderous flicker of light. In the flash, we saw a small roadside motel with a neon vacancy sign blinking in its window.

Russell and I ran to the ramshackle place to escape the deluge. We scurried up the wooden plank steps and began to bang on the locked door as hard as we could. A fat, elderly woman wearing a housedress and curlers in her hair was sprawled behind the desk, her head thrown back, her eyes shut, and her mouth wide open, snoring like a motorboat! We rapped on the window glass with our knuckles, hoping to wake her.

Finally, the ol' gal snorted and grumbled, abruptly jarred from her nap.

"Huh? Who's there?" she quizzed, leaning over the desk, squinting to see through the rain-streaked window panes. She moaned as she lifted herself from the chair, waddled across the floor, and poked her face in the window. Her nose was flat against the glass as she leered at us from inside. Then, with a frown, she opened the door. A bell jingled.

"Yeah?" she barked in a husky voice, pressing her head into the screen door with a hand up on her hip. "Wha' da ya'll want?"

"We'd like a room . . . Please." Russell stammered.

"Eleven bucks a night . . ." she snorted, scratching her stomach. "Up front." She leaned into Russell with one eyebrow raised.

"Up front?" he asked sheepishly.

I hadn't a clue as to what "up front" meant, and I didn't dare ask, but since we couldn't muster up eleven bucks to save our lives, I was sure "up front" meant we had to put out!

"Yeah!" Her eyes bugged out and her whole face quivered with excitement as her tongue greedily licked the hairs growing above her upper lip. Oh, God! We were going to have to put out for sure! I was so repulsed by the thought, I slowly inched my way down the porch to a nearby soda machine. I reached inside the change slot, hoping to scrounch up a forgotten dime. Not a cent! And just as I turned to see the old bag about ready to throw Russell off the porch, the storm-ridden sky errupted into one big blazing riot of lightning and thunder! The darkness parted, split right in two by a horrendous bolt of lightning that was heading straight for me!

My mouth opened, my eyes popped, and my hair stood on end as—KABOOM! Out from the universe descended an unleashed fury which struck the soda machine with such force that not only was I dumbfounded, I was entirely ungrounded, and tossed thirty feet in the air, landing smack-dab in the marshy earth.

The old hag screamed and Russell nearly fainted. They were sure I had died right on the spot!

"Oh, my God! Oh, my God!" Russell cried as he and the woman ran to me in the mud. I was totally speechless, to say the least! I lifted my head and groaned. I could actually see and feel the rain pouring down upon me. Oh, dear God.

"He's alive!" screamed Russell.

You'd have thought he was Colin Clive and I was the Frankenstein monster, the way he was carrying on. But then, I was pretty shocked myself. It's a good thing I pulled out my braces before we left Miami; otherwise, I would have been Southern-fried for sure!

Well, as it turned out, that little shock-a-roo was just the ticket we needed! Russell and the old woman lifted me from the sloppy ground and dragged me onto the porch to dry me off. She felt so horrible about the incident that she said we could stay the night, providing we'd be gone the next morning and not tell a soul about the freebie. We crossed our hearts and hoped to die should such a thing slip off of our tongues, and, satisfied with our pledge, the old broad pulled out a key from her trusty pocket and let us into the door marked A-6.

The room was small, with cheap linens on the bed and plastic-coated yellow-flowered curtains in the window. Russell walked into the tiny green bathroom to hang his sopping clothes to dry over the shower rod while I stood before the medicine-chest mirror, staring at my face. Russell walked back to the bed and opened his drenched bag, removing what little he had packed.

"The storm should be blown over by tomorrow morning," he said, looking back into the bathroom. I watched as he unpacked his razor and shaving cream and then took notice of his long, cleanly shaven legs.

"Your legs. They're so smooth." I said with amazement.

"Smooth as silk. First thing I'm buying me in New York is a pair of high heels."

"High heels!"

"I got the legs for 'em, don't I?" he quipped, horning his way into the mirror with an eyebrow tweezer. I watched as he painstakingly plucked the perfect arches.

"Didn't think they just grew this way, did you?"

I knew about the rituals Russell enacted to "look pretty"—I had just never considered them for myself . . . until now.

All my life I had wanted to be glamourous. From the time I first saw Lola Flores glide across the silver screen to the day I discovered

Lana Turner. The procession to the church during the Epiphany. Fantasizing about my living-room shows with Nancy Hooch. Glamour! I wanted it so badly. And there I stood, with thick eyebrows, buck teeth, and hair on my legs! I was hardly the prototype for a starlet, I must admit. And if Russell was going to primp, pluck, and puff with powder, then so was I! So with a whisk, whisk here and a whisk, whisk there, the transformation was under way, and out from all that shaving cream were unveiled two of the most gorgeous gams since Betty Grable's!

"Ooooh!" I squirmed with excitement as I ran my hands over my new and improved sinewy thighs. "OOOOWE!" I meowed again as I reached farther down to feel the silkiness of my calves.

"Wow!" Russell exclaimed, awed by their supple texture.

Maybe I'd get a pair of heels myself! But the legs were just the beginning. By morning, I was completely made over, having donned a dab of Russel's blush, with a pinch of mascara and two finely tweezed eyebrows to match. We packed what stuff we had and left the tawdry motel, leaving behind my old self in the marred reflection of the bathroom mirror.

Back to the Interstate we went, and one afternoon while hitching through Savannah, Georgia, we happened to stumble upon a very old, dilapidated neighborhood.

Although the houses were weatherbeaten and unkempt, they still maintained their splendid Southern regality. They were proud relics of the past, with large towering columns, massive porches, and graceful balconies. The neighborhood exuded such charm; it brimmed with Southern hospitality. That is, until we realized we had landed ourselves right in the middle of a black ghetto! And keep in mind, darling, that this was in 1962, when racial tension was high between whites and blacks. These people were fearsome, staring at us with scornful eyes from the rotting porches of their once graceful homes.

They watched us like hungry buzzards circling their prey as we slowly trod down that lonesome street. I felt like the wayward lamb that had wandered into a treacherous jungle of hungry hyenas. And these weren't the laughing kind, either! They had no sense of humor when it came to white boys—especially white boys who looked like white girls!

Blacks were coming of age in America, and I was there to witness it first hand! No longer were they going to stand for the stereotypical Uncle Tom bullshit. Not that I had ever instigated such a stigma— although I got the feeling that I was going to be blamed.

In Puerto Rico, I had never heard of racism. We didn't classify people by color because there were so *many* colors of people, and we accepted one another because our families were accustomed to inter- racial marriages. I myself had distant relatives who were black. Hell, I didn't know what black was until I came to the United States. To me, a "colored" person was a cartoon!

What the hell were we doing in the middle of a black ghetto in Georgia anyway? We made a wrong turn, I suppose. Honey, for all I knew, a chit'lin was a white child floured, fried, and served with greens. And I was about to find myself in a pot, if I didn't get the hell out of there and quick! Russell and I ran so fast our shadows were left coughing in a cloud of dust!

Life on the road was interesting, that's for sure. There was always something happening. Once, while passing through Fayetteville, North Carolina, we climbed in the back of a car with four Marines inside. They were nice guys, and the driver asked where we were headed.

"We're going to New York," said Russell. The driver smiled.

"New Yawk?" he said in his Southern twang. "What're ya'll going up there for?"

Russell had some flippant reply, I'm sure. I, on the other hand, remained nervously quiet, pinned between two hulks with no necks and no hair. I was wondering if anyone of them had noticed the thin line of Max Factor traced along my upper lid. And if they had, what did they think?

Well, before I knew it, we were parked outside the Lucky Star Motel and Russell was inside having a free-for-all with two of the Marines, leaving me with the two hulks in the back seat to make quaint conversation! I was scared to death they were going to "take" me as well. After all, I was an innocent child, darling! Well, pretty much so, at least. I was hardly open to a gang bang. Why, the thought of it just made me quiver. But there was no need to worry, since Russell proved to be more than enough to go around. That boy put out in more directions than a Lazy Susan!

After Russell had entertained the troops, we were once again dumped alongside the road like homeless puppies. We were broke, we were hungry, and we wound up spending a night in a car graveyard to weather another storm because we couldn't hitch a ride. We were getting tired of it all and the next day, I decided to call home.

I called my parents, pleading into the phone, sobbing and carrying on about how sorry I was and how desperately I wanted to get back home. My mother was crying into the phone; she was so happy to hear from me that she and my father both apologized, telling me that they loved me and that they would send for me. I cried and told them I loved them, too.

My parents wired money to the local Western Union office in Fayetteville so I could purchase a bus ticket home. But when I got the money in my hands, I didn't purchase a return ticket for Miami. Instead, Russell and I went back to the road and pursued our journey.

Now I was really feeling guilty! But something inside told me to take the money and run. I look back and think, God, how could I have done this to them? They wanted me to come home so badly and I turned my back on them. I defied them. But I loved them. It's just that I was so distraught and confused. I knew if I went back, it would end right back where it started, with me wanting to run away.

And so we kept running.

We had no idea how cold it could get at night in June and we were shivering in our shorts and summer shirts when a trucker in a sixteen-wheeler tractor trailer picked us up in Philadelphia on U.S. 1. The driver was a nice guy who didn't seem to mind our objectionable demeanor. Actually, no one ever gave us any trouble. Perhaps it was because we were so young and could get away with looking pretty.

The trucker drove straight through New Jersey to Manhattan, and I'll never forget seeing that incredible skyline. I felt just like Dorothy when she first set eyes on the Emerald City! I was amazed by its overpowering presence and overcome with excitement as we drove closer and the buildings grew larger. And then down we went into the Holland Tunnel and surfaced to the crazed circus on the other side—New York City.

People were bustling, horns were honking, traffic cops were whistling, and all I could do was look up. It was just as I had left it, only this time I thought it was breathtaking. The trucker dropped us off right in the heart of Times Square, and we wandered to Eighth Avenue and Forty-second Street, where we were lost among a sea of movie theaters. It was 1962, *Cleopatra* was on one of the bills, and I was desperate to see the film, but we were running low on cash, so I curbed the desire and tried to concentrate on immediate priorities— such as finding a place to sleep.

We didn't know what to do with ourselves at first. Nor did we know where to go. We were so caught up in the moment. I was terrified and excited at the same time. Here it was: New York City, what life was all about. Now what do I do?

We managed to survive, having drifted into a cheap hotel and gotten a dismal little room to flop in while we spent our days wandering the streets. We tried applying for jobs, but nothing worked out. At fifteen, it never occurred to me that I was under age or that Russell was too loud a queen. People didn't want us because we were different. It was hideous. And after about three weeks of slamming doors with nowhere else to turn but the streets, Russell decided to bail out. He called his grandmother and she sent him cash for a bus ticket home. I wanted to go home, too, but I felt so guilty about having deceived my parents that I was ashamed to call them. Besides, I was certain they wouldn't ever want to see or hear from me again. So I stayed.

Forty-second Street and Sixth Avenue was the only place I knew. One day I discovered Bryant Park, which was where all the queens and hustlers used to hang. I mistook it for Central Park—that's how green I was! One afternoon while sitting on a park bench, I met a Puerto Rican queen who emphatized with my situation and took me under his wing. He took me to his boyfriend's apartment and they put me up for a few days.

Then I met some queens from Miami who were living in a seedy hotel on Seventy-second Street and Broadway. They were all crammed into one room, and made their living on the street, hustling their young virile bodies for twenty bucks a pop. At the end of the day, they'd pool their funds to make ends meet.

Since I didn't have a place of my own, they invited me to move in. Well, the thought of selling my body just sent me into a tither! I was a nervous wreck. I didn't know the first thing about it. First of all, how does one drum up business? I could just picture myself going door-to-door. And once I did land a prospective buyer, did I have to give a free demonstration? What about a money-back guarantee?

"Listen, this ain't like selling Girl Scout cookies, you know," sneered one of my roomies.

"Yeah," snapped another, chewing on the smoldering butt of a cigarette. "You gotta sell 'em your stuff, man. But you gotta do it so no one knows dat you're doing it. See?"

Not really, but I tried. Sometimes I think I could've made more money selling rocks! I walked those streets until one or two in the morning and usually ended up at Bickford's Coffee Shop, where a person could stay as long as he wanted, provided he had a full cup. And then, when I became restless, I'd go back out and hustle some more, hanging out in dark doorways or on street corners. I was so scared. I hated doing it, but I felt I had no other choice.

One night a man, in his forties, stopped me and invited me to his apartment on Fifty-fourth Street and Third Avenue. We talked for hours! He kept telling me about a young man he had fallen in love with, how beautiful he was, and how much I resembled him. He showed me pictures and gave me coffee. And then we went to bed. Nothing wild, nothing kinky. Very innocent, as a matter of fact. Like the kind of sex you have when you're with someone for the first time, and you don't want to offend or scare them.

Anyway, when it was over he gave me fifty dollars. Fifty buck-a-roos. The big five-oh! I was so elated, I went back to the hotel thinking I had struck it rich, and we all lived on it for three days.

The experience gave me renewed confidence. I decided to just stand on the street and wait, thinking eventually someone would come along, take me home, and fork over another fifty. Darling, there were many nights I just stood, waited, and froze! It just wasn't my forte. Whenever I was approached, I didn't know what to say. I didn't know what to do. And if I scored, half the time I'd forget to take the money! And when I did take it, I gave change!

I wasn't brazen enough. I had to be harder and tougher. You know, take the money and run—to hell with putting out! Not me. If I put out, I was thrilled to get paid, because usually I was too embarrassed to ask for money and simply gave it away! I was a disgrace to the world's oldest profession. There I was, practically starving to death, freezing my ass off on the street, and allowing myself to be taken advantage of without the nerve to ask for the cash. Honey, if I made ten dollars, I was happy.

But along with that thin moment of happiness came a heavy load of guilt. My parents were always on my mind. I had hurt the two people I loved most in the world, and felt that there was no possible way I could ever resolve what I had done to them. I felt so alone, I used to cry at night thinking about them.

Eventually I left the boys in the hotel. I don't remember why, but one day I just packed up my bag and left. I became a waif, straying from one rat hole to another, sometimes left to sleep on the street. A few times I slept in the subway, riding in the last car back and forth from Brooklyn to Manhattan until the early-morning rush hour. Usually, in the morning, I'd hightail it over to Grand Central Station, where there were shower stalls in the bathroom, and for a quarter I could get cleaned up. And if I was completely penniless, I'd sleep in the station on a bench.

On occasion, I found myself huddled up in an all-night movie theater where, for a buck fifty, I could sleep until the next day. Then there was the automat, a futuristic cafeteria lined with vending machines. Inside the machines were pieces of pie, cake, sandwiches, and fruit. I'd drop a quarter in the slot, have some pie, and just hang out.

Bryant Park was a haven for colorful characters and it was in this charming little thicket that I met the Duchess. The Duchess was a tall

American Indian who claimed to be a member of the Apache tribe. He was a strange-looking fellow in his early thirties with two long black braids, prominent cheek bones, and a very affected gravelly voice that sounded as if his throat had been rasped by vodka and sandpaper.

"I am the Duchess!" he would haughtily proclaim, with his nose in the air and not a tooth in his head. The Duchess of what, I wondered. The sewer? You see, the Duchess—or "Duchie" as I usually called him (or her)—was far from grand. He survived on welfare in a fifteen-dollar-a-week hotel. Some duchess.

The Duchess was also quite proud that he gave the best head around, because, as he often declared, "I gum." I didn't know from experience, but he bragged about it so often that I just assumed it was true. So there we were, in the park, not a penny to our names, with the Duchess babbling on about how beautiful he once had been, how he could still give the best blow job in all of Manhattan, and how he had a rich boyfriend—who just happened to be out of town!

But the Duchess wasn't the only grand dame on the block. Libra and Josie, two guys in their mid-twenties, far outshined him. In my mind, they were the true stars of Bryant Park. Libra was a platinum blonde who idolized Marilyn Monroe, and Josie was his counterpart, dressing only in black.

They never paid me any attention until one night Libra saw me at an after-hours bar on Eighth Avenue and Fifty-second Street. I can't remember the name of the place now, but it was a very popular hustler joint. I used to go there every now and then to hang out and hear the latest music. "Mickey's Monkey" was the hit song during the summer of '62 and Motown was pumping out stars such as Martha and the Vandellas and the Supremes. Mary Wells and Little Stevie Wonder were also on the horizon; we would dance the night away doing the Roach and the Mashed Potato while downing all sorts of pills. Uppers, downers, Tuinals, Seconals, Black Beauties, Escatrols. Anything at all. We didn't have a care in the world, and the thought of overdosing never entered my mind. If it was there, I swallowed it. It was that simple.

Usually, after a long night of trying not to hustle (but doing it

anyway just so I could make my ten bucks), I'd hurry off to Grand
Central Station to get cleaned up. I'd go into a stall, pull my compact
out of my bag, and paint my eyelids with gold and green glitter. And
this wasn't subtle, darling. It was very bold and very noticeable, as I
had glitter all the way up to my eyebrows and was wearing lots of
heavy black eyeliner. I had obviously seen *Cleopatra* by then and was
inspired by the film!

After spending thirty minutes in the stall, I'd saunter out of there
with my hair teased up front within an inch of its life and my eyelids
looking like a Bob Mackie gown! I swear, if Wayland Flowers was
around, he would have mistook me for Madame! But I thought I looked
flawless, even though I had completely forgotten to tease the back of
my head. So the hair in back was flat while the hair in front looked
like it had exploded from an electrical shock! Well, I didn't know the
difference. I thought I was the most glamourous thing to hit the scene
since Liz Taylor! That's how I dressed when I went to the bar, and
that's how I got nicknamed "Miss Peacock"!

Libra spotted me in the crowd one night and recognized me from
the park. He thought I had beauty-queen potential, but with my hair
all teased up like the back end of a turkey, he told me I looked just
like Phyllis Diller! I was devastated, but Libra—who was a full-time
professional beautician—popped me a pill, took me into the bathroom,
and proceeded to revamp my style.

We became close friends and I would see him nearly every day in
the park. Then one muggy August afternoon when a bunch of us were
gathered on a park bench, Libra came running across the lawn with
tears in his eyes, boo-hoo-hooing uncontrollably while waving the *New
York Post*. We didn't know what had happened, but whatever it was,
Libra was completely wrecked. And then we saw the horrible headline.

"Marilyn Dead."

The city of New York seemed so quiet that day. I couldn't believe
it myself. Marilyn Monroe—dead? It couldn't be true. Surely that
evening's paper would print a retraction, saying that they had made
a mistake, that it was the wrong blonde. But they never did.

Libra used to imitate Marilyn often—not so much her mannerisms as her persona. He adored everything she represented: sensuality and glamour with a comic flair. Libra would only wear white, and, with his white hair, he looked stunning. I used to hang out with him and Josie all the time. Then Libra's boyfriend was arrested for armed robbery, thrown in jail, and sentenced to three years! Libra was on the verge of a nervous breakdown, especially since he had lost Marilyn in the same week. To heal his wounded heart, he left Bryant Park and moved back home with his mother in Brooklyn.

In September, somebody found, stole, or borrowed a car (I'm not sure which!) and the Duchess, two hustlers, and I decided to run off to Hollywood. We couldn't afford any winter coats, and this seemed the only logical thing to do before the cold weather set in. Well, on the way, while passing through Shreveport, Louisiana, the Duchess was arrested for lewd conduct in a public restroom and thrown in jail! We didn't know what to do. None of us had any money to bail him out, and besides, we were in the middle of redneck country. Any one of us could've been next, so we got the hell out of there real quick. Of course, we promised the Duchess that we'd send for him once we got settled. But that could take months, maybe years. Hell, as far as I know, the Duchess is still in Shreveport!

The car broke down in Houston! So much for Hollywood. There we sat, stranded in a strange city of redneck homo haters so homophobic they were afraid to drink from a milk carton branded homogenized! Darling, these people—if that's what you call them; I'd rather refer to them as feeble-witted little toads who don't talk at all, but simply uttered words off their thick tongues as if they were spitting up gravy. Whatever they said, it certainly wasn't articulate. And I just adore articulate people. Not these narrow-minded hooligans in dusty pick-up trucks who despise anyone who isn't white or beer-bellied!

While the rest of the entourage chose to hole themselves up in a seedy hotel, my intuition was to get the hell out of there, and fast. This bigot-infested dust bowl was no place for a frilly little glamourina such as myself. I was desperate to get back to New York, but I was out of a car, I didn't have a dime, and I was in no mood to thumb it.

I didn't know what to do at first. Then the idea struck me. I went to the bus station and hung out for a while. I met an older gentleman who took me to a cheap motel on the other side of town. He did what he wanted and, once he had fallen asleep, I reached into his wallet and robbed him of all he had—ninety dollars.

I ran back to the bus station as fast as I could, sweat beading up on my forehead and my entire body quivering from nerves, afraid that I'd be nabbed and tossed in jail. I bought a one-way ticket back to New York for sixty-seven bucks and kept the rest of the money for food.

Much to my disappointment, everyone I knew in New York was gone except for Libra, who was off living with his mother in Brooklyn. So I was back on the streets again with nowhere to go except Bryant Park and the automat. I had also completely forgotten why I had left New York in the first place, which was because I had no winter clothes.

Since autumn had arrived and I was out on the streets, I caught a vicious case of street-walking pneumonia! I became so sick and weak with a fever, I wandered delirously into St. Vincent's Hospital, where I was stripped of my clothing, thrown into a nightie, and tossed onto a gurney. I had no medical insurance and no money, so instead of getting a room, I was laid up in the hall. They didn't even put a curtain around me. I had been plucked of all my pride and put on display for the world to see. At the age of sixteen, when most kids were cramming for trigonometry exams, I was turning tricks, living off the streets, and wondering when my next meal was coming. But what bothered me the most was that I gave up the senior prom for this kind of life.

Once the fever broke, I was tossed back onto the streets to hustle for my keep or sleep in Grand Central Station. I was certain that this was the price I had to pay for the grief I had caused my parents. So I paid it in full.

I went back to Bryant Park and became acquainted with a clever young man who was a professional panhandler. He would pretend to be deaf and dumb and suck off the pity of passersby. He wasn't doing too bad with that little change cup, and when we fell in love, he took me shopping. Well, I was so taken by his generosity that I moved in with him immediately! The romance lasted a short while until we both became bored and I packed up my new winter coat and hit the streets again.

I spent a year wandering from one gutter to the next, then one night in that after-hours club, I ran into Libra and Josie again. Libra was still trying to get over his boyfriend behind bars and just the mention of his name would send him into hysterics! He was coping the best he could and had left his mother's flat in Brooklyn to live in a cute little hovel on Thirty-eighth Street and Ninth Avenue. It was awful, right in the middle of the garment district, with trucks going by at four and five in the morning with deliveries. Well, Libra was so lonely and miserable, I decided it was my chivalrous duty as a friend to move in and keep him company.

Libra was working as a hairdresser and encouraged me to pursue a career in the art of beauty. After all, I had to do *something* with my life; why not do hair? It certainly beat doing men. At least that's what I thought at the time. I was young, you know. And the thought of making the world more beautiful by becoming a professional beautician sounded thrilling. I was so excited about this new adventure, but there was one catch: It cost a fortune to go to beauty school and I was lucky to round up ten bucks a night! It would have driven me to an early grave if I had to hustle up the five-hundred-dollar tuition fee! There was only one thing for me to do and the thought of it made me cringe. For the first time in nearly five months, I was going to call my parents.

Surprisingly, they were happy to hear from me and sent me a bus ticket home for a visit. I stayed with them for a week, but my restless nature returned and my father sat me down and leveled with me. He told me I wasn't going to be happy living at home and he asked what I had planned for my future. I told him and my mother about my plans for beauty school in New York. I wasn't going to be the doctor, lawyer, or engineer they had hoped, but I would at least have a skill and they encouraged the idea.

I felt good about my choice and felt confident that I could give good perms. And one afternoon while I soaked in the bathtub, listening to the Beatles and dreaming of teasing and spraying my way into the Bouffant Hall of Fame, an announcer abruptly interrupted "I Wanna

Hold Your Hand" with shocking news. President Kennedy had just been assassinated. My dreams vanished as I lunged up from the water and listened. It was as if everything became very still and very quiet, sort of like being inside the eye of a hurricane. Everything—my house, Miami Beach, the entire world—was so quiet. The only sound for the rest of the day came from the television, with my mother, my father, and I listening to the horrible details and seeing the same newsreel over and over again.

Then when the assassin, Lee Harvey Oswald, was taken into custody and shot by Jack Ruby on live television right in America's living room, I thought the world had gone mad. Everything seemed so crazy all of a sudden. It was as if the United States was turned upside down. No one knew what was going on. No one knew what to do. No one really understood what they had just seen. The shock was too brutal, and it left the nation with its mouth open, looking like my first victim in the Hollywood School of Beauty!

Once I was back in New York, I was thrust into a head-on collision with beauty school. Soon the fall had gone and Libra and I were faced with one horrible winter, huddled up in that cramped dump trying to stay warm while a deranged Latino drag queen known as Miss Lopez was down the hall banging on the pipes, screaming, "Mira, you cheap paego! There ain't enough gas in these pipes to make a fart!" Miss Lopez was always speaking half in English and half in Spanish, depending on which half of her mind was functioning at the time.

Miss Lopez was a large, rotund character who wore horn-rimmed glasses taped to "her" face, tight sweaters, pedal pushers, and house slippers! She was tall with a big gut, bigger hips, and a flat ass, and she stomped everywhere she went. That broad was a walking earthquake. And she was big on causing scenes. One of her favorite means of self-entertainment was having these unexpected outbursts of sheer insanity, jumping up and down, waving her arms into the air and screaming, "Woooo! Wooooo!" Those were the loudest, most frightening woo-woo's I had ever heard, but nevertheless, it didn't keep me from going to Times Square with her on New Year's Eve. I figured the only way to be safe in that mob was to be with a crazy person! I later learned that Lopez had been declared legally insane and was receiving a lifetime supply of welfare checks from the government! Some people have all the luck.

The apartment on Thirty-eighth Street was too small and too cold, so Libra and I, like two cuckoos flying South, hightailed it to his mother's place in Brooklyn, where it was warm. It was a nice place; a two-bedroom railroad flat in Brooklyn's Ridgewood neighborhood. Libra's mother was a colorful woman of Irish descent. She was a big jolly gal who always had a beer in one hand and a cigar in the other. She looked just like W. C. Fields in a beehive, and she even had a little red nose.

Her name was Rosie and she worked as a switchboard operator, as well as having a side job answering phones for bookies. Every now and then I answered them, too! I remember a guy named Louie would call, and I gave him the numbers by rattling off a grocery list. "Yeah, that's three heads of lettuce, two cans of corn, five pounds of potatoes . . ."

Rosie was a blarney-babblin', beer-guzzlin' gal who loved a good time. She was brassy and rowdy, with a hearty laugh and a heart of gold; a real buxom-blond, Irish momma *and* a bingo champ. And was she a drinker! Her favorite place to hang out was at a little pub down the block. Every Friday night she'd get all dolled up for a night on the town with her boyfriend Jimbo. And every Friday, Libra would drag her into the bathroom for what they called "Sissy Magic." Rosie would go in looking like a pie-eyed souse and come out with her hair all teased, sprayed and lacquered to perfection. Her face was all powdered and painted with pink cheeks and red lips; she was so adorable, she looked like a brand new doll out of the Woolworth's window.

Once we had sent Rosie on her way, Libra and I would get all dressed up to hang out in Greenwich Village. There were still a few beatniks around playing the bongos and reading poetry, and where Sixth Avenue and Eighth Street met there was a big gay hangout. We'd go there around nine at night and hang out on the corner and talk until two in the morning.

I remember one night we were standing on the corner, talking to some of the young hustlers on the block, when I happened to see a beautiful androgynous figure standing on the curb in the distance. He or she, whatever it was, was alone and appeared very aloof, not really paying close attention to what was happening in the immediate environment. It seemed more concerned with self-presence. Libra took notice as well, and when the young hustlers caught on to our curiosity, one shot up and said, "Oh, don't pay any attention to her. She doesn't talk. She thinks she's too good."

That, dear friends, was my first glimpse of Miss Candy Darling, a dark-haired eighteen-year-old boy who would later become an underground legend.

CHAPTER 5

Les Girlettes:
Jackie Curtis,
Candy Darling,
and Moi

"**I** saw Ingrid Super-star today and she was with Andy," I remember Candy saying in that breathy affected voice, her large doll-like eyes bright with inspiration. "Andy said he was going to put me in his next movie. If anyone can make you a star, Andy can." She chewed her gum softly with her mouth closed, and rolled her sultry eyes to the other side of the room, certain of her destiny.

Candy Darling was the quintessential Hollywood blonde, desperate for stardom. She craved fame, devoured glamour, and, like a ravenous starlet on the rise, her ego was insatiable. According to the boys on the street, she was a "snot-nosed bitch," and Libra and I weren't too eager to make her acquaintance after all we had heard. Besides, Libra was always so jovial and brusque, while Candy remained demurely aloof. Getting the two together would be like mixing a vodka martini with prune juice!

I learned from Libra that there was one golden rule to follow if you were a "girl" (an effeminate boy) on the streets. You had to be nice to the male prostitutes, or hustlers as they are commonly called. The hustlers were the ones who looked after the "girls" like me, buying us cigarettes, sodas, and candy. Also, they were usually of a rough breed, and if they became angered, they could pull a knife and kill you—or humiliate you to the point where you wished you *were* dead.

One night Libra and I were hanging out outside an ice cream parlor right on the corner of Eighth Street and Sixth Avenue. Candy was there, her eyes gazing longingly at the flickering neon of the busy intersection, appearing every bit the affected diva as she carefully licked an ice cream cone while the pagans scurried about the street beneath her.

"Hey, you gotta cig?"

I turned to see a street punk leaning into Miss Darling as she basked under the city lights.

"No. Sorry," she said, doing her best Kim Novak imitation, looking away from the hustler standing before her as her eyes fixed on the dazzling panorama of lights across the way.

"Hey, I think I like you. What's your name?" he asked, moving in closer.

"Who wants to know?" Candy continued to lick at the cone.

"Hey, you think you're something, don'tcha?" The kid snapped, cocking his head and stepping back.

"I don't think. I know. Now go on, you're blocking my light," Candy sniffed, lifting her chin in the air and dismissing him immediately. Well, with one quick sweep, the kid's hand came forth and shoved the ice cream cone into Candy's face! Miss Darling gasped; she was shocked and appalled. I was a little taken aback myself, especially with that cone coming out of her nose and her eyes crossed! There she stood on the corner, having just fallen off her pedestal when I, feeling sorry for the tramp, stepped forward in her defense.

"That wasn't very nice," I chirped, stepping back into Libra's shadow to avoid getting hit myself.

Candy unlodged the cone from her nose and tried to wipe away the mess with the back of her hand, then stammered in that affected Kim Novak whisper, "Well, I never . . . How, how could you?"

"Well, he did, sweetie. You gotta be nice to the boys," quipped Libra.

Candy didn't think she had to be nice to anybody. After all, she was (so she claimed) a distant cousin to Kim Novak, which made her upscale compared to the rest of us, I suppose. Libra, on the other hand, was the Earth Mother. She loved to take little stray things under her wing and nurture them. This she attempted to do that night with Candy, which is how we all became acquainted.

Candy was born James Jr. and he lived with his mother on Long Island. They had a charming little frame house surrounded by trees and flowers in a quiet neighborhood. It was very nice, and I visited them often, usually staying till the next morning, with Candy and me talking till dawn about boys, dresses, and movies.

Candy's parent's had divorced, his father lived elsewhere, and, as far as I know, the only other male influence Candy had was an older brother who had married and left home to raise a family of his own.

Their house had three bedrooms, but the extra bedroom was made into a library and filled with stacks and stacks of fashion magazines. *Vogue* and *Harper's Bazaar* were my favorites, and we would spend hours on end talking about famous models such as Jean Shrimpton, Verushka, and Twiggy, whom we idolized.

Candy's mother was something to behold. She was beautiful, sweet, and a lovely lady. A large portrait of her hung over the fireplace mantle. It was such a striking picture, and she looked just like a movie star. It was evident where her son had gotten his good looks.

I would go spend the weekends with Candy and his mother would make us breakfast in the morning. She was big on home-cooked breakfasts and made eggs, bacon, and pancakes. It was just like being home in Puerto Rico!

In later years, I learned that behind this quaintly painted facade lurked a darker side, where the colors all ran together into a twisted, murky world of delusion. Candy's mother was an obsessed movie fan. She idolized Joan Crawford and often wrote the star letters. She loved everything about Crawford and, I have been told, she was so obsessed with the star that she tried to persuade her son to take on the Crawford persona, which is what led to Candy's descent into transvestism. Candy's mother glowed whenever James would put on makeup and imitate the movie goddesses she adored.

Young James shared in his mother's obsession with Hollywood, and all he talked about were films from the Forties. He memorized certain scenes and would emulate the star's every move and gesture. He became caught up in the films he worshipped and believed he could be just as glamorous as the Crawfords, Garbos, and Harlows of Hollywood's past. His mind became warped with fantasy; he was lost in his own real-life melodrama starring his own creation, Hope Dahl, then Candy Dahl, and finally Candy Cane—that is, until she met up with Taffy Tits Terrifik, a fat hormone queen who (according to Miss Jackie Curtis) was also known as Taffy Tits Sarcastic. Anyhow, Taffy Tits used to drag Candy all over the West Village and say, "Come on, let's go, Candy, darling." And Taffy called Candy "darling" so often that it finally stuck.

Candy was desperate to live out the dream, and it wasn't unusual for him to turn to me and say, "Holly, let's pretend we're famous movie stars and we're getting ready for a big premiere. I know, I'm Hedy Lamar and you can be my girlfriend, Zazu Pitts."

I should have smacked him! Why the hell was I always stuck being the less glamourous one in these games? I was just as gorgeous, mind you. Couldn't *I* have been Hedy Lamar just once, for Christ's sake? NO! Candy had to be the star. He wanted to be the attention-getter, the one who was adored by all, even in his dreams. To be honest, Libra and I just didn't always understand Candy. He was on another planet thinking he was Hedy Lamar half of the time. I didn't really get it at all, and for a while, I thought he was a little cracked! Let's face it—he was! But then, aren't we all?

I use the word "he" because at this time, Candy wasn't living as a woman. He just looked like a very pretty boy in makeup hiding behind dark sunglasses, his face peeking out of an upturned trench-coat collar. I guess he was trying to be Humphrey Bogart and Ingrid Bergman, all rolled into one! Who knows? I referred to this as Candy's Audrey Hepburn stage. And although he dressed as a boy at home and his real name was James, even his mother called him Candy.

Candy and I had one common interest: We both wanted to wear fabulous gowns and be glamourous. We didn't have much in common besides that, but once we had gotten to know each other, I realized that there was more to this person than the aloof exterior that shunned the world. She wasn't so bad after all.

Candy would call Libra and me from her mother's house and talk for hours about old movies. I wasn't into old films myself and neither was Libra, but we listened nevertheless and the conversation usually ended with us planning to meet in the Village during the upcoming weekend.

Usually our escapades in Greenwich Village were the same week after week. Candy would take the train in from Long Island and Libra and I would hop a subway in Brooklyn and we'd all meet at a coffee shop or on a corner and walk for hours on end, Candy jabbering on relentlessly about Lana Turner while I listened intently and Libra watched over us both. The Village was wild in those days. It wasn't the safest place to hang out, but it was the only place where we could be ourselves without much hassle.

One night around two in the morning—long after Candy had taken the train back to Long Island—Libra and I were making our usual rounds around the block when a big ol' Buick cruised up alongside of us. We both turned and looked, but couldn't see much inside, and the car drove on. Two minutes later, the same car drove around the block again. We looked again, and this time we caught a glimpse of the guy driving. He was cute, with dark curly hair. Libra turned to me and said, "He likes you." "No, he likes you—you're the blonde!" Libra insisted it was me he was pursuing, and after his fourth time around the block, I was convinced that I was indeed the one to get lucky!

Finally, the Buick pulled over and parked against the curb ahead of us. As we walked by, I was very nervous and couldn't even muster enough courage to say hello. But Libra—in all his brazen glory—sauntered up to the passenger-side window and said, "Which one do you want?" Libra wasn't one to beat around the bush—he simply mowed over it!

The guy expressed his interest in me and Libra shot me a glance and said, "You're on your own, baby." And he kept walking. I nervously got into his car and my heart began to race as we drove to a dark street. Exciting love scenes flipped through my mind like the pages from a cheap romance novel. What if he tore off my clothes, ravaged me with his jack hammer, and tossed me in the gutter? Or worse, what if he didn't?

We made small talk for a while, and after I learned that his name was Jack, his favorite TV show was "My Favorite Martian," he was twenty-two years old, and worked as a pressman for a big city newspaper, I figured he was okay to kiss. That's when I learned that he was straight and only kissed women! There I sat with my lips puckered, ready for love, and all he wanted was some head! The nerve.

Now, I'm sure you are all wondering why a straight man would have any interest at all in a feminine little thing like myself? Well, that was just it—I was feminine. So feminine, in fact, that I was usually mistaken for a girl! And for a straight man during the early Sixties who wanted to, shall we say, "release himself" without having to do it himself, a young man who looked like a young woman was the safest way to sexual gratification without the hassle of courting, condoms, or shelling out bucks to a hooker.

He asked me if I wanted to do "anything." These straight men. Hell, yes, I wanted to do something. I wanted to go shopping! I wanted to see a movie! I wanted to be romanced over a pizza pie, for Christ's sake. I didn't want to put out and be thrown out like some floozy. That was just a fantasy in my mind. I wanted to be Doris Day! And since I was shy and I wasn't entirely comfortable with the idea of "doing it" in a car with someone I had just met, I bade him farewell, hopped out of the car, and raced around the block to find Libra. We carried on like schoolgirls at a slumber party, gabbing on about how handsome he looked. Then came the dreaded question.

"What happened?" squealed Libra, squirming in his pants with anticipation. "Did you see it? Did you do it? What was it like?" Libra was spewing out so many questions I thought his mind was going to short-circuit and blow up.

"Nothing happened," I said as we made our way down Christopher Street.

"Nothing?" Libra stopped dead in his tracks and seemed to shrivel right there before my very eyes.

"Nothing," I reiterated. Libra's eyes sank.

"You didn't even feel it?"

Libra was shocked and mortified. I was a bit frazzled myself.

A week later, we were walking around the same block when the Buick cruised by again! It was the same routine, only this time when I got in the car, I was determined to feel it! If not for my sake, for Libra's! And I did. And it felt good. And so I felt it again. Oh, dear. Then I got a little reckless (the harlot in me had begun to surface by now!) and I reached inside his zipper. That cheap pulp novel was flipping through my mind again and getting cheaper by the minute! But whenever I reached in for a kiss, he'd turn away.

"I don't do that with men," he'd say.

"I'm not a man, I'm a goddess!"

I thought if I appealed to his Greek sensibilities, he'd think I was Aphrodite and take me by storm. Or at least by my body! These trysts went on for several weekends, but we never went all the way. I just couldn't—I was much too terrified. And the thought of being caught by the police—can you imagine the humiliation? Sodomy was illegal, although I really didn't know this myself. I thought sodomy was a cute little name for a poodle! Or is that Salome?

Nevertheless, one night as I was getting out of his car to find Libra, he happened to ask where I lived. When I told him, a look of disbelief came over his face. Surprisingly enough, he lived two blocks away from Libra's place, where I was staying! So we drove around the block, picked up Libra on the corner, and he drove us home. We chatted all the way back to Brooklyn and I began to like him. And since I assumed he wasn't a maniac, when we arrived home I gave him my number as I was leaving the car.

Everything worked out perfectly. Libra came home from work at five, Rosie was out until seven, and I usually strayed in from school at noon. Jack worked nights and he came over during the afternoons and we talked for what seemed like hours. We talked about everything from the weather to religion, when all along the only thing on our minds was sex! I don't know how it would happen, but we'd eventually get around to taking off our clothes, have a quickie, and off he would go until the next afternoon. I felt cheaper than a whore at a clearance sale.

After a while, once our nerves had settled, Jack warmed up. He wasn't so eager to get out of bed and the sex got longer and longer and warmer and warmer. Jack began to fondle me and hug me and treated me more like a real person, not some love doll with its legs in the air! And then one day, in the heat of passion, he kissed me. Right on the lips! That's when I knew how it felt to be truly fulfilled. The seed had been planted, the fields had been plowed, and a romance had blossomed!

A couple of months had passed and Jack, who was still living with his parents, started to talk about our moving in together. I was all for it. It was getting rather cramped in that little railroad flat, so I began to pack my bags.

Jack found an apartment in Queens underneath the Myrtle Avenue El—the elevated train. That train rumbled louder than an earthquake, and shook the building so much you never knew where the furniture would wind up next! The apartment was yet another railroad flat, which we entered through the kitchen. From there, you walked through to the dining room, past the bedroom, and into the living room. It was the perfect love nest for newlyweds.

Jack told the landlord that I was his wife since, by this time, I was wearing very subtle makeup and my hair had grown to shoulder length. I was thin and very pretty, and since a lot of people mistook me for a girl anyway, we figured no one would know the difference. Also, I thought since Jack was basically straight, he'd prefer me looking more like a woman than a pretty boy. Ah, what we do for love.

Long hair, eye shadow, and a pair of earrings seemed to do the trick, but I wanted authenticity, darling! And it was a friend of Libra's who introduced me to the man who could make it possible. His name was Dr. Benjamin, and he had successfully treated sex changes in the past. I went to see him immediately for female hormone shots, and within a few months, I was looking damn good in a tight sweater! The neighbors took it for granted that I was Jack's wife, and since my street friends had called me Howie, I changed the "w" to a pair of "l"s and added a "y." Ta-dah!

My change into womanhood was a gradual one. My breasts developed slowly and to complement my figure, I wore hip pads. I felt so comfortable with my new identity because it was easier for me emotionally and mentally to pass as a pretty girl than a funny-looking boy. When I was a boy, I got harrassed and had to endure ridicule. When I was a girl, I got whistles! No longer was there a struggle between me and society. I was gorgeous! And also, I just felt so much better inside. I gained confidence and became more outgoing. Otherwise, I was just a fag. A misfit. A thing. And I was miserable because I felt like a freak of nature. But when I put on a dress, fixed my hair, and painted my face, I became a true human being—and it was then, for the first time in my life, I felt worthwhile.

Jack was happy. He liked my newfound breasts, and best of all he loved me. And I did everything to please him. I was a happy housewife, in Queens, a role I imitated by watching Mary Tyler Moore on "The Dick Van Dyke Show." I'd get up early in the morning, make breakfast for Jack, putter around the house, and talk to Betty next door. It was just like television, the way I thought it was supposed to be.

Jack worshipped me as a woman and the only flaw in our near-perfect marriage was that I was still attending beauty school . . . as Harold! Every morning after breakfast I'd have to get dressed in jeans, a nondescript blouse, high heels, dark glasses, and take the subway to Times Square, where I'd dash into the subway bathroom, take off my makeup, change into my sneakers, pack Holly into a gym bag, and re-

sume my previous identity. Then when I got out of school, I went back
to the subway station, changed back into Holly and became a wife again!

This *pas de deux* went on for quite some time, and needless to say,
I hated it. The bathrooms in the subway were filthy, they smelled of
urine, and attracted every low-life in Manhattan! Plus, I was starting
to get confused! My life had become a revolving door to Harold and
Holly, and there were times I didn't know who was coming and who
was going! There was one day when I accidentally came into class
wearing my lipstick because I had forgotten to take it off! Then one
day I walked right past the subway bathroom, took a deep breath as
I climbed the school stairs, and showed up in class as Holly. After all,
the school was in the middle of Times Square, and everyone was so
loud and crazed anyway, I figured no one would know the difference.
Taking this into consideration—not to mention the fact that I was
studying makeup and hair—I simply thought they wouldn't mind.
Well, they did and I was promptly summoned into the director's office,
where I was expelled immediately.

Well, kiss my chocha! Who needed that drug-infested dump anyway? Jack was making a good living, so why should I learn about
beauty? What's there to study? You either are or you aren't and I was!
Case closed. And with that little load off of my mind, I became a full-
time housewife. I painted my nails, I painted my face—I even painted
the apartment!

Libra came and visited often. Jack liked Libra because he was a
good, responsible person and he trusted me with him. Candy visited
us as well, but Jack disliked her. Nonetheless, Libra and I still hung
out with Miss Darling on the weekends in the Village, and when Jack
finished work he would pick me up in the wee hours of morning and
take me home.

It was around this time that Jack told his parents he was living
with a girl out of wedlock. Living in sin was unheard of in the early
Sixties, but I just loved it! Jack's parents weren't too thrilled, but once
they met me, they fell in love. I was quite a charmer, darling. Still
am! But let me give you a quick tip—it's all in the eye makeup. I
must admit, my eyes are my most captivating feature. They could melt

a heart of stone with one soft glance, and when it came to Jack's parents, that's just what they did!

We went to Jack's parents' home for dinner often, and I became very close to them—but not close enough that they knew the REAL family scandal. But believe it or not, eventually it did come out. I forget how. But one day Jack was telling them how special I was . . . and then he told them how *really* special I was. Boy, were they floored. But after a while, the smelling salts brought them around and they just accepted the fact and it was never mentioned again. Odd, but true.

I always wanted to look like a fashion model, and Jack kept me dressed to the nines. Everytime I stepped into Macy's I walked out looking like I was the diva of Myrtle Avenue. Candy admired me for living as a woman and liked my sense of style. She would often come over to borrow something to wear and spend the entire weekend. Personally, I didn't mind, but Jack wasn't too thrilled because he thought she was a pig. "She never takes showers," he used to gripe. Well, Candy had this quirk about bathing. She was clean, it's just that she always waited until we were asleep before she'd take a bath! Back then she was very fanatical about the possibility of being seen nude. If anyone—man, woman, child, or dog—ever got a glimpse of her (or rather his) genitalia, it would send him/her into a state of devastation. Candy was so uptight she would get up at three in the morning to bathe and then go back to bed!

I really hate to say that Candy was a pig; it sounds so callous, being one myself! It's not as if we ate out of troughs, mind you, we were just born to have handmaidens. Then perhaps I should say she was a piglet. That's sounds rather cute and gets the point across nicely, doesn't it? After all, Candy never cleaned up after herself when she stayed over. She would dirty the dishes, fill up the ashtrays, and leave the entire apartment in disarray after I had spent the entire weekend cleaning! She had no shame. Once she borrowed one of my best dresses and returned it in shreds, claiming she was nearly raped.

Candy loved to get smacked around by men, and she always seemed to get the most pleasure out of it in my clothes! She loved to suffer. Her favorite song was "Ninety-Six Tears," and she would sing it right in the middle of the street in that soft, breathy voice she had perfected so well. "You've got to cwy. . . ." (She was trying to master the cockney British inflection, so she pronounced her "r"s as "w"s, and pronounced "tears" as "te-ahz.") And there she stood with a babushka kerchief tied around her head, wearing dark black sunglasses and scarlet red lipstick as she clutched her collar tightly around her neck and leaned to the right, singing to herself, "You've got to cwy . . . ," sounding like a cross between Kim Novak and Elmer Fudd!

She cried every one of those tears on the corner of Seventh Avenue and Christopher Street, and had the nerve to tell me she was going to be the next Garbo! I really thought this was a crazy woman, but we had one thing in common: We were both boys in women's clothing and we were often misunderstood by the masses. I suppose these fantasies were her way of making it better.

Soon Candy had become a full-blown transvestite and was living entirely in drag. She had finally left her mother's house (even though her mother didn't mind having her son in drag), and moved in with Jack and me for a while—until Jack had a fit and she eventually moved into a rooming house off Gramercy Park.

Candy had a friend named Semour who lived in the West Village. He had a color TV and one night Candy and I went over to his place to watch Barbra Streisand's "Color Me Barbra" TV special, and that's where I was introduced to an interesting-looking fellow by the name of Jackie Curtis. Jackie was an aspiring actor/playwright who worked as an usher at the Winter Garden Theater, where Streisand was starring in *Funny Girl*. Candy wanted to hear all about the theater, and since Jackie also shared her interest in films of the 1940s, the two hit if off famously.

Curtis wasn't in drag when we met him, and he never really wanted to be a woman, but putting on a dress was a way to get Andy's attention. Jackie, who was born John Holden, lived for a while with his grandmother, Slugger Ann, who ran a gin joint on the East Side by the same name, where Candy eventually worked as a waitress. Jackie was the madcap redhead of our trio, and she had a passion for pounding at the typewriter keys while poking her veins with amphetamines. As a matter of fact, Curtis was so taken by the drug, she decided to make it herself with a chemistry set in Slugger Ann's basement! She slaved for hours over those bubbling vials, trying to concoct the right recipe, which would catapult us all into orbit. I wasn't too trusting, however, and prefered to get my fix from a more reliable source in the back room of Max's.

But God bless Curtis! She tried her damnest, although I fear she had more success in making her own cigarettes. Curtis loved to smoke and always started the morning off with a big, fat puff. Often, she would sit before her typewriter with a cigarette in her hand, one in her mouth, another in the nearby ashtray, and a cocktail at her side. Then she'd flip on the TV, turn down the volume, watch "I Love Lucy" and type up a storm. I can't tell you how many of her plays were fabricated around the shenanigans of Lucy and Ethel! Curtis would watch and type, watch and type, filling in dialogue she couldn't hear for the comediennes on the screen.

Curtis, like Candy, longed for fame and glamour, although Curtis's glamour was truly something I shall never forget—nor shall I hope ever to see again! Jackie Curtis walked around town in ratty house-dresses, snagged nylons, and unruly hair, with her face painted up like a cartoon! But she thought she was glamourous, taking bits and pieces from the film stars of the 1940s and modeling her own deranged sense of vogue, a style that was not favored by the family. The following conversation between Curtis and her mother was recorded in Curtis's unfinished autobiography, *A Storm of Kisses*, which she began writing around 1972 while living above the Eden Theater.

"If you don't dress right, Curtis, you'll never get on TV," warned Jackie's mother.

"But I do dress right," defended Curtis. "People try to copy me, they really do."

"Oh, Curtis, please," the mother said. "What are you doing with your life?"

"Listen, Ma," Curtis barked. "What are you going to say when I win the Oscar?"

"Nothing."

"Nothing? What do you mean nothing?"

"I can't be proud of you in an evening gown, Curtis. It's okay to wear those clothes on the stage, but all the time? Why all the time? Are you *that* way?"

"Am I what way?"

"*That* way!"

"Do I look queer?"

"Curtis, you were born a man," she said emphatically. "A man!"

"Ma, how can I be shaming you? Whose kid do you know that's on the cover of every newspaper in New York City? Whose?"

"Yeah," she said. "But look at you. How can I walk down the street and hold my head up when they see you looking like the bride of Frankenstein?"

It was true. Curtis did look like the bride of Frankenstein, but she thought she was the best thing to hit the beauty scene since Max Factor! Like Candy, she lived to be famous. And I respect that now, but at the time I didn't get it. I didn't know they were "artistes." Candy was much more pragmatic about the issue of fame, while Curtis was the fearless go-getter. Curtis was shrewd, assertive, and knew that being a "star" wasn't all glamour; it was business as well.

Despite our differences (I was the least impressed with stardom), we all became close friends and frequented the Village nooks often, hanging out, drinking coffee, reading poetry, and thinking we were esoteric. We shared some of the most tearful moments of our tortured little lives together in those coffee houses. One such moment was the day Candy lost the last tooth left in her head. It was harrowing! There we were in Ratners, a big Jewish deli, when Candy started stuffing dinner rolls into her handbag. Well, she started to bite down on one and CRACK! The roll was hard as a rock and Candy gasped, immediately putting her hand to her mouth. "Oh my God, Candy, oh my God, no! Oh my God . . ." Jackie cried.

"Oh my God!" Candy said, repeating after Jackie.

"Oh my God . . . oh my good, good God . . . Oh, God in heaven!" Jackie wailed. Bellowing "Oh my God" was one of their favorite pasttimes, and this time they had reason to wail since Candy was entirely, undeniably toothless.

Often Jackie, Candy, and I would visit with friends, one of whom was a woman named Barbara who ran a cluttered little junk shop on Bleeker Street. Barbara was a gypsy beatnik relic from the Fifties who was always smoking pot, dropping acid, and feeling groovy. She was very esoteric, living in the back of her store and indulging in free love with other free-spirited souls such as Bob Dylan.

By this time, Candy was spending time with me on a regular basis. One night while hanging out at Ratners coffee shop with Candy and Taffy Tits, Taffy introduced us to an ugly, chubby-cheeked fat boy with a pug nose and big eyes who turned out to be a pain in the ass. The kid was only fourteen years old and already he was trying to get into drag! He looked horrible, particularly since he hadn't the slightest idea what makeup was all about, and when we first caught sight of him, his face looked like a paint-by-numbers travesty! We grabbed him as fast as we could and told him immediately that lipstick was for the lips only—and under no circumstances should it be used as eyeshadow! Darling, we turned that awkward, puberty-stricken disaster into a glamourina who became known as Little Chrysis, named affectionately after the Greek legend.

Little Sheba was another fat fourteen-year-old thing we met in the Village. Little Sheba was a little monster who terrorized the West Village ruthlessly. He would dress in drag, pick up guys on the street, haul them into a hotel, beat them silly, and rob them blind! He had no shame, the tramp! And barely out of puberty, too. Sheba popped pills, shot speed, and wallowed in the bowels of the gutter. There was no return for this poor lost soul. About a year and a half later, at the age of fifteen, Little Sheba was found dead in a hotel room. The poor thing had been beaten and stabbed to death. The life of a street queen wasn't pretty. This was one Little Sheba who was not coming back.

CHAPTER 6

Thoroughly Modern Holly

*T*he Sixties took off like a skyrocket and exploded into a tumultuous fury of race riots, political protests, and rampant chaos. The nation which had so long prepared for nuclear war and the onslaught of the Russians would not be so prepared for the turbulence of the civil rights movement and Vietnam.

Marilyn was dead, Kennedy had been assassinated, and the Beatles had invaded the airwaves. A wicked shift in trends began! Girls looked like boys, boys looked like girls, and in the middle of the insanity Martin Luther King was fighting for equality. Kennedy's Camelot was definitely headed for ruin.

It was one upheaval after another. Gone were the straight-laced, clean-cut Mickey Mouse Club prototypes of the Fifties, and in came the love-beaded hippies on their quest for peace. Flower power, free love, and LSD were calling to the youth of the day. And while Frankie and Annette were content to frolic on the sands in California, the real world was in despair, dropping acid while blasting Janis and Jimi, hoping to find some escape from the turmoil through the new psychedelic craze.

It seemed as if everything was affected by this maddening revolt against tradition. Boys were burning their draft cards, women were on the verge of burning their bras, and Andy Warhol was making masterpieces out of soup cans, silver helium balloons, and Brillo pads. He had turned the art world on its head with his crazy, off-beat shows and was soon to be known as the King of Pop. I can remember seeing him in the newspaper and not thinking much of the white-wigged man. I actually thought he'd be like the latest fashion trend: in one season, out the next. Little did I know.

The most popular places at the time were The Dom and Serendipity Three. The Dom was a large club that featured the Velvet Underground, a band with a tall Swedish blonde named Nico, who had a monotone voice that sounded like a cross between a truck driver and Marlene Dietrich. Nico would be singing while movies were being projected on the screen behind her. Libra and I would take speed and dance all night and, when inspired, we would take colored oils and mix them between two sheets of glass placed on an overhead projector. Our wild psychedelic designs would then be projected on the wall. We thought it was far out.

Serendipity Three was another place we used to frequent. It was an ice cream parlor/boutique nestled in the very chic Upper West Side, and was largely patronized by the fashion set from *Vogue* and *Harper's Bazaar*. The fashions were divine! The British mod look had swept the nation, and all the girls had boyish figures and short-cropped hair, lots of eyelashes and eyeliner, Kewpie-doll lips, long legs and clunky shoes. At the helm of all this madness were the likes of Mary

Quant, Yves St. Laurent, and Courreges (who revolutionized fashion with the creation of a flat go-go boot with tiny slits in the sides, a knot in the front, and an open toe).

I had an eye for fashion and a sense of taste, but I was hardly prepared to, or in favor of, trading my fabulous frocks for unflattering fatigues. Army fatigues, if you get my drift. Or perhaps I should say "draft"! It was in 1964 on my eighteenth birthday when I too was awakened to the horrendous reality of Vietnam by a letter from Uncle Sam himself. Well, if Sammy wanted to see me at the draft board in downtown Brooklyn, I best get my ass down there and make an impression. So I called up Libra in hysterics and shuddered, "Darling, the draft board wants to see me! How am I going to get out of this one? Help me!"

"Honey, you won't go to Vietnam!" Libra hollered into the phone. "Leave it to me!"

"What should I do?" I asked in a panic.

"Become a platinum blonde!"

"Become a what?"

"Don't move, I'll be right over."

And with that, Libra rushed over with vats of bleach, two Tuinals to kill the pain (that much bleach hurts!), and a bottle of vodka. Within an hour, we were so high, Libra poured the vodka on my head and nearly drank the bleach! When it was over, I felt like Carole Lombard but looked like Carol Channing.

I didn't want to get drafted, but I did want to look my best for the boys. Perhaps I'd get discovered and stage my own USO show. Move over Maxine, Patty, and Laverne! I was going to entertain the troops now with my very own boogie-woogie bugle-blowin' jamboree!

Libra accompanied me to the draft board the following morning. I arrived in hot pants and sandals, with a dab of blush for color. The minute I walked in the joint, there was one big wolf whistle. Every eighteen-year-old Italian boy from Bensonhurst had shown up, and they were hootin' and hollerin' over my outrageous getup. I was scared to death, but I had to do what I had to do.

Needless to say, we caused quite a stir. So much so that I was immediately escorted into the doctor's quarters while Libra waited outside and passed out his phone number. When I entered the doctor's office, he peered at me over the top of his spectacles and said with concern, "Hmmm, well, what do we have here?"

"Service with a smile, honey. That's how I'm going to serve my country."

"Remove your clothes please," he said, adjusting his stethoscope to his ears.

Naturally, I complied and pulled off my tank top. When the doctor noticed my chest, he stopped me from removing anything else.

"I'm on hormones," I told him.

"Well, that'll be enough. Nurse, excuse this young man from duty."

"C'mon," she said, dragging me by the elbow to her desk, where she grabbed a large rubber stamp and blotted it on a red ink pad. "Sorry, sonny—it's 4-F for you."

Oh, well, so much for olive drab and reveille. Now how the hell was I going to get this bleach out of my hair? It was useless to even try, and the only alternative I had was to buy a brand-new wardrobe to go with my brand-new image, which I proceeded to do at Macy's with a charge card Jack had given me on our anniversary. Oh, how I cherished that Macy's card. It was a prize that gave me the most pleasure and Jack the most regrets!

I ran amok through that store with no conscience whatsoever, having discovered the true joy of being a woman. I found my thrill on Blueberry Hill during these rapturous romps, and the thought of a bill arriving never entered my pretty little head. Oh, the delight! Just the thought of those overstuffed shopping bags would make my panties twitter! I didn't know it at the time, but I was a sick woman.

At first, my Macy's mania started out small. You know, a teensy toaster here, a coffee pot there. And what kitchen is complete without a blender, a mixer, and an auto-defrost Frigidaire? Down with dishpan hands! Out with beige housedresses! Forget those rollers in the hair! Darling, I was going to revolutionize the role of the Sixties housewife. If I couldn't be a real model, then I'd be a role model, and I did everything but stay in the house! "Out of the apron and into chiffon," was my motto. And back to Macy's I went, where I unearthed a monumental discovery: designer wear!

And monumental it was, particularly when they tallied the price! I ravaged those departments from top to bottom, and came home with boxes stuffed with blouses, skirts, dresses, stockings, scarves—and another toaster! This one was a deluxe model that not only toasted the bread, but sliced and diced it into tiny croutons. Oh, the joy of modern-day conveniences! I even bought myself a five-hundred-dollar cerise suede suit, which came with a blue silk charmeuse blouse sprinkled with matching brown paisley. It was a stunning outfit, borrowed continually by Miss Candy Darling. As I said earlier, Candy admired my taste in clothes . . . so much that I had a hard time getting her out of them!

I loved to shop and I paid no attention whatsoever to the prices of these little expenditures. Well, when the first bill arrived, I didn't know whether to have paramedics on hand to save Jack's life or the police on call to save mine! Instead of relying on outside sources, I got myself dolled up, made a fabulous gourmet feast in my new toaster oven (I was very creative that way), and greeted Jack at the door with a big smile and an even bigger martini. He, of course, knew I was up to something, and when I nonchalantly broke the news that we were two thousand dollars in the hole, I realized I should've made that martini a triple! Jack combusted right on the spot, so powerfully I thought there'd be nothing but a charred little mound left in his brand-new chair.

Once I had doused the volcano with another drink and tempers had quelled, we both came to a somewhat rational, sensible decision. He thought it was sensible. I thought it was a bit too rational. But I went along with it nonetheless, to save my life as an insatiable charge-o-holic: I was going to get a job and pay the bills myself! Oh, the horror of it all. Gone were the days of posing glamourously in my designer wear by my Frigidaire. I was going to become a career girl.

I was pissed off! There I sat, my butt stuck to the vinyl of the kitchen chair, chained to the table like a fallen queen, my face being eaten alive by the classifieds! Believe me, I've had more fun reading a cereal box. But since this was the only way I could possibly redeem myself, I perused the available opportunities eagerly, although I was quite perplexed as to what I could do. I just had to do something! And then I saw it! There it was in black and white . . . my calling:

"Help Wanted."

Well, it sounded good so far.

"Experienced Dog Groomer. Full time. Excellent salary. Apply in person. La Rue's Dippity-Doo Doggie Boutique."

How fabulous! What could be more fulfilling than spending the day with man's best friend? How hard could it be to groom a dog anyway? After all, I was a near-graduate of the Hollywood School of Beauty. If I could glamourize a woman, then a dog would be a piece of cake! Half of those broads were beasts anyway! So I sat there and chewed on the thought for a while, picturing my name scrolled in pink across a frilly lavender smock with pink earrings and rubber gloves to match. What an ensemble!

"Scrub a dub-dub, three poodles in a tub!" I would sing to the little pooches as I lathered them up in a flea bath. Just imagine the possibilities! A bouffant for a Lhasa, a beehive for a poodle, and bumper bangs for a Pekinese. And the thought of bleaching the shit out of a shitzu just made my day! I could do their nails in frosted pink and tie their tails with bows to match! I was going to revolutionize dog grooming and turn haggard hounds into prize-winning prima-doggies!

Then I thought, "How on earth would I put lipstick on a dog?" They have no lips! At least, none that I've ever seen. Nor do they have much of an eyelid, and the bottom of their nose is a mouth! Darling, these creatures are completely wretched looking! No wonder they're covered with fur! And their tails . . . how on earth does one style a tail? Should I tease it, curl it, or hide it? Worse yet, what if it's not a tail at all, but a mere stump! Then I pictured myself trying to coif a pit bull, but all I could forsee was shooting it to put the poor thing out of its misery.

Well, so much for being a dog groomer! Perhaps I'd be a better air-traffic controller? I could wear one of those cute little blue uniforms with the wings pinned to my lapel while blowing a whistle and waving two flashlights. And what kind of experience does one need to be a traffic cop in the sky? I'd blow a whistle, wave my lights, shake my can, and jiggle my jugs as I helped those handsome airline pilots down to a smooth landing right into my braless bosom!

My eyes were nearly crossed from looking at those classifieds and my pencil was worn to a little nub. Should I be a dental assistant, dairy clerk, or donut dunker? A sales woman, fry cook, or organ grinder? No matter how exciting, dismal, or demeaning the jobs seemed, they all required experience; the kind I did not have. I was helpless with despair. I didn't need a job, I needed a cigarette! And I needed it fast. Well, just as I struck a match to light one up, there it was! Smacking me in the face from the inside cover of the worn matchbook were the blessed words "Want A Job? Become A Key-Punch Operator!"

What the fuck was a key-punch operator? I didn't care. I was so desperate, I would have punched Mother Theresa. I read onward. "If you want a high-paying job that's rewarding and fulfilling, the Magoo Key-Punch School is for you!" It didn't sound all that exciting, but with the right wardrobe it might be glamourous. I began to wonder. Could this be the answer to my frustration? Was this the skill I had been looking for? I, too, could be among the movers and shakers of the city, leading a fast-paced exciting life in a glamourous high-rise as a key-punch operator. And before the vision had a chance to dissipate in my head, I dialed the number immediately.

What a mistake! Five weeks into the course, I wanted to punch myself. The only rewarding moment I could foresee of this job was going home! So I punched out of class and went back to the classifieds. Jack wasn't too pleased, but I told him I'd find a job if I had to steal one to get it. So I trudged on, scrutinizing the paper, pounding the pavement, and wracking my brain. Finally I sat back, threw my arms in the air and sighed, "Holly, Holly, Holly. Out of all those years in school, what is it that you excelled in most?" And then I thought harder.

Surely there must've been something I had learned that could be applied to the working world. After all, I didn't spend all of my time with a towel on my head singing to Connie Francis records! Well . . . maybe I did.

As a last resort, I stumbled into an employment agency and pleaded for them to place me into any position except on my ass and in the street!

"Well, I don't know," minced the snooty, hatchet-faced prune as she mulled over my application through the wire-rimmed spectacles resting on the tip of her aquiline nose. "You can't type, take shorthand, work a switchboard, use a Dictaphone or a ten-key punch. What can you do?"

I almost blurted, "I can go to lunch and shop at Macy's, bitch," but I refrained. And I thought again. Hmmmmm. I began to bite my nails, which hadn't been filed in weeks, and that's when it hit me: filing! I knew the alphabet! I could become a file clerk. Honey, if I could file my nails, I could file anything—and within the hour I had a job at JC Penney's on Seventh Avenue and Sixty-first Street, filing my way into oblivion. I felt like a new woman as I embarked on my new career.

Every morning I'd go through the drudgery of getting showered, painted, and plucked just in time to race out the door to catch the early-morning subway into Manhattan. Rush hour is not a pretty picture, especially when *I* was trying to be very pretty. I put my life on the line every time I boarded that train and became trapped among the thousands of other drones crammed together like cattle. I held on to the riding straps for dear life because if I was to let go—WHOOSH! Like a small leaf that falls into a babbling brook, off I would go with the pushes and shoves of the moving crowd. And God only knows where I'd wind up.

By the time I got out of that sardine-stuffed monorail monstrosity, I had been goosed, groped, poked, prodded, thunked, pinched, squeezed, bruised, and insulted! I would leave my apartment looking great, but by the time I surfaced into the city from the depths of hell, my skirt was twisted, my blouse was unbuttoned, and my hair was in such disarray that I looked as if I had been mugged. This wasn't a ride—it was an assault!

Needless to say, when I stumbled into the office I was ready to throw back a double. Going to work was an exasperating experience, but doing the actual job was even worse! Then again, things were working out, and my life as a little Sixties yuppette was smoothly rolling along until one dark day in the elevator. While making idle conversation, a woman asked if my real name was Hollis. Hollis? What the hell kind of name is that, I thought. I had never heard of it before, and to me it sounded rather masculine. For days afterward I came to work in a shroud of paranoia and silk chiffon, wondering to myself if she knew about my true gender. People thought I was in mourning.

Well, truth be known, trying to find an exciting career in filing was like finding peanuts in a piccadilly plant. There ain't no such thing! So one day I went to lunch, tossed back a cocktail, and never went back. I was tired of working in that stuffy office with the same old girls, so I resumed the role of a glamourous housewife. Little did I know that Jack would one day say, "Holly, it's time to get another job!" Didn't he know any other line? That's right, the Macy's bills were piling up again! So back to the agency I went.

It didn't take long for me to find myself buried under tons of tissue paper that represented every kind of currency in the world. Yes, I had landed yet another glamourous filing clerk position, this time at American Express. And I was up to my head in drachmas and yens.

Meanwhile, on the other side of town, Candy had landed herself a file clerk position at an investment firm on Wall Street. She did well and later became the front-office receptionist. We usually met in Battery Park for lunch with our brown bags or, on occasion, she'd sneak into my office and we'd go eat in the employee cafeteria, where we chowed down on Stouffer's dietary delights.

On the weekends, we would hang out in the West Village at Rienzy's Coffee House on MacDougal Street, where we'd listen to poetry readings and become very esoteric, drinking coffee and tamarind juice until our bladders were about to burst. Candy was going through her intellectual phase, and everywhere she went, she carried a copy of Tolstoy's *War and Peace*. Personally, I think she hollowed out the center and used it as a makeup bag! I mean, she hardly looked like a book worm. Her translucent skin was powdered white, and her lips were painted a bright fire-engine red, the latest from the Revlon "Fire and Ice" collection. While the rest of the women were wearing very pale pinks, Candy was out to carve her own niche in the world of fashion: part Bohemian and part Vampira! She had a unique appearance, to say the least, and in all honesty, there were times I was embarrassed to be standing beside her. When she wasn't wearing my clothes, she usually wore a tight black skirt, black fishnet stockings, sling-back pumps, and that same old trench coat tied so tightly around her waist I was surprised she could breathe! Naturally, her collar was turned up, which added mystery to her persona and made her resemble Audrey Hepburn in the movie *Funny Face*.

Once again, I grew tired of my job. Tired of the same old girls, tired of the same old gossip, and tired of handling other people's money. So, I went out to lunch, threw back a cocktail, and never went back.

Shortly thereafter, I found myself on the seventh floor of Saks Fifth Avenue as a salesgirl in the Seventh Heaven Boutique. I was very impressed with myself, being a Saks girl, even though all I did was sell useless trinkets—you know, fountain pens made of ostrich plumes, marble eggs, and other expensive junk with which people clutter their lives for no good reason. We also carried one-of-a-kind designer dresses and scarves.

After a while, Seventh Heaven was becoming retail hell. Then one day, while strolling through personnel, I noticed an opening for a house model. Sashaying through the store in fabulous frocks was definitely my calling, especially since I had known no other aspiration in my life than to be a model and to ride on a Rose Bowl float. So I applied and got the job.

Well, there I was! Sauntering around the fifth floor pushing the exclusive collections of Oscar De La Renta, Geoffrey Beene, Yves St. Laurent, and Sophie Gimbel. (Sophie was the wife of the Mr. Gimbel who owned Saks, so Soph had her own salon.)

Now that I was a model, I felt it imperative to look my best at all times, even in slumber. For you peons out there, that means I slept in my makeup! I wasn't about to take it off after I'd spent hours putting it on. I did, of course, have touch-ups about four or five times a day.

My eyes had the creased look, very Garboesque. I would put the eyeliner right on top of my eye where the lid creased, and I wore big false eyelashes with a ton of mascara on them. My head was well stocked in hairpieces and falls, something no fashion models of the Sixties could be without, and I had more hair piled on my head than any one woman should be allowed!

I loved the women's fashions of the Sixties, but no matter how much I accessorized with my big plastic clunky jewelry, no matter how glamourous the gown I wore, I couldn't get over the painful shame that lay hidden in my panties. Yes, I had everything a woman of the day could desire: a beautiful husband, a fabulous wardrobe, every electrical appliance imaginable, a Macy's charge card, and a glamourous career. What I didn't have was a muff! And I'm not talking about the kind that keeps your hands warm, either. And although I didn't dwell on the fact, it usually came to mind after I'd made my rounds and returned to the dressing room with the rest of the girls. They'd all be getting gussied up, smoking cigarettes, and chewing the fat while I struggled to make my winkie stay dinky, pulling it back and strangling it between my butt cheeks! What a pain in the ass!

Every day was different. Some days I'd put on a different dress every half-hour and model it through all the departments on the floor. Then there were days when we had private fashion shows for exclusive clients. It wasn't as glamourous as I thought, having these chi-chi old broads pawing at me and trying to find the price tags cleverly hidden under my armpits!

"Oh, you're too skinny," they would whine. "Are you sure you're wearing the right size? That doesn't fit well in your rear at all."

How much of this abuse could I take? I was getting tired of these cranky old broads with more money than God pushing and pawing and then bitching about the price. That's when I realized that people with money weren't always happy and I swore that such misery wouldn't happen to me. Not that I was going to spend the rest of my life poor, mind you. I just felt that when my haul came in, I'd know where to shop. And with that little notion filling my head, I went to lunch, threw back a cocktail, and never came back.

I landed modeling jobs at various fashion houses including Morris Metzger's, where I modeled sportswear for buyers—usually fat old men. Smelly cigars rolling between their lips, they often groped me, acting as if they were interested in the fabric when what they really wanted was a quick fondle! They even came into the dressing rooms where the girls were changing just to get a quick peek, the pigs.

Then, after I had downed a cocktail and kissed modeling good-bye, I became a file clerk in the Hounds Department at the American Kennel Club. It was here that I became tight with an alcoholic lesbian named Carol. Together we would go to lunch at the bar, around the corner on Madison Avenue, and get loaded. We would then go back to work, stick our heads in our files, and fall asleep. One day I was napping on a stool that I used to roll around on, and as my snoring head sunk deeper and deeper into the file, my body rolled further away on the stool. Then BAM! The stool shot out from under me, and my head jerked out of the file as I was thrown to the floor.

Carol came running over, picked me up off the floor, and hugged me to her double D's.

"Oh, Holly! Are you hurt?" she asked, holding me tight.

"No, I'm okay. Just a little shaken, that's all," I managed to say, smothering in her bosom.

Carol had just broken up with her girlfriend and was feeling a little lonely when she decided to turn her desires toward me. Well, I hated to break the poor dear's heart, but I thought if I leveled with her about my true gender, she'd realize that I wasn't the woman for her. So I revealed the big secret, and much to my surprise, she craved me even more!

She invited me over for dinner one night, and we were drinking and smoking grass when the next thing I knew we were in bed! If you're confused, imagine how I felt. I might have had some delusions before, but now I was really snapping! I was assuming the female role with Jack and the dominant lesbian role with Carol. It was like the time while I was going to beauty school, when I'd leave the house as a woman and get to school as a man. My mind was in a whirl again, and having a penis wasn't helping any.

The thought of a sex change haunted me, and Jack—who had been saving for the big day—was close to having the thirty-five hundred dollars it would take to pay for the operation. The time was getting closer and my nerve was getting weaker. I was plagued with second thoughts. What if they make a mistake? No operation is one hundred percent foolproof. What if they goofed? What if I didn't look real? Or what if it didn't feel real? What if I came out looking like a freak?

I even thought of Jack. What if he didn't want me anymore? Maybe he was a frustrated homosexual who couldn't make up his mind. What if *I* didn't want *him* after I got the operation? Day in and day out, these thoughts congested my mind and, to make matters worse, when I finally fell asleep after lying awake worrying, I was terrorized by nightmares.

Just as I was dosing off I'd feel a strange sensation, as if I was on the edge of a very high cliff. Everything around me was very dark, and suddenly I would drop off into the abyss. I'd be falling slowly into the darkness, descending deeper into the bottomless space, screaming as loud as I could. It was weird, because I knew I was in bed and I knew Jack was beside me, but I couldn't stop falling, no matter how loud I screamed.

Finally, I would lunge up from the bed in a cold sweat, shivering with fear, and scream. Jack was always dumbfounded and thought I was losing my mind.

"Why didn't you help me?" I yelled. "Why didn't you wake me up?"

It was horrible. For a while, I was having the dream everynight, and I became so terrified of having another that I'd stay up watching TV until I finally nodded off from exhaustion. These dreams continually haunted me until years later, after I had become "Holly Woodlawn."

A sex change, I thought, would put an end to all of my problems. I wasn't much of a man, and I was so much more comfortable being a woman. Also, I thought it would bring Jack and me closer. Our relationship had become tainted with sexual frustration because Jack never wanted to touch my penis. And after all of the female hormone treatments, my testicles had shriveled and I couldn't have an orgasm. I couldn't even masturbate because I could barely achieve erections, and when I did, I'd work myself right up on the edge of a climax and then poof! Nothing would happen. It was terrible.

This frustration led to my getting my thrills in other ways, such as picking up strange men while hitchhiking into Manhattan—and even that started to take its toll. I was feeling guilty for fooling around on the side, and I was unhappy with my inability to be satisfied sexually. Finally, no matter how frightened or unsure I was, a sex change seemed like the only way to go.

I was fairly ignorant as to how a sex change would affect my sex life—although I had heard about several transsexuals who seemed to lead normal, happy daily lives. Pat Moran was one of them, a notorious transsexual from New York who often cruised through Times Square in a sports car to pick up male hustlers. Another was Coccinelle, a famous French transsexual who was the star of the Crazy Horse night-club and an entertainer with the Folies Bergère in Paris during the 1950s. Then there was Lady April Ashley, who became the scandal of London society when it was learned that her title was contrived not only from marrying a lord, but also under the knife of a surgeon! And what all-American, red-blooded woman-to-be wasn't aware of Chris-tine Jorgensen, who had about as much spunk as June Cleaver! She was such a nice lady, but hardly a role model for me. I wanted to be notorious and gorgeous, not prim and proper.

I was definitely influenced by these miracles of modern-day science, and since the operation worked for them, I felt certain it could work for me. Of course, I was entirely ignorant as to what the medical procedure entailed, nor did I have a clue as to the pain involved. When a man becomes a woman, he undergoes a series of operations. The first step is to remove the testes. The second step is to remove the muscle tissue from the penis. The nerve endings are left intact, and the penis is turned inside out and plugged with a long, narrow shaft. The flesh heals around the plug, thus forming the vaginal canal. After the plug is removed, cosmetic surgery is performed to construct the labia and clitoris—not to mention the insertion of breast implants and a lifetime supply of hormone treatments. Then the doctors toss you out on the street and say, "Good luck, honey!"

At the time, though, when I was certain I was going to have the operation, I never once felt like a woman trapped in a man's body. I felt more like a man trapped in high heels! I was never miserable with my body, but for some strange reason, I played up the notion that I wanted to have "it" cut off.

One Saturday afternoon while deliberating the issue, I wandered into the salon where Libra was working to get a "do," and he introduced me to a new hairdresser named Enrique. Enrique was a shy, tall, skinny kid from Cuba with short, dark blond hair and a very feminine face. He was not a queen by any stretch, just very androgynous, with a soft voice and the most beautiful feminine hands. Enrique wanted to become a woman and asked me if I could give him some pointers. Immediately, I introduced him to the doctor who was treating me with hormones. Well, the next time I saw Enrique, he had blossomed into a blonde named Julie and became a hit with all the straight men because they loved her exotic looks, her flavorful accent, and her helpless femininity.

Julie lived in an apartment that glowed with wall-to-wall candles. She had pictures of saints plastered everywhere, and at first I thought she was very Catholic, but it turned out that she was practicing Santeria, a white voodoo intermingled with Catholicism practiced in the Caribbean.

Julie not only practiced voodoo, but she swore up and down that she was a medium. I didn't believe her at first until one night she went into a trance, started doing the hee-bee jee-bee dance, and brought down her guardian spirit, a two-hundred-year-old Cuban slave woman named Michaela who smoked cheap cigars and drank rum. Michaela was incorrigible, and often possessed Julie's body without warning and drank, smoked, and carried on something fierce. And the worst part of it was that Michaela hated Julie in drag. She would become violently upset, screaming that she wanted Enrique. Then Julie, possessed by the spirit, started ripping off her dress. This always scared the shit out of me, and there were times when I thought about calling over the boys from St. Patrick's for an emergency exorcism! It was terribly frightening, but once Julie had undergone a complete sex-change operation—which she later did in 1968—Michaela left her body entirely.

Julie's first big dive into womanhood happened when she and Libra moved upstate to work as beauticians at a chic little resort in George-town. Julie left New York as a man and arrived at the resort as a woman! It was the first time she was experiencing life entirely as a female and she was loving it!

While Jack was hard at work saving money for my vulva, I was out carousing! I would take the train upstate on Friday night and party with the "girls" the entire weekend, dancing in cheap bars and picking up straight men. The men always thought I was loose, but after I had gotten them all hot and bothered, I wouldn't put out. I was a nice girl, I couldn't go all the way. At least not yet, anyway.

One night Libra's boss lent us his Ford Fairlane so we could race through town, blow the horn, and burn some rubber. There we were, out on the town for a night of frolic, with Julie in the back teasing her hair, Libra in the front smoking a cigarette and popping downs, and me clinging to the wheel for dear life. I was painted to the hilt, but my eyelashes were so thick that I couldn't see a thing! We were having a riotous time, nonetheless, smoking, screaming, and laughing as we blazed our sordid trail down Route 96. My chin was pressed to the steering wheel as I squinted to read the road signs as they whizzed by, while the two maniacs screamed directions: "Turn here! Go there! You passed it! Where are you going?"

In a fit of sheer frustration, I let go of the wheel, threw my hands in the air, and told them to drive! Well, I can't remember what happened next, but the road was yanked from beneath us and we were tossed, turned, and spun into a tither! When we finally came to our senses, we found ourselves stuck on the edge of an embankment. Julie had been thrown from the backseat into the front and was in a heap with her hair on the floor and her legs in the air, with Libra underneath her demanding to know why I had stopped in this God-forsaken pit in the middle of nowhere and if could someone please find his cigarette. I didn't understand how I got my head stuck in the steering wheel, but an even bigger question in my mind was how to get it out.

Somehow we managed to ooze ourselves out of the pile of wreckage and tried everything we could to get it back on the road, but it was no use. There was no budging it. So we left the car in the ditch and we three glamourinas hitched a ride into town, planning to return the next morning to try again. Well, when we returned the next day, we didn't find a car at all. It was gone! And all that was left in its place was a black mound of charred steel. We were shocked. Libra had forgotten about the burning cigarette he had dropped in the seat during the accident, and the car had gone up in flames.

I, of course, immediately hopped the next train back to New York and never laid foot in Georgetown again!

In the fall of 1966, Jack forked over the dough for the big change. I was not about to go through this alone, and since Jack had to work, Julie, who was back in Manhattan, was going to travel with me to Johns Hopkins Medical Center in Baltimore to lend her support during this trying time. I was leaving New York and coming back a new woman! I was more than thrilled—I was petrified!

When I arrived at Johns Hopkins, however, I was told that I had to wait a year for my womanhood. It wasn't that there was a terribly long waiting list the doctor explained, but that I had to live in drag for a year.

"But I've been living like this for four years!" I insisted.

"That may be the case, but we have to keep you under psychological analysis to prove that you can live with the change," he said seriously, folding his hands on top of his desk.

The nerve! I had been living as a woman long enough. I deserved my own snatch, but they refused, and so, in my despair, I went on a mad shopping spree! And after I had blown the wad that Jack had slaved to save, I thought that if I returned home pussyless *and* penniless, I'd soon be lifeless for sure. So, in my fear, Julie and I took a cheap little apartment in Baltimore and hid there for a month. When we returned to New York, I moved into a rooming house and eventually called Jack. I apologized, confessed my sins, and pleaded for him to take me back. I felt bad for Jack because I had run out on him, and I felt worse for myself because I was out of money.

Meanwhile, on the other side of town, Candy had teamed up with Jackie Curtis, and they were doing their second production of Curtis's play *Glamour, Glory, and Gold*. They had done this production previously, but then the lead role of Nona Noonan was played by a real woman. The show was such a success they decided to go for a second run. Candy had recently finished a show called *Give My Regards to Off-off Broadway* (written by Tom Eyen, who also wrote *Women Behind Bars* and *Dreamgirls*) and her reviews were so impressive that the director, Ron Link, cast her in the starring role for the show's revival. Candy was so excited, she bleached her hair at a salon called Valley of The Dolls on Tenth Street and was never the same again!

Glamour, Glory, and Gold was an insane folly, and I was given a featured role as a showgirl. Most of the actresses doubled up on parts, while the male roles (all ten of them!) were played by a kid named Robert DeNiro. If they only knew what lay ahead for that young lad. I had a scene with him in which he played a Jewish producer; I was auditioning for him and he felt me up. I think he felt up the whole line of us, actually. It was a ball!

DeNiro's mother owned a print shop and she printed all the programs and posters for the play. When Link ran out of money, DeNiro was given the original artwork as payment. Actually, this poster caused quite a ruckus among the stars. Candy and Jackie were having hissy fits because they both wanted their names to be bigger on the poster, but since the printing had already been done, there was nothing Link could do. So, Candy and Jackie, their feathers ruffled, tossed their roles to the wind and haughtily walked away from the production. Well, birds of a feather gotta stick together, so I walked too.

Then one day, while I was at home mulling through my recipe file, I received a startling phone call from Candy.

"Holly, Andy's been shot!" she cried on the other end. "It's horrible."

"What? Who got shot?" I asked, horror-stricken.

"Andy! Some crazy woman walked into the Factory and tried to kill him!"

I couldn't believe what I was hearing, but it was true. That afternoon—June 3, 1968—a disgruntled Factory player named Valerie Solanis barged into the Factory and fired three slugs from a .32-caliber automatic pistol into the King of Pop. She then shot a Factory visitor, Mario Amaya, and attempted to shoot Andy's business manager, Fred Hughes. The news carried over the airwaves worldwide, and it made Andy a bigger celebrity than he had ever dreamed.

Valerie was mentally disturbed and Ondine, one of the earlier Superstars, had once said the bitch was cracked and Andy was nuts for ever letting her into the Factory to begin with.

But who was to know that this nut was any different from the rest of the lunatics who hung out in the Factory?

Although I didn't know Andy personally, Candy worshipped him, and when I learned of the attempt on his life, I felt terrible. Miss Darling was in hysterics, calling me on the telephone and keeping me posted throughout his surgery.

"Oh, Holly, it's horrible. The doctors are having to put together his entire insides. They don't know if he's going to make it." And then she'd start bawling again and tell me she'd call me later. I turned on the television set. During the news, Viva, one of the biggest of all Superstars, flashed onto the screen to comment on the shooting. It was a horrible tragedy. Andy's life was at stake and so was Miss Darling's career. As I said, Candy idolized Andy, and she socked all of her faith into his making her a star.

During all this trauma, Julie had taken an apartment on Thirteenth Street with another hormone queen named Tamara. Tamara was a crazy Cuban who worked as a belly dancer in straight bars around Manhattan as well as upstate. Julie loved to tantalize straight men, and got the idea of becoming a stripper. Tamara gave her some pointers, but told her that her tits were too tiny.

"A big bust means big tips, doll," said Tamara, who jiggled her generous double-D's for dollars at Wanda's Strip-O-Rama in New Jersey. Well, Julie was destined to become a star jiggler herself, and traveled to Yonkers for a new pair of honkers. Julie couldn't afford to stay in a hospital, so she had the job done on an out-patient basis. I went with her to lend my support, and when it was over, Miss Julie was in such pain she couldn't breathe! Whenever the cab hit the slightest bump on our way home, Julie would scream and faint.

When I finally got her home, she had to lie on her back for a week, and when the bandages were finally removed, one tit was going East and the other going West! Then, to make matters worse, Michaela, that crazy drunkard of a spirit, came down and tried to rip out the silicone! I had to tie Miss Julie to the bedposts so she wouldn't do herself any harm.

When Julie was fully healed, Tamara tipped her off about a bar upstate that was hiring. Julie packed her pasties and hopped the bus to fame and fortune as the star slut of Syracuse. Every weekend I hopped the train to visit. Julie was making loads of dough, and all she had to do was shake her can and jiggle her jugs. And the best part of it was that she was having fun. Well, during one of these weekend jaunts, while she was showing me around town, we ran across a bar with a sign in the window that read, "Go-Go Girl Wanted. Apply Within."

"Holly, why don't you take the job?" Julie grinned.

"Me—a cheap go-go dancer?" I gasped.

"Yeah! Go on," she encouraged with an elbow in my ribs.

"Oh, how fabulous!" I gushed, jumping into the air. We ran into the bar, where I applied and was hired on the spot.

The next day, I ran out to the five-and-dime and bought everything I needed for a cheap getup. I wore bikini panties with fluorescent flowers I had made out of crepe paper, strategically placed around my crotch to hide any flaws in my character. It really wasn't that difficult to pull off, since all I had to do was tuck myself between my legs.

When they turned the black light on, I lit up like Las Vegas! I had a little neon garden of flowers growing between my legs, and little fluorescent flowers adorning my nipples while I danced to the Bee Gees' "To Love Somebody."

I loved my work—and it beat being a file clerk, that was for sure.

Go-going on the weekends became my new career, and I always came home with no less than two hundred dollars in my pocket.

The bartenders would give me some change, I'd play five songs on the jukebox, and that was my set. In between sets, I'd be hanging out with the guys at the bar, while Julie was in the next town, stripping for the local Lions Club!

It was during these weekend trips that Jack had begun to see another woman—and a real one, at that! When I found out, I decided it was best for us to separate for a while, so I packed my bags and moved upstate with Julie.

One night while dancing in the bar, I met this goofy-looking guy named Virgil who swore he was head over heels in love with me. He was around twenty-one years old and lived with his parents in a huge house on a pig farm. He was very nice, always bringing me candy and flowers, and soon I got to liking him myself. Well, we were becoming quite chummy when suddenly he invited Julie and me to spent the weekend at his folks' farm. I was charmed by the invitation and accepted.

Julie and I showed up on their front porch conservatively clad in our picture hats and chiffon dresses, looking about as prim and proper as two Sunday-school teachers! I knocked on the wooden screen door and was greeted by a dowdy middle-aged woman in a pink housedress and an apron. Her graying hair was combed back in a chignon and her eyes twinkled like the stars as she welcomed us with open arms.

"My lands, you must be Holly!" she exclaimed, fanning herself with her hand, she was so taken aback by my overwhelming beauty. "Virgil said you were a beauty, and merciful heavens he's right!"

I quickly introduced that cheap pig-slut friend of mine, Julie, and hightailed it into the kitchen, where our tummies were entertained with fried chicken, biscuits, and sweet potato pie. Well, while I munched on the yams, Virgil fondled my gams as he sat conveniently beside me at the supper table.

Virgil's parents were very friendly and making such a fuss over us that I began to think something was weird. Then I discovered that Virgil was going to ask for my hand in marriage! I was plucked! I just wanted a roll in the hay—not a walk to the altar! Besides, this kid hadn't the slightest idea about the devastating truth behind my womanhood. And devastating it would have been, since this was one very strict Christian family. To think they had the nerve to imagine I was a virgin!

The parents also had no idea how Julie and I earned our living. All they knew was that their son, Julie, and I went out every night and had a good time. Well, one night Miss Julie got bombed out of her mind and came home with a strange man. Those two carried on something fierce and exhausted themselves to the point of passing out. When Virgil's mother walked into Julie's room the next morning and found them together, butt-naked and in bed, all hell broke loose. I was awakened by shrieks, and two minutes later we were tossed out of the house with them screaming "heathens, harlots, and whores," behind us.

Back on the road in my hot pink deVille, I parked myself for a three-week stint in a cheap dump called Willie's Go-Go Palace, located in Amsterdam, a small town near Syracuse. I wasn't twirling my ta-tas and busting my buns to a jukebox anymore. This time I was go-going to a live band and a light show in my very own cage!

I was a wild go-goer, jiggling my ass in the hungry faces of those jeering, whistling, redneck bumpkins whose tongues longed to lap my gyrating loins. Julie and I used to drag men home and carry on with them like cheap Babylonian women, and these men never found out the truth about our womanhood. But then, these straight men can be so damned gullible. Usually, after giving me a ride home, they'd park the pickup and want to make out, but I'd simply say, "No, darling, I can't put out on the first date. I'm not that kind of girl."

I'll say I wasn't that kind of girl!

"But how 'bout some head?" I would offer. I'm surprised I wasn't beaten, raped, and burned at the stake for my wicked, lascivious ways.

Then one night I met this cute twenty-two-year-old, and I wanted him so badly. Oh, I was going mad with desire! He was so adorable, with beautiful brown hair and big brown eyes, broad shoulders, and a sweet smile. I seduced him, but I told him that he couldn't dare touch my womanly jewels because I was saving those for marriage; however, my other assets were available for his appraisal. And praise 'em he did! I was rotten to the core and sore for a week!

After our passionate romp, with me contorted in an assortment of precarious positions, struggling to hide my deepest, darkest secret in my hands (and succeeding), I discovered that this kid's father owned a donut factory and they were seeking a Miss Donut to ride in the local Homecoming parade. Well, naturally I was more than happy to volunteer, since all I ever wanted out of life was to be a Rose Bowl queen. And although this wasn't the Rose Bowl, it was a parade and that was close enough in my mind. So there I was, propped up on the backseat of a Chevy convertible with a tira on my head and a sash across my chest that read MISS DONUT—1968 And as I waved to the adoring throng of thirty people, I realized that I had achieved a monumental crowning glory: a year's supply of free donuts. It was the thrill of a lifetime.

We had so many donuts in the house that Julie and I would invite the good ol' boys over for a late-night snack after a hard night's work. Well, we had so many men traipsing in and out of our apartment for our good-morning hospitality, the landlady had gotten the insane notion that we were prostitutes. Imagine that! We weren't selling it; we weren't even giving it away. We were honest, hardworking *artistes* having a few laughs with the local fellas. We couldn't take off our panties because we were ladies . . . so they thought. And if they knew otherwise, we could have been shot and hung by our g-strings!

Julie and I were so insulted by this sordid accusation that we packed our donuts and moved on to the nearest metropolis, which happened to be Albany. Julie landed another stripping gig at Bo-Bo's Bar & Grill while I go-go'd down the pike at Barbarella's Disco Den. What a hellhole that dump was! I had to dance on a pedestal to the drunken crowds of college boys from the university in the next town. After each set, the boys would invite me to their tables for drinks, and I would hang out with them until it was time to hoist myself back upon my pedestal. Well, one night I met this real hot kid from New York

City and we hit it off. We downed a few drinks, shared a few laughs, and when it was time for me to go home, he offered me a ride.

Well, the ride ended at a cheap motel on the outskirts of town. No sooner had we gotten into the door when he locked me into a wet kiss while his hands roamed down my back. He groped clumsily at my breasts as I clung to his back, falling victim to my rapturous whims. Suddenly his hands moved under my skirt and started to reach inside my panties. I tore myself from his arms and told him I couldn't go any further.

"Hey, c'mon, baby," he whined, touching my shoulders with the palms of his hands.

"No," I said angrily, pushing him away. "I can't."

"Sure, you can," he persisted, pulling me against his chest and smothering the nape of my neck with kisses.

Well, something came over me—and I think it was that last cocktail I downed at the bar. I decided to be honest with this boy and let him know the truth of why I couldn't go all the way.

"Look," I said, peeling myself away from him. "There's something you gotta know. I . . . ummm . . . I'm not a woman. I mean, yes, I am a woman, but I'm not a whole woman. But I'm not a man. Well, most of me, that is."

He stared at me for a moment with a confused look on his face, shook his head and said, "What?"

"I mean I'm not a woman . . . down there," I said, looking down at my crotch.

"What are ya?"

"I'm a man."

"You're a man?" he laughed. "You mean you gotta dick or something?" He leaned in for a closer look. "You're pulling my leg, aren'tchya?"

"I wish I was, but I'm not."

"Holy shit!" he exclaimed as he fell back onto the bed. Then he lifted his head back up. "Prove it."

When I did prove it, I was rather surprised by his response. He actually liked the idea that I was part man, part woman and pulled me down into the sheets with him. He began sucking on my nipples while he fondled the fire that burned between my silky legs.

We poked, plowed, licked, and kissed ourselves into a frenzy, and when it was over, he promised never to say a word about my "stash," so to speak. The next day when I returned for work, I got some very unflattering looks from the boys at the bar.

"Set me up, boy." I winked at the bartender as I planted my can on a stool.

"Yeah, sure," he said, giving me the once-over as he prepared my vodka stinger.

"Hey, liven up fellas! What's wrong—did somebody die?"

Louie, the elderly man who owned the dump, hobbled over to me. "Hey, Holly, I want you to come to the back room. There's something I gotta talk to you about." I thought, Oh shit, he wants me to put out on a box of beer. Well, I uprooted my well-planted can from the stool and sauntered into the back room. Louie lit a cigar and puffed.

"There's a guy out there who says you're a guy, Holly," he said, billows of smoke flowing through his wrinkled lips.

"Me? A guy?" I laughed off the possibility. "How could that be? Louie, I'm up on that stage every night practically naked."

"Well, I want to believe you, but this guy is out there making bets that you're a man."

"Well, so? He's wrong! What—Does that mean I'm fired if I don't pull down my panties?"

"No," Louie said, chewing on the end of the cigar.

"Well, then I'm going up to do my set."

And I left the back room and climbed atop my pedestal to dance, whereupon I felt all eyes staring at my crotch. These men were no longer the hootin', hollerin' hooligans I adored. They were a pack of threatened wolves, their eyes squinting to see if there was any trace of manhood lying beneath my flowered bikini. It was nerve-wracking! How dare they believe such a rotten story about a girl like me! After I finished the song, I jumped off the pedestal, ran out of the dump, and took a cab to the bar where Julie was stripping.

I refused to go back to Barbarella's, and word got around town that I was a man. Julie freaked out, and we decided to leave town, but I said, "Listen honey, I ain't leaving town without my check. They owe me a week's pay." The next day we went back to see Louie to get my check, whereupon I told him I was quiting.

"Hey, you can't stiff me. I need a dancer! I ain't paying ya unless ya dance."

"I'll dance for ya," chimed Julie. Louie gave her the once-over and approved. She was a stacked broad and her bases were far more loaded than mine.

"Yeah, okay," he said, clinching the smelly cigar between his teeth. Well, Julie threw back two vodka stingers, hopped up on the bar, and began to twirl her tits faster than the propellers on a WWII bomber! The men were going crazy and she was eating it up. She bumped and grinded herself into a stupor, to the point where she actually fell off the bar! She landed on her back on the floor, but she was so bombed she didn't feel a thing and kept on twirling, occasionally squeezing her mounds of siliconed breasts as she writhed in ecstacy beneath the men, her tongue licking her luscious wet lips. The men were cheering and whistling, and the look on Julie's face was pure delight. She had definitely discovered euphoria.

Julie had a ball, I had my check, and the next day we packed our bags and boarded a train for New York City. I had called Jack and told him that I was tired of living upstate and that I was coming home. Besides, I missed him.

Jack was only going to be in town for a few weeks, however, because he had planned a vacation in Mexico with one of his friends. I said I didn't mind his leaving and that I'd take care of the apartment while he was gone. Once again, I had become a career girl, having landed myself a respectable job at a dress shop in the neighborhood. I spent my days helping housewives choose their wardrobes, but at night I became bored and restless. After all, there's only so much television a person can watch! So one night I ventured into Greenwich Village to hang out at a bar and hear some music. I met up with some other queens who shared my interest in fashion and we hit it off! Well,

I had such a good time that I decided to go back the next night. And the next night. And before I knew it, I was going to the bars night after night, drinking, popping pills, and dancing my life away. Since I had the entire apartment to myself, I often brought home a slew of friends, which wound up in a wild party—we wrecked the place.

One afternoon after one of those uproarious all-night soirees, I started digging through the day's mail and accidentally opened an envelope addressed to Jack. Well, my heart stopped and the organ sounded as I read the shocking letter concealed inside that filthy, stinking card. "My darling Jack," it began. "I have missed you terribly these past few weeks. How I long to feel the caress of your kisses—" My hands began to tremble and my knees began to shudder as I became weak with the burdening, sorrow-laden truth. Jack was in love with another woman. Oh, I was woe-striken and miffed! Just because I had dabbled in a few Jezebelian delights didn't give that cuckold the right to do the same. At least not in my mind. I became incensed with jealousy and threw wild parties every night. No longer would I just sip the ambrosial nectar of Aphrodite—I was going to drown in it!

When Jack finally came home, the place looked as if it had been struck by a tornado, and there I was lying amidst the rubble half bombed with a sneer on my face.

"What the hell happened in here?" he demanded.

"Thought you'd come home, huh?" I snapped, pulling myself out of the pile and staggering across the floor for the draw. "I know what you've been doing. You can't fool me."

"Look at this place. It's a goddamn mess. What the fuck—"

"Fuck you! I know all about your goddamned girlfriend you got on the side. I know what you got going on, so fuck you!"

I screamed, kicking old newspapers across the soiled floor. I knew he had stopped loving me long ago, even back when I was in upstate New York—I just didn't want to face it. Jack suddenly became very cool and he simply told me to leave.

"Get out, Holly. Just go." I couldn't believe what I was hearing.

"Leave? You're kicking me out?" I questioned, still in a shocked state.

"Go on, Holly. It's over. There's no use in sticking around anymore."

"You can't do this to me. I, I don't have any place to go."

"You'll work something out. Just go."

"You can't just kick me out, Jack. Come on. You can't."

Jack headed back to the bedroom and I followed, pleading for his forgiveness.

"I'll clean up the mess, I promise. Please, Jack . . ." But he wasn't listening. He didn't care, and why should he? It was over. Kaput. Fin. I, of course, wasn't that convinced until he began throwing my clothes out of the bedroom window and onto the front lawn!

Well, that romance left on the last train out of town, leaving me behind in a trail of dust with two arms full of silk and chiffon. I thought he'd at least have the decency to throw me a hanger. Silk wrinkles so easily, you know. But he didn't, and off I plodded into the wilderness of Queens, heading for Greenwich Village. I felt just like Charlie Chaplin at the end of a one-reeler, when he walks off into the horizon, twirling his cane as the film fades to black. I was indeed a little tramp.

CHAPTER 7

Les Miserables

*W*ell, there I was, like a rat in the gutter, sweating out the blistering fever of summer. Out of a house, out of a husband, and out on the street! I thought I'd never be homeless again, but as I soon came to discover, life can be unpredictable. And so are husbands! Jack discarded me like a worn-out rag. What did he think I was, a cheap dime-store floozy he could throw aside after the fun was over? A floozy maybe, but I was never cheap. Macy's could vouch for that. Yet I was tossed to the wind without a dime to my name, despair in my pocketbook. Needless to say, I was blown away! Like Mary Poppins, I sailed off with only the clothes on my back, into a journey unknown.

Libra was nowhere to be found, although I had suspicions that her puckered puss was pushed between the bars of the cell that housed her jailbird beau. Though we were friends, Libra and I had strayed and our interests had changed. She was in love and I wasn't. So piss on her. I had no time to listen to those sobs over a petty thief who had stolen her heart and was doing time in the hoosegow. She could put it to music. I had my own opera of sobs. I either rustled up a place to stay or spent the night munching grubs in Bryant Park! And if you've ever tasted a grub, you'd know why I was crying.

Julie was also out of the picture, having moved back upstate, living in Albany as a housewife. She had met a man while stripping in a cheap tavern, fell madly in love with him, and started saving her tips for a sex change. The way she wiggled, jiggled, and gyrated, I'm sure she had quite a stash. At least she had the sense to know what she wanted and the nerve to go out and get it. I wasn't sure anymore. I had been a street kid, a housewife, a floor model, a go-go dancer, and the only Miss Donut ever known to Amsterdam. But something was definitely missing from my life, and on this particular eve, it was dinner!

On the glamourous side of this tawdry tale, Candy and Jackie were both hanging out at Max's Kansas City, fully immersed in their grand and fabulous selves. Since Candy was the only person to whom I could turn in this time of distress, I thought I might rely on her for a helping hand—but instead got a kick in the ass. Miss Darling was too busy doing an Off-Broadway stint with Miss Curtis and was too consumed by her own glamour to be bothered by my beggary. I always knew that bleach would one day take its toll, and boy, was she shortchanged.

Candy's brain had been pickled by peroxide and filled with notions that she was the next blond goddess to rule filmdom. She idolized those vintage movie-star personas, but instead of becoming a snappy Carole Lombard–Joan Blondell type, she became a weak, submissive jellyfish. She thought this frail and useless put-on was sexy; I thought it was a pain in the ass. Not that I was overly tormented by this ridiculous facade. She was far too busy with rehearsal to acknowledge my pleas, and didn't even offer to take me in for the night! After all the times I took her in during the weekends? After all the encouragement I gave her to get a job? After all the times she borrowed my clothes, ate my food, and turned my home into a filthy sty, she had the nerve to turn me away?! She sure did. I should've smacked the blond right out of her hair!

Miss Curtis couldn't have been much help either, but we weren't that close at the time, so I didn't ask. Besides, she too was very busy under the lights of the stage. She and Candy were both very much into devoting their souls to the art of acting, and both were trying to prove to the Warhol crowd that they were worthy of Superstardom. I had no interest in this bullshit, particularly since I could hardly stomach the affectation (or shall I say affliction) of the "thea-tah." But then my mind had embraced the notion that one day I was going to grace the cover of *Vogue*, my latest aspiration since I had already been in a parade.

I scrounged around and eventually moved in with some other queens I had befriended at the Stonewall, this little gay bar on Christopher Street across from Sheridan Square, right in the hub of the West Village. The Stonewall was a popular after-hours watering hole, but because of the frequent police raids on the gay bars at this time, the place was very careful when it came to allowing people inside. It had the set-up of a Roaring Twenties speakeasy. To enter, you knocked on the door and waited for the bouncer to answer. If you looked okay, you would be admitted.

Inside it was very dark, with a long bar to one side and go-go boys in bikinis dancing on either end. It had a dance floor and a jukebox. The place attracted an eclectic bunch: butch guys, preppy boys, older men, a few lesbians, and a few so-called straight men sprinkled in between. Well, at least their wives and kids thought they were straight. Anyway, it was these straight patrons that attracted me. I wasn't interested in gay men because I thought I was a woman and I wanted to be treated accordingly, unlike some of the other girls who could put on pants and become a man. I was a woman regardless of what I was wearing.

Also, there are different degrees of transvestism. There are some men who are very straight and only have sex with women, but get excited over wearing panties and a dress. Then there are those men such as myself, who want to live as women and go to the extreme of shooting hormones and undergoing electrolysis treatments so they can look real. Looking real was very important in my mind, because if there was any question that I was a man in drag, I could be arrested, and worse yet, I could be killed by homo-hating hoodlums! It was during this period of the mid-Sixties when all the "girls" in the West Village were starting to come out of their closets. Or their dressing rooms, as I like to say. So I felt right at home.

Anyway, me and the girls were holed up in a tawdry little rooming house on West Tenth Street and Hudson in the West Village, near the river. We were all piled into one room, fought for mirror time in the community bath down the hall, and formed our own soriety: Phi Kappa Drag!

Life had definitely taken a step in the right direction. I slept during the days and partied throughout the nights, popping pills and dancing until dawn. I was twenty-two and no one enjoyed her youth more than I. It was a carefree existence, free of stress and the everyday pressures of the working class. I didn't have a job because I didn't want one. Besides, I could happily exist on handouts from friends, and who had time for work anyway? I was far too busy reading *Vogue* magazines and dreaming of my future as a beautiful model. After all, it was the dreams that kept me afloat during these hard times. And by hard times, I'm not just referring to when I was broke and in the gutter, but the times when I wondered about where I was heading. Or who I was. And whether I should have gotten a sex change. I didn't know, and I didn't want to think about it. And so I kept dreaming, hoping one day I would know the answers.

Usually, all the "girls" would pool their pennies to pay the rent. Sometimes I had money, sometimes I didn't, but we all looked out for one another and made sure no one was stuck out in the street. It was back to the same old routine of living hand-to-mouth, and too often the hand was empty.

Miss Liz Eden, a notorious transvestite hooker, lived down the hall. She was continually turning tricks with a guy who would come in to see her from Queens.

"Sonny's coming! Sonny's coming and he's gorgeous!" she would scream down the hall, and all the girls would flutter about like chickens in a hen house. Sonny was a straight man who had a wife and kids, but every now and then he popped up at Miss Eden's door for a sampling of her charms. Eventually, he professed his love and said he'd do anything for her. Well, she of course pounced on the opportunity and told him she wanted a pussy. And not the kind with nine lives, if you get my drift. So Sonny robbed a bank to get her one. Boy, was he a fool for love. The story made the headlines and became the inspiration for the film *Dog Day Afternoon*.

There were always straight men traipsing in and out of the building, to drop their drawers as well as some dough. If one of my roomies had a trick coming over, the rest of us would hide upstairs or down the hall until services were rendered. Then after the trick was turned, we'd spend the money on makeup and get all gussied up for the Stonewall, hunting for straight men who would dump their girlfriends after the date and come to us for a night of frolic!

Most of the "girls" were unreadable, which meant nobody could read—or rather tell—their true gender. And then there were the black and Puerto Rican queens who were very readable, meaning they would hang out the windows of our seedy hovel and snap their fingers at the people walking by. And this was not one little snap, darling. It was a whole slew of snaps that came out of a hand that waved up, down, and to the sides while a barrage of verbal abuse peppered with "Miss Thing" and "Motherfucker" hurled from their torrid tongues.

"Reading" was a form of cutting a person down to size, and these girls never missed a chance to get their fingers right in an unsuspecting face and snap away. The Puerto Rican queens in New York City were the most vicious. If the snaps didn't do the job, they'd use a knife. These girls were psychotic. They ran in packs, and I made sure I stayed clear of their path. They carried razor blades in their hairdos and knives in their panties. I heard all sorts of horrifying stories about these psycho queens from hell terrorizing the Lower East Side. One night a poor queen was walking the street alone in the wrong part of town when a sultry Puerto Rican approached.

"Oh, girl, ju so pretty." She smiled. "Ju skin is so pretty and white, baby."

"Oh, thank you," said the queen, taken in by this brush of flattery, when suddenly the spik gingerly reached behind her head and pulled a razor out of her wig! She slashed the queen's face repeatedly and scarred her for life—all because she was too pretty.

They were very sly, these Puerto Rican queens. They would not take shit from anyone. One night on Fourth Street in the East Village a car filled with straight guys began to taunt a Puerto Rican queen lounging outside of a closed liquor store.

"Hey, faggot!" one guy hollered as the car pulled alongside the curb and stopped in front of the queen. "How'd you like your ass kicked?"

The queen stared at them, expressionless, then shot up, "Ju tink I'm a faggot? Huh? Ju calling me a faggot?"

One of the guys got out of the car and approached him. He was far bigger than the queen, at least six feet tall with the build of a football player.

"Yeah, I'm calling you a faggot."

And as he stepped closer, the queen shouted, "Yeah, well, take dis, motherfucker!" The queen pulled a knife out of his pants and plunged it repeatedly into the guy's stomach.

I never messed with these psycho queens, and stayed as far away from them as possible. It was strange. All of us queens were walking the same path in life. Who would've expected such rivalries? But our living conditions were wretched. We were all living like rats on top of each other. And rats have to protect themselves and their territory. And so the Puerto Ricans formed these little gangettes that terrorized the gutter.

I had my own gang to run with, so to speak, except that we were a bunch of mad queens who invaded the Stonewall every night and had a ball. Well, one night I met a guy named Peter—this scrawny, dark, curly-haired man with a little mustache, big eyes, and thick lashes. Peter was a very intelligent man with a macabre sense of humor, a very quick wit, and a tongue as sharp as a machete. Little did I know that the reason his wit was so quick was because he was on speed! Well, he had another quick-witted friend named George—a tall, darkly handsome gentleman from the South who was the closest thing to Rhett Butler that I've ever known. They were a stimulating couple and, since I was just thirsting for some stimuli myself, we hit it off splendidly.

George and Peter lived on the Lower East Side, a section of town I never went near because it was a dilapidated haven for junkies. George hung out with the Warhol crowd, and had been known as Silver George in the early Factory days. I didn't understand the reason behind this nickname until later, when we moved in together and he painted and foiled the entire apartment silver. That was when his true colors came out!

George loved to tell glorified tales of Andy and the Factory, and I used to sit for hours listening to him talk. One such story was about a photographer called Billy Name who lived in a Factory toilet! Another story was about Edie Sedgewick, who was so fucked up on drugs she'd wobble in and fall face-down on the Factory floor with Andy's only response being, "Wow. There goes Edie."

George babbled on and on about rampant drug use, illicit sex, the famous people that were in the center of it all, and how everybody pitched in to help Andy make his silkscreens. Some even helped sign his name! Well, after hearing about all this lunacy (and wanting to hear more!), I understood why Candy and Jackie were so enamoured. I also knew I wanted to be part of the insanity.

During one of my sojourns to George and Peter's apartment to gorge on Factory tales, George went into the bedroom and came out with a syringe in his hand. At first I was confused and thought, "What's he going to do with that?" And then when Peter pulled a bag of white powder he called crystal meth from out of a ratty sofa cushion, I thought I was going to keel over! I had no idea that these boys shot up. They were so casual about it, talking on about the Factory as they prepared their speed "fix," and before I knew it the needle was in George's arm! Peter asked if I wanted some and I was speechless. Darling, taking drugs with a needle was heavy-duty junkie stuff. That was the big time as far as drug use was concerned, and in my mind a junkie was the lowest form of life there could be. I finally made it clear that I wanted no part of it.

"Oh, come on," pleaded George. "You can't become a junkie off of one hit. Besides, it's not heroin."

"I don't know . . ." I was a nervous wreck.

"Go on, try it. It's wonderful!" insisted Peter.

I had no idea how to shoot up, nor was I too keen on being jabbed by a needle. But that ol' what-the-hell spirit came over me and I consented. Well, they shot me up with speed, honey, and it was the most fabulous thing I've ever felt in all my life! A warm rush flooded my body, causing my brain to burst into a blazing riot of fireworks. The entire room lit up as thoughts raced through my mind and I talked and talked and talked, spewing forth every idea that had ever entered my pretty little head. I felt so good, I moved in and became quick-witted myself.

George and Peter thrived as a professional couple, but instead of being yuppies, they were more along the line of "yuddies"—Young Urban Drug Dealers! George dealt in speed and Peter, sly fox that he was, had managed to rake in Social Security benefits for life because he had been declared legally insane. I thought it was a grand scheme and soon I was on welfare, too. It was easy to get welfare then, since all a person had to do was stand in line, plead for help, and sign on the dotted line. Today there's so much red tape it's not worth the hassle.

Welfare, Häagen Dazs, Crystal Meth, Vitabath, and a scrub brush were the essential elements in the tiring life of this speed queen. I would shoot up and clean the apartment for hours on end. I don't know why, but whenever I shot up, I turned into this crazed scrub woman. The only problem was, I'd start scrubbing in a corner and thirteen hours later, I was still in the same corner, scrubbing away! I was maniacal. Then there were those tranquil moments when I listened to the Moody Blues while jotting down my esoteric thoughts in a blank book and shoving spoonfuls of chocolate-chocolate-chip ice cream into my gaping mouth. Or sometimes I'd just jibber, jabber, gab, and blabber until I simply passed out from too much talking! Too often, I'd start a conversation on Monday and talk until I passed out on Friday. And I was so heavily wired that when I came down from the high, I landed hard. It was if I was a strand of pearls that had broken and was strewn out all over the floor. I was a mess, and when there was nothing left to hold me together, I simply collapsed from exhaustion and slept for days.

Well, one night during our Methedrine madness, George introduced me to one of his strange toothless little friends named Norman. We were all so quick-witted that night and having such a good time that Norman insisted, "You must meet Ondine! He would love you! You must meet Ondine!" And he insisted on it all night long.

I didn't know much about Ondine, except the fact that he was a Warhol Superstar who had starred in several of Warhol's earlier films, including *Chelsea Girls*. Finally, one night this Ondine character came over. He was rather strange in demeanor, he talked with a stutter, and it took him forever to complete a sentence—but it was well worth the wait when he told me that I was so beautiful that I too should be a Superstar.

"Y-Y-Y-You got t-t-t-to meet An-Andy," he said, and I agreed.

George also thought it would be a good idea for me to meet Andy, and one afternoon he called the Factory to arrange an introduction. Andy invited him to bring me to the screening party for *Flesh*, the latest epic among the Warhol works of cinematic art featuring my cohorts Jackie Curtis and Candy Darling. Finally, I was going to the famous Factory, which at this time was housed in a loft across from Union Square Park.

When we arrived for the soiree, an elevator took us up to a loft, where we were greeted by a dead-as-a-doornail, black-and-white Great Dane that had been stuffed and stashed outside of the door. George rang the bell and announced us. Inside, huge photos of Viva, Joe Dallesandro, and Tom Hompertz lined the silver-painted walls, and opposite them was a large picture window with a small balcony overlooking the park.

The place was packed with plastic people nibbling on cheese, drinking wine, and making idle conversation among themselves. Not a friendly crowd, really, but you know how those artist types can be. So self-absorbed. Anyhow, in the midst of this coiffed crowd I saw a white tuft of what looked like a teased-out cotton ball! Before I had the chance to really dwell on the matter, George grabbed my arm and said, "Come on! Let's say hi to Andy." And with that we headed right into the mob and straight for the tuft.

"No, I can't!" I panicked and pulled away. "What am I gonna say?"

"Say hi, he'll love you," George reassured me.

"Stop it," I pleaded. "How do I look?"

"You look fine," he said as we elbowed our way toward the star-maker himself, with nothing in our way but my terror. And as we became enveloped in the false smiles and gay laughter. George extended his hand to that strange little man in the center of it all. He was dressed in a black turtleneck, blue jeans, and a gray tweed jacket. His face was a purplish white, with a bumpy nose and a quirky smile. But he had a glint in his eyes which seemed to enliven this otherwise bland visage. He was strange, but he was cute.

"Hi, George," Andy said. "And what's your name?" he asked, turning to me.

"Oh, this is my friend Holly," said George. "Holly, this is Andy."

"Oh, you're so glamourous." He smiled, taking my hand. "You should be in one of our movies. Do you have a last name?"

"Uh . . . No." I smiled.

And he stood back with surprise and said, "Oh?"

To which I retorted, "But I'll have one the next time you see me!" He laughed, then turned away, dissolving back into his own queer placid facade, leaving me to wonder if I'd made a good impression.

Moments later, George introduced me to Nico, the lead singer of the Velvet Underground. She was also very strange. "Hahlo," she bellowed in her deep monotone voice, her face expressionless. She was at least six feet in height and dressed as if she was six feet under! But then, all those avant-garde types seem to wallow in the gloom-glam funeral look. She wore tight black pants and a pullover turtleneck with her long, straight white hair framing her very pale face. She never said another word the rest of the night, and remained by the window until the film was screened.

Jackie and Candy were there in all their hyped glory, and both acted hideously cold toward me. I didn't know what their beef was; perhaps they were threatened because I was on their turf. Or maybe they were afraid I was trying to push my way into the Warhol scene? Who knows? Our friendships were up and down so many times it was like riding a carousel. Sometimes we loathed one another and sometimes we loved one another. We shared laughs, tears, makeup, and drugs. But when it came to sharing the spotlight, it was every broad for herself!

Flesh launched Candy and Jackie's careers as Warhol Superstars, but when I saw the picture for the first time that night, I thought, "Oh, brother. What a dull piece of shit." It was all about Joe Dallesandro, a gorgeous young stud, and all the people who are after his body. I didn't think it was much of a movie at all. Where was the glamour? The excitement? Or the big musical number? This wasn't entertainment, it was real-life crap. Although I didn't care for the film itself, I did like Candy and Jackie's performances. They were very comical, particularly because as they talked back and forth about movie magazines, Joe is seen standing before them getting a blow job! It was the first time I'd ever seen Jackie in drag, and I thought she looked okay . . . sort of.

Something good happened to me that night. Although I was bored with the film, I was enticed with the possibility of being in a movie. I saw the attention Jackie and Candy received, and once the film premiered, they were the toast of Max's Kansas City. They were thrust into the spotlight of fame and became the social sweethearts of the underground. Their fame also transcended into the mainstream, as they were fawned over by celebrities, artists, and socialites. And there I stood in their shadows, envious as hell. I saw what they had and I wanted it, too. What did they have that I didn't? Not only was I just as pretty, but I had been a woman longer! And I was Miss Donut of Amsterdam; it was time I dusted off my tiara and put it to use. The big question was how.

Well, one night while frying high on speed, George, Peter, some other friends, and I decided to create a last name for me. The female Superstars who stuck out most in my mind also had the most captivating names: Ultra Violet, Viva, and International Velvet. Well, I wanted to captivate a little myself, but I wanted a name that was catchy yet glamourous. And we tried everything. We thought I could really shine if I was named after a planet and came up with Holly Star and Jupiter Moon. Then we decided to actually steal from legendary film stars, and came up with the doozies Holly Taylor and Holly Lamarr. When someone suggested Holly Buddy, I knew we were getting desperate.

As fate would have it, the TV was on and Peter was watching a rerun of "I Love Lucy." It was the episode where Lucy is riding the subway with a loving cup stuck on her head. Well, in the subway background was the word "Woodlawn," since Lucy was supposed to be riding the Woodlawn train—which, incidentally, was the train that traveled to the Bronx and made its last stop at the Woodlawn Cemetery.

Peter spotted the word and his hair curled, his eyes popped, and his finger pointed as he up and shouted, "That's it! The Woodlawn Cemetery!"

"What the hell are you screaming about?" asked George.

"The Woodlawn Cemetery! Holly, you can be the heiress to all that land. And who's gonna contest? They're all dead!"

I had no idea what Peter was ranting about, and just assumed he had gone over the edge with too much speed. But when he finally bridged "Holly" with "Woodlawn," I got the picture. And it was divine! Yes, I could be the heiress to the Woodlawn Cemetery. Darling, with all that marble, I could build a palace and use the crypts as powder rooms. But most importantly, I could be Hollywood's namesake! After all, it was the film capital of the world, and what could be more glamourous? Finally, I had a name I could give to Andy.

That was in the infamous summer of 1969, which shall plummet into the annals of history! Everything happened that year. I became Holly Woodlawn, the hippies flocked to Woodstock, the gays rioted, the men landed on the moon, and Miss Jackie Curtis got married! She had planned her wedding for the same day that the men were to land on the moon because she thought it would add to the occasion. Leave it to Curtis! That broad would've flown to the moon for her honeymoon if it meant more publicity.

Curtis lived for publicity. She was a hoopla hound, and one day while I was standing outside of Max's minding my own business, a cab sped by with Curtis's head hanging out the window. She was waving a copy of *Screen* magazine, screaming at the top of her lungs, "Page seventy-nine! Page seventy-nine!" She had gotten a write-up and she was telling the world.

Jackie was very proud of her Superstar status, but she was ecstatic when her stardom was validated in print. So thrilled, in fact, that she hauled her clippings with her everywhere in a shopping bag! One night at Max's she barreled over to George Cukor with her shopping bag in hand, reached inside, pulled out a news article, and shoved it under Cukor's nose.

"Hey, George, look at this," she said between puffs of a cigarette. "This town loves me. Listen, you gotta use me in one of your movies."

To announce her engagement to Eric Emerson, another Warhol Superstar, Miss Curtis staged a press reception at a penthouse apartment on Fourteenth Street and Sixth Avenue, obviously not Jackie's residence, but that of a close friend. George, Peter, and I bustled right over to the lively gala, which had every weirdo in town on hand to celebrate. Many of those who were invited were members of the theater groups with which Jackie had been involved. And what a crowd! I wasn't there for more than five minutes when I was struck by a vision and began to choke on my chablis. All I could see was a pile of bright orange hair that had been tied up into a little boom-boom on top of the head of a tall, skinny woman who had accidentally stumbled into me.

"Excuse me," she apologized, dislodging her elbow from my stomach. She had a snip of a nose, a well-defined chin, and she was a sight to behold in a profusion of brightly colored chiffon flowing in the afternoon breeze.

"You look brilliant," I told her. She had a build like Olive Oyle and the face of a Renaissance painting. She reminded me of Katharine Hepburn in *The Mad Woman of Chaillot*. And as we talked, I learned that her name was Ruby Lynne Reyner and she was an actress with the Playhouse of the Ridiculous, a theater group headed by John Vaccaro.

I liked Ruby Lynn. She had some style, and we hit it off like two pigs in a puddle. Through her, I was also introduced to Marie Antoinette, another member of the Ridiculous cast. Marie had the presence of an old soothsayer Indian woman who always had a smile on her face. She must've been smoking some peace pipe! And she was always laughing when she talked. It wasn't a loud laugh. It was more of a sly little cackle. She was ho-hoing and ha-haing all over the place.

"Good to see you. Ha, ha, ha. How have you been? Ho, ho, ho," she'd say.

Penny Arcade was another acclaimed actress of the troupe. She reminded me of a bawdy British bar wench. She was a small, round, street-smart brunette with sensuous white skin and dark hair, and she oozed sexuality.

Then there was Baby Betty, four feet, nine inches of fully packed woman. She was always dressed in black, with black nail polish, black hair, and an adorable little face that had big bright eyes that twinkled. She looked like a chain-smoking Betty Boop.

Jackie was all over the place, schmoozing with the press and greeting her guests, and while I munched on a cracker and sipped from my replenished glass, Miss Curtis came over and asked if I'd be a bridesmaid in the wedding. Well, I was more than thrilled. Not because I was part of the wedding party, but because this wedding promised to be a media bonanza! And since I was a star on the rise, I felt it was high time I became acquainted with the press myself. So I expressed my honor, accepted the invitation, and immediately my mind began to twitch as to what I should wear.

Well, being the broke low-life that I was, I walked into a fabric store and ran out with a bolt of gray chiffon! I didn't mean to steal the entire bolt—I would've only taken a few yards—but I couldn't get anyone to help me cut it. And I had no time to wait around for busy store clerks. I had a dress to make! So I jumped into a taxi and fled, leaving the irate store clerks behind in the fumes.

When I got home and unrolled the fabric, I discovered there were at least thirty yards in the bolt! I was chiffoned out, to say the least, and busily created myself a long, flowing Grecian gown with beaded trimming for the wedding. I also whipped up scarves, pants, a blouse, and a pair of curtains!

Now that I had all these fabulous new creations to wear, I decided it was time to learn more about this theater craze. George and Peter also felt I was in need of some theatrical culture, and took me to see a play by a Mr. Charles Ludlum. They said it was an experimental piece called *Terdsinelle*. I was very excited about it and envisioned it to be some fabulous Elizabethan drama about somebody—a woman, I presumed—named Terdsinelle. Surely it would be something I could savor.

Well, there we were in a warehouse-turned-theater watching this play, and I wasn't understanding a goddamned thing that was going on! What was this insanity on the stage? And why was this woman called Black-Eyed Susan ranting and raving while sitting on the toilet bowl? And where was this Terdsinelle woman anyway? When I expressed my confusion to Peter, he gave me the queerest look and then laughed. He leaned into my ear and softly whispered a shocking revelation. This play was not about a woman named "Terdsinelle"—it was about "Turds in Hell!"

I was plucked! I mean, whoever heard of a play being written about turds? I supposed that's why it was experimental. Well, after my mind had been cleansed of the misconception, I soon realized that this wasn't bad for a shitty play. It was about turds, you know, and it was so creative and avant-garde, I decided I wanted to be a turd, too. Progressive theater was so daring and adventurous. What could be more fun?

Ondine was very much involved with progressive theater, and so I expressed to him my desire to conquer the stage. I, too, wanted to yuk it up with the muse Thalia . . . and amuse a few others while I was at it! Ondine encouraged my thespian ambitions and took me under his wing to nurture my newfound passion. I felt just like I was Christine and he was the Phantom. Imagine, me, Holly Woodlawn . . . an actress. I immediately saw myself in all the classics, everything from the early morality plays to the Greek tragedies, Shakespeare, and beyond.

I was in a twirl, with mad little fantasies reeling through my head like previews in a movie house. But my onstage wizardry would have to wait, as I had no time to dabble with dialogue. It was happy hour, and I had to dabble in a cocktail! And so off I went to the Stonewall to raise hell, wreak havoc, and romp to my heart's delight.

The Stonewall was right across from Sheridan Square, between Waverly and Christopher Streets. The Square was a well-manicured lawn surrounded by an iron fence, with a statue of Colonel Sheridan in the middle. It was a very nonthreatening, friendly atmosphere frequented by panhandlers, bums, and drag queens.

The West Village was an eclectic neighborhood. The Women's House of Detention was just around the corner between Greenwich Avenue and Sixth Avenue, and all night long the lesbians bayed at the moon or hung out the windows, bellowing sweet nothings to their lovers on the grounds below. Also, a variety of antique, thrift, and specialty shops filled the area. McNulty's Coffee Shop was on Christopher Street, right off Bleecker—which is where I occasionally hung out. It was the hubbub of liberated New York.

Hanging out in the Village became a nightly ritual. Sometimes I'd go to the bars and the coffee houses, and then sometimes I'd just sit on a doorstep with friends and drink a bottle of wine. Pagan Pink Ripple, of course.

The Stonewall was frequented by a lot of unique people going through major gender changes. We flocked there because it was a place where we were fawned over. We were treated like women, and as far as we knew, we were women. The black "girls" tried to look like the Supremes and the white "girls" tried to look like the Shangri-Las. Our breasts were fabulous and we had the best makeup, but the gay boys gave us the derogatory label "hormone queens," which I found to be deplorable. A "hormone queen" is a man who is so serious about passing as a woman that he has taken estrogen. I hated the term, but you know how our society is when it comes to labels.

For a while, I dated a policeman who had no idea I was a man. I met him one night while walking down MacDougal Street with Miss Candy Darling. He was an undercover cop, and he used to corner kids who were smoking grass, take their dope, and then ask me if I wanted to smoke it with him! We used to make out in his car while he was on duty. He was handsome and young (about twenty-five) with dark hair. He never knew a thing about me, although he thought Candy was weird. He would see her wearing that trench coat, babushka, and cherry-red lipstick, and acting very evasive and aloof, and he'd say to me, "You know, your girlfriend is really strange."

To which I would retort, "Of course, darling, she's an actress!" I liked him a lot, but he wanted more of me, which, as you and I know, wasn't available!

June 26, 1969, was a hot, muggy Thursday night. The humidity in the air was unbearable because every queen in the city was in tears. Judy Garland was dead, and her funeral would be the following afternoon at Campbell's. Poor Judy.

That afternoon I ran into Candy Darling, who was on her way to Campbell's for the final viewing, clutching to her chest a worn Judy Garland album cover. "It's such a shame," she said softly, wiping a tear from her eye. "Judy, gone. It's so sad."

Yes, it was sad. I went to the Stonewall that night, but left early, wandering through the thick humidity, feeling it cling to me as I thought to myself, "Judy's dead. Wow." She died of a drug overdose and I felt bad for her, but it didn't stop me from tampering with the same stuff. I felt it would never happen to me; overdoses were for "other people."

When I returned to the Stonewall the next night, there was so much commotion—sirens blaring, people screaming—I thought a bomb had gone off. The cops were everywhere, and a chill shot up my spine as I drew closer, fearing the worst. I wedged myself into the mob for a closer look and heard a raspy voice scream, "Asshole!" A street queen named Crazy Sylvia had just broken a gin bottle over a cop's head! I couldn't believe my eyes. Suddenly, the mob (which largely consisted of gay men) began throwing bottles and stones against the door that the young cop had been guarding.

A tall, skinny street queen named Miss Marsha called to me from the crowd. "Holly, girl!" She screeched and waved her bangled arm into the air, flagging me down. Miss Marsha was black as coal, with an orange-brown wig that usually sat cockeyed on her bobbing head. Her skirt was tied in the back where the zipper had been ripped, her blouse was tied into a halter, and she always wore house slippers with her stockings, which were rolled down around her shins. Usually, whenever I saw Miss Marsha sashaying down the street, I quickly dodged to the other side to avoid contact. But this time the crowd was too thick and I was stuck. And she had already spotted me, so I couldn't hide. I was doomed.

"Oh, Miss Thing!" She waved again, pushing and shoving her lanky hips my way. "Honey, dawlin', get over here, child! Mmmmmm, girl, the queens are holdin' the cops hostage. Here, have a drink!" And she handed me a bottle in a rumpled brown bag. "Drink it, dawlin', it's the Pride of Cucamonga!"

And so I was introduced to the Pride of Cucamonga at only $2.98 a gallon. Little did I know it would be my chosen fruit of the vine in leaner days to come.

Miss Marsha was the Hedda Hopper of Christopher Street, and she was always in the know, doling out the filthiest tidbits of gossip I had ever heard. No one knew where she came from, no one knew where she'd been, and to tell you the truth, no one cared! But you could always find her on a corner spilling the beans on someone. Once she filled me in on what was happening, she snatched the Pride of Cucamonga out of my hand and darted back into the crowd, shaking her bubble butt and rolling her bugged eyes while ranting, raving, and screaming at the police, "Oh, dawlin'! Oh, honey! Let me tell you—"

These were the Stonewall riots, and Miss Marsha was the debutante! The media coverage brought the riots nationwide attention, making it the greatest single event in the history of gays. Personally, I think some queen took too many Tuinals, started ranting and raving, and before he knew it, a revolution had started! When people are feeling fabulous, they don't want to take any crap from anybody, particularly the cops. And it was a hot night, Judy was dead, and the cops were out busting balls. Well, they went too far this time, and before they had a chance to get a grip on the situation, it had snowballed into the gay movement.

The Stonewall riots became a milestone for the gay community not only because it was the biggest gay riot in history, but because it was the first time Miss Marsha got on TV! Darling, she made the six o'clock news, and she appeared so worldly for a girl of the gutter. Even her wig was on straight. I'm surprised they didn't erect a statue of Miss Marsha on top of Sheridan's shoulders, waving a pint of Cucamonga in honor of her carryings on.

As a matter of fact, the Stonewall created such a sensation, I'm surprised Curtis didn't stage her wedding outside the bar! Instead, she had the taste to tie the knot on the rooftop terrace of an apartment building, but it was a circus nonetheless. The groom, Eric Emerson, never showed up, but Miss Curtis was not one to be stood up at the altar, particularly with the paparazzi on hand. So, while she desperately ran around trying to round up a last-minute replacement, I drank wine and cut the cheese while chatting with John Vaccarro, founder of the Playhouse of the Ridiculous.

John was a short, skinny man who reminded me of the hunched-over troll who hung out under bridges in fairy tales. He was floored by the fact that I was a man, and he was so taken with my presence that he offered me a role in Curtis's latest play, *Heaven Grand in Amber Orbit*. Honey, I walked in as a bridesmaid and was going home a star! I was destined for greatness and cheap wine.

In a last-minute attempt to salvage the joyous event, Curtis asked Stanley Falconspeed, a handsome blond who worked as a maitre d' at Max's, to fill in. Stanley agreed, and the press had a field day as the two exchanged their wedding vows in front of a porno producer who had become a self-ordained priest!

After the affair, we went to Max's, where we reveled in the festivities of a lavish reception. It was very nice of the owner, Mickey Ruskin, to lay out the spread, and everyone was there, including Andrea Whips Feldman, who was taken out bodily, screaming that she was Andy Warhol's wife. By this time, I was feeling quite fabulous myself. So taken was I by the matrimonial bliss that I congratulated Jackie and then immediately took off with her husband! We hightailed it to the Tenth Street apartment I was occupying and continued to celebrate. Curtis had the wedding and I went on the honeymoon! Funny how those things happen.

Nineteen sixty-nine had proved to be a very exciting year, and my social calendar was filling up fast. I was invited to Woodstock, but who wanted to go to a pig farm with a bunch of hippies and have a hootenanny? I didn't want to expand my mind, I wanted to expand my chest! Besides, the only mushrooms I liked were sauteed, and I was having far too good a time at Max's, dropping acid and pillaging and plundering my way to the high reaches of Superstardom.

For a while there, I was living with Wayne County (a.k.a. Jane County, who later became a popular transsexual rock and roll star in Germany) and Lee Childers, an aspiring photographer. We were going to Max's every night and dancing until dawn, although I was laying off the speed. One night some friends of Lee's stopped by on their way home from Woodstock as they headed back to Georgia. Well, they stayed for three weeks! You know how hippies can be—they're worse than bugs. You let a few slide in, and before you know it, the whole house is infested with them!

One of the hippies was a fifteen-year-old kid named Johnny. One night after returning home from a night of revelry with Jackie, Rita Redd, and my dear drunken friend Estelle, I came in to find this Johnny kid sitting on my bed playing his guitar. He was wearing a tie-dyed T-shirt, a leather wrist band, and sandals while strumming this sad little song, singing quietly to himself. It was so precious that I was touched, but when I entered the room, he stopped. "You don't have to stop because of me," I said, sitting beside him. He smiled, but didn't say much because he was very shy and seemed a little nervous. I sat down beside him and noticed that one of his eyes was a little crossed and I said, "Mmmm, one of your eyes is wondering what the other one is doing." He laughed and we became friends.

The following night I came staggering in after I had dropped some acid. Well, by now this little nature boy looked like Tarzan! He was playing the guitar again and I asked if he wanted to loosen up. He said yes, so I took the acid out of my purse and let him have a little taste. He, of course, had no idea about my true gender, so I had to give him something to ease the shock. Well, we both got loose and moved into the bedroom, where I swooped in for the kill! This man-child was straight, but very open and experimental. It was a beautiful evening and once again I had fallen in love.

Then Miss Curtis moved in, the pig!

Not long after, I joined the Playhouse of the Ridiculous. Rehearsals were beginning for *Heaven Grand in Amber Orbit*, which focused on the freaks in a circus sideshow. I now had a purpose in life: I was an actress and I was in rehearsal. Treacherous rehearsals, I might add. Vaccarro showed no mercy and was an advocate of suffering for one's art. I was originally cast as Princess Ninga Flinga Dung, the princess of song in the sideshow. My character had no arms or legs, and I had to do the role with knee and elbow pads. One night I couldn't find the knee pads and had to rehearse without them. John showed no mercy, screaming at me because I couldn't make my mark on time. I was trying the best I could, but my knees were bleeding and they hurt. Finally, I apologized and explained that I was in pain and that I couldn't make my mark any faster. John puffed up like a bull frog, gloated, and proclaimed at the top of his lungs, "There is no *I* in the Playhouse of the Ridiculous!" And with that, I was promptly reduced to being in the chorus!

Every day after rehearsals, Ruby Lynn, Jackie, Rita Redd, and I would flock to Max's business buffet. Rita Redd was a Harpo Marx look-alike with cute little dimples and curly red hair topped by a Harpo hat! She was a real do-gooder, and she could never do enough, so Curtis pounced on the opportunity and made Rita her own personal slave. Jackie read that Barbra Streisand carried shopping bags wherever she went, and since Jackie was forever confusing herself with Miss

Streisand, she decided she should do the same. The only difference was that Jackie's arms got tired, so she coerced Rita Redd into shlepping them!

Now that I was an actress, I really played up my looks for these little afternoon buffets. I always wore long baggy pants with flared cuffed bottoms, a white cotton turtleneck sweater and my silver platform shoes. My curly hair was a wild frenzy of frizz decorated with an enormous red silk rose, while my eyes were thick with black mascara and lots of bushy, black eyelashes. My lipstick was pale pink, and my wrists were heavily adorned with bracelets and bangles that clinked and clanked wherever I went. I sounded like a clunky, out-of-tune wind chime.

Now that I was in Jackie's play we became closer friends, and I often would tag along with her and hang out at the Factory.

"C'mon, let's go to the Factory. I need some money," she'd say, and off we'd plot to harvest what she could from Andy's bank account. Curtis knew to show up at three in the afternoon, because Andy would be there to cut the check. Joe Dallesandro and Paul Morrissey were also there and very nice, although Joe usually didn't say too much. He looked so normal, he always seemed out of place among truly wigged-out Superstars like Curtis and Andrea.

Fred Hughes, Andy's art dealer at the time, was also in attendance. Fred acted as Andy's filter, and anyone who wanted to see Andy generally had to see Fred first. Fred was Dapper Dan, very classy with dark, slicked-back hair, and an impeccable wardrobe of tailored suits. He was just like a leading man from an old movie, and he was the first gentleman who ever kissed my hand upon being introduced. He was divine.

The Factory was a gathering place for many important film impressarios, artists, and celebrities of the day who wanted to hang out and see the menagerie of nuts roll in and out. Once Jackie and I walked in and Lina Wertmuller and Rainer Werner Fassbinder were there lunching. Jackie, of course, was fawned over and photographed with them because she was the latest sensation in the Warhol stable of oddities.

Another time, during a visit to the Factory, Jackie introduced me to this little Italian kid named Jeff who was working for Andy as a gofer.

Not long after our introduction, Jeff ran into me at Max's and told me that he had been fired from the Factory. I don't remember the reason, but he was very upset, cursing the entire bunch.

"I've had it with the fucking Factory. Fuck Andy. Fuck 'em all, they're nothing but a bunch of shitty exploiters anyway."

"Yeah, well . . ." I didn't care if they exploited me or not, I just wanted to be in a movie!

"They use people and fuck them over," he accused again. "That's what they did with Edie. She's fucked up and it's because of them."

A couple of days later, I ran into him again and he asked me if I wanted to go uptown with him because he had to go pick up a camera. I didn't have to rehearse, so I went along. We entered a camera shop and the next thing I know, he's charging a two-thousand-dollar camera to Warhol and telling the clerks that I'm Viva! I looked at him and I said, "What are you doing?" And he said, "Don't worry. I do this all the time." Yeah, right. He was so nervous he was quivering! The store clerk looked at us and said that he would have to verify the charge to Andy's account. There I was, not knowing what to do, thinking, "Oh, my God. What have I gotten myself into now?" when Jeff bolted out of the store and fled. Well, I ran out of the store as fast as I could and kept running until I collapsed in an alley from exhaustion. I felt used and betrayed. I couldn't believe this little punk made me his moll, and then ran out on me when the heat was on. The nerve!

In September 1969, *Heaven Grand in Amber Orbit* opened on Forty-third Street in a small funeral-home-turned-theater. I'd spend hours preparing for my role as Cuckoo the Bird Girl, who was featured in the chorus as a Moon Reindeer Girl. While getting dressed, I'd grease up my entire body with petroleum jelly and Johnny would help sprinkle my body with glitter. I had glitter everywhere—in my hair, my ears, my nose. And I'd wear a black mink bikini with different shades of chiffon shreds hanging from it, along with red glittered lipstick, green glittered eyeshadow, and green glittered antlers on top of my head. I was a something to behold and a sight no one would miss.

The Moon Reindeer Girls' opening number was a song called "Antlers," which was sung to the tune of "There's Nothing Like a Dame" from the musical *South Pacific*. The lyrics were as follows:

> Antlers—we've got antlers.
> We got antlers in our nose,
> We got antlers in our hose,
> We got antlers in our panties,
> And antlers in our toes!
> What ain't we got?
> We ain't got ulcers!

Rogers and Hammerstein it wasn't, but we were written up in *Newsweek*! Also, a writer by the name of John Heyes did a feature on me for an underground news rag. My first big interview. Well, I couldn't say I was a nobody, so I took the opportunity to use the media to my best advantage and lied through my teeth. I told him that I was a Warhol Superstar and they ran the story with some shmaltzy Art Nouveau photos taken by Lee Childers. I thought, what the hell? If I wanted to be a Warhol Superstar, I'd better just go out and grab it.

When Paul Morrissey saw the issue with my face plastered on the page and me giving an interview as to what it was like being a Warhol Superstar, he was amused. "Who the hell is this Holly person?" he thought as he approached Andy with the article. Andy was a little leery, and ever since the Valerie Solanis incident, he had every right to be cautious. He had guessed that I was the one behind the camera heist, from the description he received from the camera store, and because of this suspicion, Andy wanted no part of me. But Paul, who was fascinated by my nerve, had a hunch that I would be good on the screen.

Word was going around Max's that Andy and Paul were preparing to shoot a new film about junkies living on the Lower East Side. I knew I'd be perfect for a part, but I didn't know how to get one. Paul was still curious about my acting ability and he knew I could be reached at Max's. So, as fate would have it, one night after the show, when I staggered into the back room, I was summoned to the great round table, where I was asked to call the Factory the following morning and ask for Paul. There were no details given, but I knew something was up. Why else would Paul Morrissey want to talk to me? I just knew it was that stupid camera incident. Didn't they know I was innocent? That damned mishap was going to haunt me until the day I died.

I didn't want to call the Factory! But Jackie Curtis kept on saying, "Holly, at least call 'em. If they wanted you arrested, they would have arrested you. Paul's shooting a movie. He wants you. I know he does. So call him already," she insisted. "And if they don't want you, ask 'em if there's a part for your sister here."

Curtis and I were always sisters when she needed something.

So the next day I very nervously rang the Factory and Paul answered the phone. "Ha-ha-hi, Paul, th-this is Ha-Holly," I stammered.

"Hi, Holly, I'm glad you called," Paul began eagerly. "Listen, we're doing a movie this weekend and I was wondering if you'd like to be in a scene?"

Without asking where, when, why, or how much, I heard myself screaming, "Yes! I'd love to! What do I do? Where do I go?"

"Well, can you be at my place this Saturday at one o'clock?" I quickly grabbed a pencil and scrawled the directions on the wall so I wouldn't lose them. "Sure, no problem. See you then." I quietly hung up the phone and shrieked with glee. Finally, it had happened. I was so excited I danced all the way from Fourteenth Street to Forty-fourth Street, singing to fruit vendors, flower carts, prostitutes, and junkies —right up to the theater entrance, where I flew into the air, performed an entrechat, and fell into the arms of the stage manager. "Oh, Noah," I said, beaming. "I'm gonna be a star, a Warhol Superstar, and, and, and—" And then KABOOM! Noah dropped me on the pavement.

CHAPTER 8

Plucked From the Gutter and Tossed on the Screen

*W*e began shooting on a cool Saturday afternoon in October 1969, and I slaved for hours on my face and hair, in a stunning effort to look my best for the audience. And stun them I did! Looking back at the film today, I'm a little shocked myself.

I had no idea what to wear, nor did I have any real idea about my character, so I threw on a lavender dress (a hand-me-down from Jackie Curtis) and an old racoon coat.

I arrived at Paul's brownstone, which was located on Sixth Street between Second and First Avenue on the Lower East Side, at one o'clock sharp. I was nervous as hell and brought Johnny, the littlest hippie, with me for moral support. Paul brought us into the kitchen, where I was introduced to Jed Johnson, the film's gofer, gaffer, grip, and editor. Since there was no one else around, Jed served as the picture's entire crew.

Andy never came to the sets during filming, and he only saw the footage when it came back from the lab. His reaction was always exactly the same: "Oh, it's great!" No matter what he was seeing, it was always "great." Years later, Jackie Curtis told the story about how, during the filming of *Women in Revolt*, she demanded that Andy shoot all of her scenes and, in doing so, Andy loaded the film backward. Miss Curtis was obviously out of her mind when she spun that yarn. Andy never got behind the camera and she never made such a demand because Paul would not have allowed it.

That afternoon when we were preparing to shoot my first scene, I was also re-introduced to Joe Dallesandro, the film's star. We had said hello to each other before during my jaunts to the Factory with Jackie, but this was going to be our first time interracting with each other and I was nervous.

Joe was nice, but very quiet. I never feel entirely at ease around anyone unless there's some sort of emotion shown toward me. Whether it's love, hate, hot, or cold, I need to know where I stand when I meet someone. And with Joe, I couldn't tell what he thought about me and at first I felt uncomfortable. I didn't know if he thought I was crazy, I didn't know if he liked me, I couldn't feel any vibes whatsoever. He just seemed indifferent to me. So throughout most of the filming, I was very careful around him. I didn't want to scare him or offend him in any way. And most importantly, I didn't want to get slapped! Also, I respected him as a fellow actor and so I did my job the best I could.

After filming began that day, I became a bit more comfortable around him. He was very nice to me, always bringing me Olde English 800 and Miller High Life beer, which later gave Paul Morrissey the idea that I should use the bottle as a sex toy. There were no limits to what we would do for the sake of art! I remember Joe was very helpful on the set, and he was always pitching in to sweep the floor or help with the lights. I was surprised by his down-to-earth attitude because here he was, this gorgeous Andy Warhol Superstar, and he wasn't the least bit affected.

Paul was trying to make me comfortable by describing my character and the scene. At this point, Paul didn't exactly know where the film was heading, nor did he have a title. He just told me that it was a story about a junkie (played by Joe) who lives off my character in a sleazy pit of an apartment and hops from girl to girl, trying to get money for heroin.

Once everyone had become acquainted and my nerves had settled, off we went to the set. I was expecting a soundstage, but what I got was Paul's basement, which was supposed to be my apartment. Jed set up two lights, one on the left and one on the right, and then began to load the film into this clumsy old 16mm movie camera. As crummy as that basement appeared, once the lights had been set up, it changed my entire perspective of the dump. I suddenly felt like I was on a movie set, and the butterflies were aflutter in my stomach again. But it was exciting and I loved it.

"The set" consisted of an old wrought-iron bed, an old bird cage, and Joe's dog. In the middle of the room was a lobster trap that was supposed to be a cocktail table and an old sink that I'm saving for people to pee in, which was another one of Paul's brilliant notions. He was very quick with his ideas. He would come in, set up the scene, and hand out a few choice lines, as well as his directional ideas, but the rest was pure improvisation. It was that simple. We didn't need scripts—we had faces then!

Since *Trash* was about a junkie's quest for heroin, or "junk" as it is commonly called on the streets, Paul decided that my character should be a symbolic version of Joe's addiction; therefore, Paul had the idea that my character collected junk out of garbage and sold it for money. I must admit that the characterization was not far from home, as I had wallowed in the gutter on numerous occasions. I also dabbled in drugs and I lived in squalor, but the similarities ended there. I had a taste for the finer things in life, like booze and pills, and I was not interested in collecting garbage. Also, I wasn't the least bit attracted to Mr. Dallesandro, not that I didn't find him good-looking. He was too good-looking! Not to mention that he had a wife and a child. Besides, I had my little Johnny, who was more fun than a barrel of monkeys and more virile than a stable of stallions!

The first scene opened with me lounging in what is supposed to be my unkempt basement apartment while Joe moves the sink across the floor. After the sink is moved, Joe lies down on the bed to nap and I become upset, because I'm in the mood for love and he's in the mood to snore. Well, like any woman whose libido is on the verge of a nervous breakdown, I go off into a fierce tirade, screaming at him for nodding out every time I want to talk, accusing him of roaming the streets looking for dope, and abusing my hospitality.

"Hey, stupid. Hey, fuck. Get the fuck off my bed!" I scream. ". . . You're a mooch, motherfucker. A mooch!" (Brilliant dialogue!)

Well, the camera kept rolling, so I kept on ranting and raving. All my bundled nerves had sprung loose, and this wild woman's personality just burst out of me. I never knew I had it in me, because basically I was a very shy, demure little thing . . . well, most of the time. But I just yelled, screamed, and carried on nonetheless, and before I knew it the scene was over. No retakes, no cuts, no changing camera angles, and no makeup person to powder me down. So this is how a Warhol movie was made, I thought. I loved it! I'd have a swig of beer, Paul would turn on the camera, and we'd perform. What could be more wholesome and natural? Ah, ptui with Stanislavski. This was the true school of acting, felt from the heart of my festive soul. Bring on the beer! I felt like the best thing since Sarah Bernhardt, having completely forgotten my lady-like decorum to become this sleazy, scheming, money-grubbing, cock-sucking, low-life bitch. What a juicy role.

The shoot ended at four that afternoon and I signed the release. I was so thrilled, you'd have thought I'd just signed a major studio contract! Paul thanked me, handed me a check for twenty-five dollars, and told me to call him the following week so I could see the rushes. Then Johnny and I flew out of there on cloud nine and skedaddled over to Max's, where we celebrated to our hearts' content. To hell with the cheap all-you-can-eat pigeon-wing buffet, honey. We ordered real food—a whole carafe of their best wine with two orders of lobster tails and steak, appropriately known as Surf and Turf. Twenty-five bucks sure went a long way in those days.

As we sat down in our banquette, Andrea Whips Feldman, who

was now calling herself Andrea Whips Warhol, spotted us from afar and screamed, "Holly, dahhhhling!" And then she fell over, obviously festooned in her festivities.

"Goddamn it!" she screamed, picking herself up from the floor, brushing herself off, and heading our way. Andrea was blond thunder with a voice that sounded like a cross between screeching tires and Zsa Zsa Gabor. She, too, was a Superstar who also was going to have a part in *Trash*, but according to Andrea, it was her movie and she was the star.

"Everyone, I'd like to make an announcement!" she hollered above the voices of the maddening crowd as she approached our table. "Everyone, listen—hey!"

No one was really paying her any attention at all, and she began to fume.

"Hey, shut the fuck up! Don't you know who I am? I'm Mrs. Andy Warhol. Now shut up!" she screamed at the top of her inebriated lungs, quieting the room. "This is Holly Woodlawn and she's in my new movie. Holly, I'm gonna make you a star, baby. I'm gonna make you a Superstar because I'm Andrea Whips Warhol."

The crowd, mostly friends, cheered to appease the drunken lush, and as she luxuriated in the applause, security moved in to haul her off!

"Hey! HEY!" she hollered, trying to yank her elbows from the clutches of the two men dragging her out into the alley. "I'm Mrs. Andy Warhol! I'm a Superstar! Don't you know who I am? Hey!"

Well, so much for Mrs. Andy Warhol. But then, Andrea was always screaming, yelling, and carrying on that she was Andy's wife. Once she went off the deep end at the Factory, screaming that she was Mrs. Andy Warhol and smashing typewriters on the floor! I always thought her outbursts of insanity were a part of her glamour; I had no idea that the girl was actually born with a fruit cocktail between her ears.

And speaking of cocktails, as I nursed my martini, Johnny sat across from me trying to rebuild my self-esteeem. I had begun to think that I had done a horrible job of acting earlier in the day, but Johnny defended my ability.

"You were good—really, Holly," he said, picking at his bread.

"Are you kidding?" I snapped. "I was horrible!"

I honestly thought I was terrible, but then who is satisfied with their first on-screen performance? Besides, I looked so ridiculous in that dress. I looked like Miss Biafra! And the hairdo that I put so much time in creating looked like it had been set by the A-bomb. Not to mention that my teeth were so buck that I couldn't close my lips, and there was a small cavity in the front that looked like the black hole of Calcutta! Oh, the horror!

I was terribly distraught because I wanted to be taken seriously as an actress. Most of the Superstars were just crazy people who were famous because they were strange. Many of them weren't even recognized as having talent, but rather shock value. They just reached out to the world and said, "Look at me. I'm fabulous!" And most everyone bought that shit and thought they *were* fabulous. Or at least interesting. But I wanted to be the first Superstar who was recognized for talent and not lunacy. I didn't just stand before a camera, yelling and screaming. I had tried my best and I flopped. Or so I thought.

Trash was a great contrast to the Factory's earlier productions, which were fairly pedestrian. Andy turned on the camera, it rolled, and when it ran out of film, he turned it off. How much imagination does that take? And people said this was art? It was crap.

Paul Morrissey was the one who revamped the Warholian style of filmmaking; he added narratives that gave the films structure. He was also a conscious director, which resulted in *Trash* becoming the first Andy Warhol production regarded as "mainstream."

Later in the week, I decided not to call Paul at the Factory to see the rushes because I was too embarrassed. I didn't want to see myself on the screen, particularly at the Factory with a room full of people. So I decided to chuck this experience and go on with my life in the theater, but Johnnny kept pestering me to call.

"Holly, go on, give him a call," he pushed. "You probably did a great job, but so what if you didn't? At least they'll have free wine."

Well, that's all I needed to hear. I picked up the phone and dialed, but all I could think about was how humiliating this was going to be.

"Hello, is Paul there?" I asked the woman who answered the phone.

"May I asked who's calling?"

"Uh, tell him it's Holly. Holly Woodlawn."

I cringed, fearing she'd scream that I stunk and hang up immediately, but suprisingly the voice seeemed to brighten.

"Oh, Holly, hi. Hold on."

Oh, my God. They were actually going to take my call! I couldn't believe it. She must've thought I said Holly Soloman, the art dealer. Paul picked up the phone.

"Hi, Holly. Listen, your scene looks great. You want to come by, say, tomorrow and see the rushes?"

"Oh, yeah. Sure."

"Yeah, well, uh, come on by tomorrow afternoon around three-thirty. We're going to have another screening. And listen, do you think you'd be available to do another scene?"

Did he say what I thought he said? I wondered. And then I made him repeat the question. I was stunned. He actually wanted me back for another scene. Oh, I wanted so badly to blow him off with a casual "Let me check my calendar and I'll call you in a couple of days" routine, but instead I became flushed and pounced on the opportunity. After I hung up the phone, I kicked up my heels and screamed, "They want me back!"

Johnny and I went to the Factory to see the rushes later that week and I was floored. There I was, on the screen, looking like Broom Hilda! I looked heinous. I had spent hours getting dressed for that shoot, and I looked as if I had just rolled out of bed. I was mortified. And to think I thought I was so beautiful, walking around in these thriftshop outfits with this frizzed-out hair that looked like a fire hazard. I knew I should've invested in a full-length mirror. But despite the holes in my teeth, my ratted hair, and my lanky body, I was funny. The audience attending the soiree actually cracked up at my scene, and I laughed a bit myself. Perhaps I did have talent after all.

Attending the rushes at the Factory had become a big event. It was like an art opening, with big-name producers, directors, and museum curators dropping in to see the latest bits of film. A lot of the superstars would get all dressed up, since it was a chance to mingle with the jet set. By this time, Andy and I had become more sociable, and he would tell me how glamourous I looked and how good I was on film. And I, so deeply moved by his admiration, asked him to pay my rent!

Actually, it was Miss Curtis who gave me the idea. Johnny and I were stone-cold broke, with nowhere to turn but the streets, when Curtis pulled me aside in Max's and said, "Ask Andy, he'll give it to ya."

"I can't, Jackie. You know me. I get afraid. I feel weird asking—"

"Oh, go on!" she butted in. "He owes you, Holly. He's gonna get rich offa you. Please, I do it all the time."

Ain't that the truth. Curtis was forever dipping into the pot at the end of Andy's rainbow, and it never fazed her. I, however, felt so demeaned until one day I had no choice. I either asked Andy for a handout, or Johnny and I were evicted. So I went to the Factory and Andy gave me a three-hundred-and-fifty-dollar check for my rent and an additional fifty dollars for food. I was very grateful and took it to Max's, where Johnny and I cashed in and celebrated. And, of course, we once again bypassed the cheap buffet.

My second scene was filmed a week later. This time I really wanted to look good. So I wore my camel-hair coat with the fox-fur collar, and went all out to arrange my hair. I also took a black jersey dress that I had redesigned by cutting off the sleeves and shortening it a titch above the knee.

Again, I had arrived with Johnny in tow, and while we were hanging out in the kitchen waiting for Jed to arrive, Paul asked Johnny if he had any acting experience. Johnny had none, but Paul had the idea of my picking up a boy on the street and bringing him home on the pretense of selling him dope. But what my character was really after was sex! Johnny thought it sounded fun, so Paul ran upstairs and brought down a suit jacket for Johnny to wear. He was going to play a preppy young school lad seduced by a depraved harlot. You see how impromptu this film was? Paul just plotted as we plodded along!

In the scene, I bring Johnny home while Joe is sweeping the floor. The basement was actually clean this time! I get money from Johnny and run out of the apartment to cop some dope down the hall while Johnny waits with Joe. When I return, I simulate shooting Johnny up with a hideous horse needle, and then proceed to ravage the poor boy's body.

At first, I was taken aback because Johnny was my real boyfriend, but he actually became this preppy school kid right before my very eyes. He was an extremely good actor and he knew just how to play the scene, so it was very easy to react to him. The day's shooting went really well and Paul always claimed that this scene was his favorite in the movie.

Well, the rushes were so fabulous I was asked back again! People in the underground art scene finally started to recognize me as a worthwhile performer. They'd come up to me at Max's and tell me they saw me in the rushes at the Factory and start stroking my ego. One night, Johnny and I were walking past the bar and this cigarette-scorched voice cried out, "Holly!" And I turned to look and there at the bar was Miss Sylvia Miles, with her shimmering blond hair and thick black eyelashes and those bright white teeth stretched into a flawless smile. She certainly had good reason to smile, since she was flanked by two handsome young men.

"I just saw rushes at the Factory and you are marvelous!" she said, beaming. My God! Sylvia Miles had just told me that I was marvelous? I couldn't believe it. She had just been nominated for an Academy Award for *Midnight Cowboy* and she's telling me I'm good? It was the ultimate approval.

The scenes were only shot on Saturday or Sunday afternoons, and filming only lasted an hour or two at a time. We never filmed one day after another. After Paul saw the rushes of an earlier scene, he thought up the following one. By the time the third weekend rolled around, my head was swimming with compliments from viewers of my earlier rushes. I began to take this acting stuff more seriously than ever before and I was really doing my damnedest to act. I was playing the scene with a woman named Diane who was supposed to be my pregnant sister and whose child I have decided to raise once it is born. I reached deep down into the trenches of my soul to pull out something Lee Strasberg could have been proud of and I fell flat. I lost my spontaneity and became very blahhh. I guess I went so deep into the trenches I got lost!

Diane was very nice, but very misunderstood. People thought she was a witch because she always dressed in black, had an interest in mysticism, and played with crystals. At the time, she was pregnant with a baby by an Israeli man named Achem. She had a white face, frizzy hair, and buck teeth, and everybody swore we were sisters!

There's a scene in which I catch Diane and Joe making it on my bed and I have to scream at her and throw her out of my apartment. I felt so bad because she was such a sweet person, but I laid into her anyway. It didn't do any good. She had the nerve to smile at me all throughout my tirade. I think she thought it was funny that I had turned into a beast so quickly.

Then there was the big location scene. I was so embarrassed. We drove around in Joe's van, scouting locations in the worst part of the Lower East Side on Avenue D. It was the height of junkie land, and the lowest pit of hell. Finally, Paul spotted a pile of rubble near a gutted tenement. There was a mattress and a chest of drawers on the street, and Paul got the idea that I should haul the mattress and the drawers back to my humble home.

While the camera was set up inside the van with Paul and Jed, Joe and I were outside among the hoodlums. I don't know about Joe, but I was fearing for my life with these mad junkie Puerto Ricans lying in the gutter shouting "Mira, baby, mira!" And then they'd suck their lips together and taunt me with smooch noises. "Come here, you like this, Mammi?" they teased while they rubbed their crotches. I thought, "Piss on you, motherfucker! I'm a movie star!" It might've been a cheap movie being filmed in a low-life part of town, but it was a movie nonetheless. "I am an actress, not a puta!" I proclaimed, proudly standing my ground on two legs that had kicked higher and wider than any chorus girl's around.

As we were shooting the scene, a gust of wind swept my hat right off my head! Well, during the rushes later in the week, many of the viewers gasped. My hair looked to be very short in the scene, not the wild fury that it had been in the past, because I had tastefully pinned it up into a French twist.

"She wasn't wearing her wig," I overheard someone whisper. My wig? I never wore a wig in my life. But apparently this person thought I had been stripped of my character. Oh, darling! If I was going to be stripped of anything, it would have been my morals! Which is exactly what happened one afternoon when Paul got the idea that my character was so sexually frustrated that she'd masturbate with a beer bottle! It was an infamous romp that plummeted into the anus—I mean annals!—of cinema history and would hopefully be forgotten by all. I had tried to forget myself, but there wasn't enough dope in the world to fry that memory from my mind.

It all started with Joe, Paul, and I sitting around waiting for Jed to finish loading film into the camera. Paul was tossing around ideas and he came up with a doozy. He wanted me to jerk off Joe. Well, I was shocked! I was apalled! I was a serious thespian of the stage and screen—I was not about to do pornography!

"Well, I don't want to show it," reasoned Paul. "We can just make it look like you're doing it off-camera."

Joe and I were positioned so that all the audience could see was my hand moving up and down the inside of Joe's blue-jeaned leg. I felt so stupid with my clenched fist beating off the thin air.

Joe's character, however, couldn't get an erection because he was supposed to be strung out on heroin, so Paul suggested that I remedy my sexual frustration with an empty beer bottle! I was shocked again, but being an actress dedicated to her craft, I obliged. The action was, of course, simulated and it was a true circus act. I was positioned on the mattress with nothing on but my pink panties, a sheet, and my frosted white nail polish by Revlon, with the sheet glamourously arranged so that nothing could be seen of my supposed-to-be-naked naughty parts. And I just went for it!

So there I was in a fetal position working this beer bottle up and down between my legs, having a jolly ol' time while trying to hide my panties, show off my manicure, and look glamourous, all at the same time. I felt like a flying Wallenda! Honey, that's when the true actress inside of me took over. I was wallowing in this role like a pig in caca getting down and dirty. The mattress was flopping, the springs were sqeaking, my hips were grinding, and I was bouncing myself up and down, higher and higher to make the squeaks louder and louder. Then I "climaxed" and faked a tumultuous orgasm!

Joe was lying passively on the floor and I, having just made a complete asshole of myself, felt completely demoralized. Mine was such a sad character, having to resort to such extremes in search of affection. I groped at Joe's arms and legs and made him promise that I'd never have to do this again. As the scene played out, I became so emotional that I began to cry and Joe took my hand and held it. He held my hand and he squeezed it. I was touched emotionally and I felt so good, because this had been the first time Joe had ever shown any warmth to me—ever. I finally felt as if I had won his friendship. Up until then, I didn't know where I stood with him, but after that scene, I felt as if a wall had come down between us—a wall that I'd put up to hide my insecurity.

When I was asked to commit sex acts with a bottle, it didn't dawn on me that I could possibly be embarrassed by this performance in the future. As far as I was concerned, I was doing it for art and to hell with what people thought. But I soon realized that what I thought were wonderful and fabulous acts were just crazy antics to get attention. Later, after I had seen rushes of the scene, I thought, "Oh, Lord. What have I done to myself?" I was so humiliated. There I was with my ass to the wind, having an orgasm with a beer bottle! Just the thought of it made me shrivel, but what made it even more embarrassing was that people actually thought my beer bottle charade was real!

"How did it feel? Didn't it hurt? Weren't you afraid?" were the usual questions.

If they had paid attention, they would have noticed the shot where my panties show, thus blowing the whole illusion.

Then there were those who thought the scene was touching, which eased my humiliation. Some even said it brought a tear to their eye.

"Well, *au contraire*," I would jokingly toss off. "It brought hemorrhoids to my asswans." And they took me seriously, which I suppose is the reason many thought I actually shoved a bottle up my ass!

We finished the last scene on a weekend the following spring with Michael Sklar playing a welfare social worker infatuated with my shoes.

I tried to con him into giving Joe and me welfare by faking a pregnancy, but the scheme falls through when—in a fit of anger—I stand up for my rights and a pillow falls out of my stomach.

Michael was my first experience with a professional, unionized actor. He had a portfolio, a résumé, and an eight-by-ten glossy to boot! I was very impressed. He was involved with the original Second City troupe and he was a very funny guy. When we weren't filming, we would be yukking it up in the back, but when we did the scene, he suddenly became this pain-in-the-ass welfare worker who didn't like me at all. I was so intimidated and at a loss for words, until Michael made a crack about the Negroes cranking out babies every nine months to get on welfare. Well, honey, I was livid! Beverly Johnson was the top model of the year and he's talking about Negroes cranking out babies to get on welfare? The NAACP was going to picket this movie for sure! I became so upset by this racial slur that I actually began to take him personally. I was no longer Holly Woodlawn playing Holly Santiago in a movie. I had made the transition, and this was real. Needless to say, we got into a big uproarious fight, with everybody yelling, screaming, and carrying on.

The scene had to be shot five times! Michael wasn't easily satisfied and my pillow didn't easily fall out on cue. He was always striving to bring more into his character. The more he strived, the more I strived, and so when it was over, I hated his guts. Previous to this, nearly all of my scenes were filmed with one take. I mean, come on. There was only one camera angle, goddamn it. He had said the same line five times! On the sixth take, I was convinced he was going for nuances!

Although Andy never came to the set while we were filming, he often commented on my performances during the rushes. "You're going to be a big star," he told me before the film was completed. And to think I believed that crap. It was as if Zeus had handed down the last thunder bolt and said I was bound for divinity.

CHAPTER

9

It Should
Happen to You

*A*fter filming was completed and I got the twenty-five-dollar check in my hot little pawpaws, Johnny and I scurried over to Max's and cashed it instantly. Once we had gotten the bread, we raced over to the seedier part of Chelsea—Seventeenth Street and Ninth Avenue, to be exact—and came face-to-face with a dark, towering brownstone. Inside this foreboding, grafitti-marred edifice lurked a friend of Little Chrysis's who dealt heroin.

I sauntered up to the steel door and rang the apartment bell. "Who is it?" grumbled a voice. I leaned into the speaker and lowered my voice, "Chrysis sent me." The loud, menacing noise of the buzzer sent a chill down my spine. It was so abrupt and shocking, if I didn't

Three years old—Puerto Rico, 1950.

Six years old—with Mommy and
Uncle Virgilio, New York, 1952.

With Mommy and Aunt Chalo, the Bronx, 1952.

My father and I with the rest of the monkeys of the neighborhood.

At age 35. Back in New York after an extended busboy engagement at Beni Hana in Florida. No, I did not like this identity!

Eleven years old—while attending South Beach Elementary, Miami Beach, 1958.

The gang from the factory on "The David Susskind Show," 1970. *(left to right)* Michael Sklar, Taylor Meade, me, Andrea Feldman, Paul Morrissey, Susskind, Geri Miller, Jackie Curtis, Bruce Pecheur, Ondine, and Talley Brown. *(Fred W. McDarrah)*

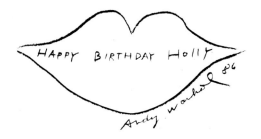

HAPPY BIRTHDAY Holly
Andy Warhol 86

A birthday card from Andy Warhol.

Playing to the pin light. *(Jarry Lang)*

Jackie and I during "Cabaret in the Sky" at Lincoln Center.

Advertisement for my show at Reno Sweeney. *(From the collection of Jarry Lang)*

Divine and I during the run of Neon Woman. *(From the collection of Jarry Lang)*

Divine and I at a pagan party in Provincetown during *Neon Woman*. *(Ron Link)*

Me with Casey Donovan *(left)* and Scorpio *(right)* at NYC's Ice Palace. *(Gene Bagnatto)*

With John Sex *(left)* and Michael Musto *(right)* during a production of "The Sound of Muzak" at Club 57. *(Gene Bagnatto)*

WORLD PREMIER! ALL STAR CAST of the Decade!!!

Theatre for the New City Bartinell/ Field
Present:

HOLLY WOODLAWN* in
"TINSEL TOWN
TIRADE"

The New Musical by HIBISCUS

Directed by Jeffrey Shock
Music Lyrics Ann & Fred Harris
Starring Penny Arcade Dun Fudeaway Hibiscus
and The Screaming Violets
Luke Warm Joyce Mandell Giovani Lash Lame
Geretta Giancarlo Angles of Light

Opens April 2nd   Info 212-254-1109

VOICE MARCH 9, 1982

In the ad for "Tinsel Town Tirade" with Hibiscus.
(From the collection of Jarry Lang)

Cabaret still, 1978. (*Kenn Duncan*)

Me in Esther Williams's bathing suit from *Jupiter's Darling*, Fire Island Pines, 1974. *(Jarry Lang)*

Trying to be androgynous. *(Jarry Lang)*

Candy Darling. *(Ron Link)*

Candy rehearsing "Vicissitudes of the Damned" at La MaMa in the West Village. Circa 1972. *(Bob Gruen)*

Jackie circa 1970. She autographed
the photo during a mad rush of
speed freak lunacy.

Jackie thinking she was James
Dean for a day. (*Bob Gruen*)

Jackie circa 1970. A woman
of the Seventies just speeding
away. (*Jack Mitchell*)

Last photo taken of Jackie Curtis. (*Bob Gruen*)

Jackie and I during "Cabaret in the Sky" at Lincoln Center. We were singing "Just in Time" and Curtis had never looked better. (*Bob Gruen*)

Me in *Broken Goddess*. (Dallas)

The night I bombed at the Continental Baths.
(Bob Gruen)

During my androgynous phase, just before I bombed at Bimbos. *(Jarry Lang)*

(Jarry Lang)

Pre-*Trash* opening while I was living with Johnny next to the Hell's Angels. *(Laura Rubin)*

Famous People in Bathtub Series. *(Donald Herron)*

Me today. *(Julia Sloan)*

know better I would've thought someone had just fried in an electric chair. I grabbed the coldness of the steel latch, pulled opened the door, and entered the building. The door slammed behind us. This dump had all the charm of a mausoleum and we had the willies. We clung to each other like Hansel and Gretel as we softly crept down the ominous hall to the elevator cage. We summoned the car, got in, closed the gate, pressed the button, and rattled, jiggled, and joggled ourselves to the third floor, where we stopped with a jolt. We escaped the clamoring contraption and began to search the murky interior for Apartment 3F, constantly looking over our shoulders for fear that some ghoul would creep up on our heels and say, "Boo!" Or worse yet, we'd be murdered by some psycho in a housedress and hauled off to a fruit cellar!

Once we had found the apartment, I knocked on the door softly. We waited a moment. Then we waited another. And just when I raised my hand to knock again, the door opened just a crack and I saw the chain lock that prevented it from opening further. Through the opening peered a tall, skinny, black Puerto Rican drag queen, her hair squeezed under a stocking cap and her sleepy eyes giving me the once-over. I handed her a ten-dollar bill, which she snagged immediately, handing me a small baggie in exchange. Then the door slammed in my face. No hello, thank you, or good-bye, which was fine because who had time for congeniality in that eerie tomb?

We stashed the dope in our pockets and fled like bandits to our dilapidated tenement on Third Street and Second Avenue. It was a dump, really, but compared to that pit we had just escaped, this place looked like a chateau! It was an old, narrow, five-story brownstone from the Twenties, with a black fire escape that scaled the facade and large French windows peering over the street.

Johnny and I charged up the rickety wooden stairs into our palatial fourth-floor flat, slammed the door behind us, and went through the ritual of locking, bolting, and barricading the door. It was quite an ordeal, with an array of locks that extended from the top to the bottom of the door frame. We did everything but slide a dresser in front of it! After all, we were living in a dangerous neighborhood and one had to take precautions. A crook would need a bomb to get past all of those locks!

The Hells' Angels owned the building right next door, although the big black butch momma who was renting the joint to us didn't happen to mention that fact, between puffs of her pink cigarette, when we were signing the lease. There was a sea of motorcycles outside my window, with leather-clad hoodlums on top of them. One of the gals who used to hang out with the boys looked real fierce. She was a tough cookie—you know, the gum-smacking type with blond hair, black roots, and tattoos; with breasts the size of canteloupes and biceps to match. Her name was Wanda, and I think she made her living beating people up for loan sharks. At first, I was terrified of the entire pack, but once we became acquainted, I found that they were actually very nice. One of them even helped me upstairs with my groceries! It turned out they were very protective of the neighborhood, so it was like having a pack of guard dogs prowling the grounds. I became very fond of them, and they became affectionately known as the Harley Girls.

We had a lovely jacuzzi in the kitchen—an ancient bathtub, crafted of porcelain but smothered under four thousand coats of paint. The tub had a tin cover that fit snuggly over the opening, turning it into convenient counter space! It was on this tin cover that we prepared for our blissful journey into the fabulous realm of Ga-Ga Land. It was our launchpad, so to speak.

Johnny reached into the cupboard over the tub, pulled out one of the Welch's jelly jars we used for drinking glasses, and began to fill it with hot water while I went to get "the works." These were all the necessary tools, which we kept rolled in a Baggie and hidden in the cuckoo clock we'd found in the trash and hung near the stove. My hand, quivering from a rush of adrenaline, reached for the big hand on the clock and pushed it to twelve. Or was it one? No, it was three. Oh, shit! I had no time for cuckoo combinations, darling! I needed my fix, so I pulled open the clock's back side, reached in, and pulled out the Baggie, unrolling it as I made my way to the tub.

I laid out the works—a makeshift syringe (we made our syringes out of eye droppers), a bottle cap, a bobby pin, and a wad of cotton —neatly across the tin cover. Johnny took the bobby pin and spread it apart, wrapping it around the bottle cap so the head of the pin could be used to hold the cap over an open flame.

The heroin came in small wax-paper envelopes no bigger than two postage stamps. I took one envelope and carefully unsealed it while Johnny ran hot water over the needle in an effort to sterilize it. I dropped some water into the bottle cap and mixed it with the dope, then lit a match and held the makeshift bobby pin–bottle cap contraption over the flame. This was known as "cooking the stuff," which we did to get rid of the quinine with which the drug was cut. Cutting was like an additive, sort of like adding bread crumbs to a meat loaf. Heroin was always cut differently. Sometimes it was cut too much, sometimes it wasn't cut enough.

I was a pretty good cook when it came to heroin. One would think I was whipping up an exotic soufflé, I took it so seriously. You have to cook it just right, darling. You can't have the flame too close to the cap, nor can it be too far away—and God forbid should you overcook it! I don't care what you call it—dope, stuff, or smack—if you scorch it, then it's crap! And I had a very sensitive palate, even when I was shooting up.

So, there I was, fancying myself as Julia Child slaving over a hot bottle cap, when the stuff began to bubble. I let it bubble a little bit, but not too much because what the hell can you do with all that froth? Plus, darling, the big fear with shooting up was getting an air bubble caught in your bloodstream and dying of a heart attack!

Johnny took a small wad of cotton and put it in his mouth, getting it good and wet, and then rolled it into a ball and stuck it in the bottle cap. Then he took the "spike" (that's what we called the needle) and pushed it into the cotton, which had by now absorbed the heroin. The cotton was put into the bottle cap to absorb all the impurities and to insure that no air bubbles would travel into the syringe. Impurities and air bubbles could kill us, for God's sake! So we had to be careful. We, of course, didn't like to think about the deadly possibilities while we were fooling around with the stuff! But then, what junkie does?

I was not a junkie in the least, I had convinced myself. A junkie is someone who is entirely dependent on the drug. One actually becomes the drug, and one's entire existence becomes an effort to get it. I never lived for it, darling. I just couldn't wait to get home to do it!

I used my orange ribbon scarf as a tourniquet, tying it tightly around Johnny's arm. He clenched his fist several times, causing his veins to become engorged and rise from his flesh. I watched with anticipation as he searched for the main vein, then poked the needle into his arm. Once the needle had penetrated, I slowly released the scarf, allowing the blood to travel inside the body of the syringe. I myself preferred to lie back and savor the moment, allowing the substances to frolic and mingle before I pushed the party upstream. Once the blood had mixed with the heroin, then it was slowly shot back into the vein.

The high from heroin was completely opposite to that of speed, giving me a nice, warm feeling. It mellowed me out to the point of being completely useless. All I could do was lie on the mattress and listen to the Beatles sing "Let It Be."

The thing I loved most about heroin is that I could drift off into a semiconscious state and have the most beautifully vivid dreams. I would hear everything going on around me and then I'd float off into my own little euphoria. Then I'd come to my senses and find myself slumped on the mattress, holding an unlit cigarette. I'd hold it for a while and then I'd slowly bring it to my lips, but then off I'd go, back to the Red Sea! Meanwhile, my finger was on fire from the match I had lit ten minutes ago! If I ever got around to lighting that cigarette, I was damn lucky to get a puff before it burned down to the filter. Or I'd just forget about the cigarette completely and answer a question someone had asked me forty minutes ago.

While speed energized my sex drive, heroin erased it entirely. I usually became nauseous as soon as I shot up, so sex was the last thing on my mind. Not to mention that I was very lethargic. I tried having sex on heroin once and it took me four hours to get out of my panties!

One thing we had to be careful of was overdosing. Honey, in those days, I brushed death more times than Jackie Curtis brushed her hair!

The scary thing was that if I overdosed and died, Johnny would get nailed by the cops on a drug rap, since he had been taking the stuff as well. So I told him that if I ever keeled over, he should simply toss me out the window.

"No, one'll ever know!" I reasoned. "They'll just think I'm some dead drag queen and haul me away."

It's obvious I wasn't thinking with a clear mind.

Luckily, my lifeless body never did meet the pavement with a thud, and Johnny always seemed to catch me in time before I drifted off into eternal oblivion. I was always being summoned out of my journey in a tub of cold water with ice cubes up my ass and under my balls. I mean, who the hell wouldn't wake up from an overdose after such an experience? It was totally humiliating and all I could think about was how did my makeup look and why the hell were they doing this to me? They were ruining my high and bringing me down, momma!

"Don't leave me, Holly!" I remember Johnny screaming. "Don't leave me!"

I ask you, where the hell was I going in this condition? Are these people crazy? And then suddenly I felt more cold water being slapped into my face and my head being shaken. Johnny's cries were echoing from somewhere far away now. I didn't know where. I didn't care. I was lost on an island in the clouds and it was very agreeable. So soothing. So warm, as if I had become a fetus again and I was floating in my mother's womb. I opened my eyes and looked down to see myself being walked naked across the floor by Johnny. He was screaming something, but I didn't listen. I was too busy floating higher and higher into the midst of euphoria.

The worst part of an overdose was that once I had been revived, I was still flying high because I had just given myself one big flawless shot. The problem was that my trip was such a harrowing experience for Johnny and resulted in such turmoil that I had ruined his high entirely. Oh, the guilt I suffered.

Since our dope came from the street, we were never certain of its quality. Sometimes it was good and sometimes it was bad. Sometimes it was cut with quinine, so we were never sure of its grade or potency, and it was very easy for us to overdo it and find ourselves teetering on the edge. Also, the more I did the drug, the more drug I needed to get high. Johnny and I always took the same share and usually split a ten-dollar bag. We were cheap dates and thought ourselves to be on the lower rung of strung out. So it never took much to nearly kill us!

In November 1969 John Vaccarro cast me in the chorus of his latest play, *Cockstrong*. I was thrilled to be on the stage again and managed to get Johnny a job as an assistant to the company. I'd rehearse with the company during the afternoons in Vaccarro's loft in the East Village near St. Mark's Place. Once we had wrapped for the day, I'd flutter off to Max's with Johnny in tow for the five o'clock business buffet.

I would sit in the front and order a carafe of white wine or I'd occupy a banquette. I was now Miss Holly Woodlawn, and Miss Darling appreciated neither Miss Curtis or myself at this point because she had become a snotty blonde. She had also grown green with envy over my success with *Trash*, and was rather miffed that I was now a rival.

In the evenings, I'd walk into the back room resplendent, dressed in big hats and feeling like Juliet of the Spirits in my little red-ruffled strapless minidress, my silver lurex fishnet stockings, and my high heels. I had to look my best, since rumor was getting around that I was going to be the biggest sensation to hit the underground screen since Viva.

Well, I might've impressed the impressarios at the Factory, but I wasn't doing so well on the stage. After two weeks in rehearsal for *Cockstrong*, I was thrown out of the company.

"There are no stars in the Playhouse of the Ridiculous," proclaimed Vaccarro, shaking from head to toe, inflamed with anger. I had made the mistake of showing up to rehearsal late once too often and Vaccarro exploded into his usual tyrannical tirade, screaming at the top of his lungs, "I will not put up with psychotic drag queens! Get out! Get out, I say! Out!"

I did not consider myself a drag queen, nor was I about to be called psychotic.

"You don't tell me to get out. I quit!" I stomped, seething with venom. "And I'm taking my husband with me!"

And I grabbed Johnny and stormed out of the theater, never to return. Miss Curtis was floored by my outburst because nobody had ever walked out on Vaccarro, much less screamed back at him.

"Yeah! Good girl! You told him right off," she applauded that night at Max's. Incidentally, Miss Curtis had been tossed out of the company herself about a year earlier. Not only did Vaccarro toss her out of the company, he tossed her out of her own play! The nervy bastard.

The frigid November winds ravaged the lingering autumn, leaving the barren trees to fend with the bitter December frost. And there I was, out of the chorus and into the gutter, freezing my tits off. As the winter of 1969 peacefully fell upon our wayward souls, the blizzards gracefully draped the city with an angelic cloak of snow that lay in drifts along the Village streets, which hummed with the music of Christmas. And while the freezing air bit at my blushing cheeks, the falling snow teased my hungry mouth as the flakes curled upon my tongue like slumbering nymphs born from the merciful womb of heaven. Ahhh, the poetic thoughts dope put into my head. I always felt like Emily Dickinson.

Johnny had landed a job as an office boy with a Madison Avenue advertising agency, and I began passing the time with my dear friends Estelle and Crazy Sylvia, the cop-bashing queen from the days of the Stonewall. Crazy Sylvia was a cross-eyed lunatic Italian who would put anything in her mouth and swallow. She also drank rot-gut pickle wine that she brewed in a still and bottled in a flask, which she kept strapped to her thigh and sold for fifty cents a jar! She was wild, often caught up in a whirl of nonstop chatter, flipping and flapping her hands about like a crazed seal, always gesticulating as she spoke.

Often we would find ourselves trudging through the snow, heading for the East Village to hang out with our friend Kevin, the straight-laced, very preppy, blond, blue-eyed, fifteen-year-old kid who once helped Judy Garland hide her pills. He shared a suite in a hotel with his father and attended high school during the day, but during his Christmas vacation Chrysis, Crazy Sylvia, Estelle, Curtis, and I all piled into Kevin's bedroom, shot up heroin and speed, and just hung out until it was time to watch "Dark Shadows."

Johnny and I withstood the weather as best we could, huddled in our dilapidated hovel until the snow melted away. Spring trickled in and illuminated the grimy, rain-streaked window panes, peering into our lives like a cat sniffing a mousehole.

Soon, spring leapt into summer and the hot, humid months that lay ahead were unbearable. Gone was the sweet smell of the fresh morning rain and in its place was the repugnant stench of the rat-infested garbage that lined the gutter and alleys of the city, poisoning the air like an opened grave. The humidity and the odor made us so miserable that we resorted to shooting heroin and drinking vodka to ease our suffering, but the drugs did more harm than good.

The skies had darkened and so had my mind, which had been clouded by the excess of alcohol and drugs. I lost any sense of being rational and was prone to emotional outbursts. Also, I had grown hideously jealous of Johnny because everywhere we went, someone was trying to seduce him. I was afraid I'd lose him, and I resented him for my insecurity. Although he wasn't interested in anybody else, my heart had been laced with mistrust, and one summer night during a rainstorm as Estelle, Johnny, and I lay on the living-room mattress coming down from our highs, I lashed into him like a maniacal beast and exploded into a frenzied fit of sheer insanity.

"I saw him looking at you! Don't tell me you didn't know it!" I fumed, sloshing my drink across the floor. "You don't love me. I know you don't love me."

Estelle tried to calm me, but I was out of control, running around the room, blithering and bantering while I beat my breast. Suddenly, I grabbed a coffee cup and bashed it against the brick wall, causing it to shatter. Johnny bristled with fear and I, feeling quite dramatic at this point, slashed the jagged edge of ceramic across my left thigh. It was quite a performance, darling, one that surely would have garnered an award from the Sarah Siddons Society should I have done it on the stage.

Blood gushed everywhere! It spilled down my leg and onto the linoleum like a train of red taffeta gathered around my feet. Johnny, white with shock, ran out of the apartment to escape the horror. I ran after him, my mind numb to the pain as I chased him down four flights and onto the street with Estelle screaming behind in panic.

My bare feet sloshed through the cold, wet rain as I trailed him down Third Street, yelling his name. Just as I caught up with him at a stoplight, Johnny ducked into a waiting cab and locked the door.

"Please don't leave me!" I screamed as I beat on the rain-streaked window with the palms of my hands. "Please——" But the light turned green and the taxi sped away, leaving me in a cloud of exhaust and a puddle of water.

I heard my name being screamed frantically and I turned to see Estelle running down the street, arms flailing, lungs shrieking, and legs churning a mile a minute.

"Holly, you're bleeding to death!" Estelle cried as he grabbed hold of my weakened body. "We gotta get you to the hospital."

The throbbing wound had begun to permeate my senses, although it really didn't seem to matter. I felt myself fall against a lamppost and cry, "I don't care! My husband is gone!"

That night made no sense whatsoever. I was so confused and disheartened, I didn't care if I died in the gutter. Estelle, however, flagged down a taxi and hauled me off to an emergency room, where I was stitched up like a rag doll, full of stuffing and nothing else.

Johnny wound up staying with a friend in an apartment building behind mine. It was hell having him so close, because I wanted to call him so badly, but I was so afraid of what he'd say. Finally, on the day before he was leaving for Atlanta, I went to see him, but he refused to come back. He told me I was the only person he'd ever loved, but that he was afraid. The scene was just too much for him, which I understand now. After all, he was only sixteen years old. I was a world-weary twenty-four.

We talked long about what had caused all this turmoil in our lives. We were so happy at first—what happened? The only logical blame we could lay was on drugs. They had prompted the most horrible, emotional breakup I had ever endured. Sure, I had my friends. I had my life. And I had Max's. But I felt so alone. I'd lie on the mattress and listen to Johnny's records, which only added salt to the wound. My Tarzan man-child had gone with the wind and left me holding the vine, alone, with nothing to keep me warm but a few scratched records, an empty wine bottle, and a clock whose cuckoo had flown the coop.

CHAPTER 10

Madcap Mania at Max's Kansas City

*A*hhh, the privileged life of a Superstar. I'd usually wake up around noon and have breakfast, which was served in a syringe. Methedrine, melba toast, and a strong cup of coffee were always an eye-opener, and got me ready for the rigorous task of dressing for the night ahead. This was quite an undertaking, and required hours of painting, plucking, stretching, and tucking. And that was just my face. When I did my hair, I caused quite a riot with the teasing comb; puffing, poofing, pounding, and poking.

Jackie Curtis would often join me during these afternoon endeavors into beautydom, and we would carry on incessantly like two contestants on our way to a pageant. We were very serious when it came to makeup, and our faces became our art. There were, of course, occasions when Curtis had shot too much speed and came out looking like a Picasso, with one eye on her cheek and the other on her forehead, but she was a masterpiece nevertheless. And who was I to talk? I plucked both my eyebrows and penciled in McDonald's arches on my forehead. I don't know what possessed me, but I thought I was the best thing since Marlene Dietrich.

"You have the face of the Seventies!" proclaimed Truman Capote one night at Max's, swaying before me with a cocktail in hand. He was quite tipsy, that Truman, and I was genuinely touched by his kind expression, until I later learned he said the same to Miss Darling on the very same night! I was quite pleased with the compliment nonetheless, and to think it was coming from the creator of my inspiration, Holly Golightly. I was elated. Picture perfect, that's what I wanted, as if I'd been torn from the pages of *Vogue*.

Curtis and I were outrageous hussies, so naturally our makeup was put on to last. Darling, our faces had the durability of aluminum siding! Well, actually, Jackie's more than mine. Every now and then I'd have to take the trowel out of her hand and say, "Hey, hon, this is makeup you're putting on. It's not stucco."

Once Curtis and I were happy with our freshly painted *facces*, we jumped immediately into our garb and hightailed it to the ol' Max's hellhole. Max's was like a carnival: cheap and tawdry, yet glamourous and entertaining. It was a beehive abuzz with activity and, with Johnny gone, it became my ticket to escape the misery that had fallen upon my little heart. It was going to take more than Elmer's glue and tape to put me back together. I was a woman without a man, and I felt no better than Humpty Dumpty! I ask you, what is Jane without her Tarzan, Eve without her Adam, or Harriet without her Ozzie? They are lesbians! And I was not about to become a part of that again, at least not for the moment. I was far too busy wallowing in my own self-pity, which seemed to subside once I had romanced the bartender into sliding me a cocktail under the table.

It's a strange feeling, looking back at it all. It's as if I walked into the place when I was twenty-three and didn't walk out until I was twenty-five. That was one helluva party we had going in that back room! Hell, the commotion was so loud, I couldn't possibly concentrate on my depression, and after throwing back a white wine or two, my sorrows were lost in the pulsating rhythm of excitement that had now engulfed me. The bacchanalian madness aside, Max's was perhaps the best group therapy I've ever known!

Max's back room had become more of a home to me than my own empty apartment. I even got mail there! And being a wounded woman whose heart had been stomped in the mud, I wasn't about to stay in an empty apartment with James Taylor on the record player. I would've thrown myself out the window for sure! At Max's, however, the people were alive and they were having such a good time yucking it up, I just tossed my worries to the wind and lifted my glass for a refill.

During the winter of 1970, I got a telegram at Max's from the Academy of Motion Picture Arts and Sciences. It was addressed to Holly Woodlawn, % Andy Warhol, % Max's Kansas City, and regarded the upcoming Academy Awards.

I had taken the film industry by storm, and George Cukor, smitten with my performance and touched by my persona, had launched a campaign to prompt the Academy of Motion Picture Arts and Sciences to nominate me for an Academy Award. Soon orange buttons reading HOLLY WOODLAWN FOR BEST SUPPORTING ACTRESS were being distributed all over the place and a petition supporting the nomination was also circulating, boasting the signatures of such luminaries as Ben Gazarra, Joanne Woodward, and Cukor himself.

I desperately wanted to have an impact on those Hollywood yahoos and immediately called up my friend Jacques Kaplan and asked if he knew of a fur that was looking for a good time. Jacques said he had several in need of a night out on the town and invited me over to pick one up. So I raced to his studio and met the love of my life, a big, black beast that fit perfectly. It wasn't a mink or a fox or a chinchilla, darling. Those were far too humdrum. This, my dear friends, was a full-fledged, banana-fed gorilla—with a vine to match! I went ape and felt just like Queen Kong.

Unfortunately, the Oscar nomination never came to be. Rumor had it that the Academy rejected the nomination on the basis of my gender, but recently I learned from the curator for the Academy, Danny Woodruff (who incidentally was also Cukor's former assistant), that my cross-dressing had nothing to do with it. According to Danny, Cukor was making an attempt to write in my nomination after the other nominations had already been announced. It was and still is against the Academy's policy to do so and therefore I was ineligible.

Max's was located in a remote area of Manhattan, at 213 Park Avenue South. It was a bustling arena for every imaginable life form —both high and low—that had crawled in New York and beyond! The back room had banquettes lined against the wall, and tables clothed in red with a bowl of chick peas on top. The place was a haven for both weirdos and artists, although it became difficult to distinguish between the two. Every night the stars, freaks, druggies, and creatures of the avant-garde flocked together for those dusk-to-dawn sprees of delirium. Among the revellers were Tennessee Williams, Truman Capote, Mick Jagger, Robert Mapplethorpe, Patti Smith, Bruce Springsteen, David Johansen, Judy Garland, David Bowie, Dennis Hopper, the three J's—Jimi, Janis, and Jim—as well as countless others, some who shined brightly and some who were simply burnt out.

Max's got its name from the Kansas City cut of steak, which was supposedly the best cut of steak available. No one knew who the hell Max was, except that the owner of the joint, Mickey Ruskin, liked the sound of Max's better than Mickey's. I can't say I blame him. Mickey's Kansas City? It just doesn't have the same ring.

Mickey Ruskin was a dark, towering figure with a sunken face and black hair, who hovered over the crowd like a sullen vulture. At least that's how I perceived him. I never once saw that man smile, and I always got the impression that he hated me, even though he let me run up the tabs like crazy. But then, he always knew Andy would pay the bill.

And there we have it! The real reason why I liked to hang out at Max's. Besides the fact that I was continually fawned over, the pure and simple fact that Andy would foot my bill was the motivation behind eating that goddamn business buffet! Andy had a tab at Max's, and I would run it up like crazy and sign his name to all the checks. I was hesitant about signing the checks at first, but then Jackie Curtis took me aside and straightened the kinks in that hairpin.

"Listen," she insisted, a smoldering cigarette hanging out of her painted lips. "Andy's gonna make a mint offa you. Every time one of our films is shown, he gets money and we don't get a dime. You gotta cash in while you're hot, hon. Sign the check."

Curtis had a point. After all, *Trash* was doing quite well at the box office and the publicity Andy got from my shenanigans alone was worth a mint. So I signed the checks, and I continued to sign them. One afternoon, however, after I had gobbled up a large ice cream sundae and downed two glasses of Pouilly-Fuissé, I learned that Andy had put a halt to all house charges. There I sat with what was left of a pleasantly nursed cocktail and a pleasantly pleased appetite when a young man named Philip, who had just started working there as the maitre d', announced the wretched news to my face.

"We can't charge this. I need cash."

I was simply aghast. I had no money, I had no welfare, and— goddamn it!—I still didn't have a husband. Oh, life can be such a kick in the face at times. Well, what was I to do but flippantly shoo away the horrid possibility that I, Holly Woodlawn (star of stage, screen, and Max's Kansas City), would be forcibly pulled kicking and screaming from my pedestal and reduced to washing dishes because of a flimsy little tab! I was not going to be mortified, especially in that pithole. I was going to sign the check and Andy was going to pay for it and there were no buts!

Well, Philip, who had never met me before, took my word that I was indeed a Factory starlet and that it would be all right for me to sign. Unbeknown to me, Philip nearly got fired! All over a lousy ice cream sundae and two glasses of wine.

Years later, Philip told me that Mickey Ruskin dragged him into his office the next morning and screamed, "You approved Holly Wood-lawn's check last night? You're fired! No one pays their bills over there [at the Factory], especially her!"

I had been plucked, to say the least. Luckily, Philip was only fired for a few minutes and was allowed to continue his job after Mickey's immediate anger had quelled. After that, I stopped signing Andy's name to the checks because I didn't want to abuse the privilege. Instead, I wheedled my own tab and let the bills pile up until Mickey pulled me away from my cocktail, dragged me upstairs to his third-floor office, sat me down in a chair, and dropped a stack of unpaid bills in my lap.

"These are piling up, Holly," he'd say, looking at me scornfully.

"Ohhhhh, all right," I'd wince. I hated these confrontations. "I'll take care of it," I reassured him, knowing that I'd have to muster up the nerve to go to Andy and plead for him to cut a check! Usually that was the only way I'd show up at the Factory. Otherwise, I didn't care to hang out there because it was nothing more than a big, boring office.

One afternoon, I discovered that my cup, which had runneth over in the past, was now dry as a bone. And so my dear friend Estelle and I decided it was time to fill 'er up at the Factory. We got all decked out in our finery, me in my gorilla fur and Estelle in his fake fur, and made the procession to the great one's till. As we neared Union Square, we saw Andy duck inside the Factory building. My heart jumped because I knew I was in for a handout (or a haul, as I call it).

Estelle and I entered the building at 33 Union Square West and took the elevator up to the stuffed Great Dane that guarded the door. I buzzed the intercom and Pat Hacket, the Factory's receptionist answered.

"Hi, Pat, it's Holly."

"Oh, hi, Holly. Andy's not here right now," she said.

"Oh. Well, that's okay. I just wanted to come up to say hi."

"Well, why don't you come by tomorrow? He should be in around two. Why don't you stop by then."

This was the ultimate brush-off. I had just seen Andy walk into the building moments before.

"Yeah, sure," I said, feeling like an idiot. Who did she think she was fooling? Little did I know that Andy was avoiding me due to a few drunken tirades I had made to the Factory upon learning that *Trash* was a million-dollar hit.

Every now and then, usually after too many drinks, I would feel like an exploited fool. But then, all the Superstars were Andy's fools. We acted like lunatics on film and he made millions off of it. Sometimes I felt cheated and sometimes I didn't, but when I did, I would become totally unraveled and incensed with anger. So, to release my frustrations, I'd march over to the Factory, snort flames, stomp my feet, and carry on like a mad banshee. "That goddamn son of a bitch is making millions off of me and I'm living in poverty!" I screamed.

Well, the entire Factory was alarmed by these disruptions (particularly after the Valerie Solanis incident) and decided to ignore me for a while until I cooled my heels. But I was tired of being ignored, and since Estelle and I had just seen Andy walk into the building moments before, I really felt like a fool.

Then Estelle turned to me and said, "Hey, listen, Jackie showed me where the powerbox is in the basement. If they're going to fuck with you, let's fuck with them."

"Yeah!" I said with a glint in my evil little eyes, and down the elevator we went to the dark recesses of the basement, where we shut down all the electricity to the Factory. Then, having not fully recovered from this spree of mischief, I decided to climb the fire escape, which ran alongside the now-darkened windows, and terrorize the hell out of them.

"It's Valerie!" I screamed, banging on the windows with my fists. "I'm back and I know you're in there. I'm gonna getcha—and your little dog, too!"

Andy had two nicknames, one of which was "Grandma"—because of his snow-white hair—and the other was "Drella," which was a combination of Cinderella and Dracula. I think a lot of the Warhol entourage thought Andy was taking from them, living vicariously through them. Sucking from them what he wanted and then casting their drained souls aside. Once he looked Jackie Curtis square in the face and said, "You're using me." And she shot back, "No—you're using me."

One of the most striking examples of this trend was Edie Sedgewick. Andy was impressed by her wealth and her social status, but I don't think he really cared for her as a human being. She had charisma, energy, and an old family name with old family money behind it. She fit well in his menagerie of dancing bears, but like a toy a child has grown tired of, she was put on the shelf and replaced by another. I, of course, paid no attention to such details at the time. I was far too concerned with having a good time.

"'Scuse me! Pardon me! Get outta my way!" I pushed and plowed my way through the line at that fucking business buffet like a JAP at a Bloomingdale's clearance sale. But what I was really doing was falling victim once again to Max's barbecue ribs and chili. Boy, was that the worst crap I ever had! You could taste it in the back of your throat for three days if you weren't careful to subdue the flavor with a bottle or two! And to think Curtis and I ate it day in and day out. And let's not forget those chick peas. They were hard as rocks, but we ate them nevertheless. Ugh!

The chicken wings weren't much to bark about either. They were scrawny little things, and since Max's was located right across the street from Union Square Park (directly opposite the Factory), which happened to be a very popular pigeon hangout, it really made me wonder if these little wingettes came from chickens at all! Nevertheless, I stuffed them into my mouth more often than not, until my plate (and a few others') was spotlessly clean.

So there we were, featured players in this insane circus of the underground. There was never a dull moment at Max's; even the bathrooms were overrun with lunacy. People were getting fucked, giving head, shooting up, selling smack, and taking a dump, all at the same time.

One night during one of my midnight escapades at Max's, Eric Emerson (one of Andy's beautiful blond discoveries who hung around the Factory like a horse) and I went upstairs and caught ourselves in a fit of passion after shooting Methedrine. We were voracious when it came to speed sex, which was quite the rage back then. It's far better than cocaine sex. Speed sex just goes on for hours. We got together several times afterward during those sweltering summer afternoons. Eric would stomp around naked in his cowboy boots while cracking his whip! Sort of made me want to jump up and scream, "Yeeeee ha!" Now I know how Dale Evans felt when she mounted Trigger!

One of the regular sights in the back room was Andrea Whips Feldman. Every night she'd crawl on top of a table, scream, "It's showtime!" and belt out "Give My Regards to Broadway." What a voice that one had. I swear, she had more frogs in her throat than a Louisiana swamp. Andrea was a self-proclaimed star, and she had her act down pat, screeching at the top of her lungs while taking off her clothes. By this time, she was usually being hauled out the door, except for one night that is forever engraved in my memory.

Miss Andrea was drunk out of her mind, teetering on the edge of the table while sloshing a drink around as if it were a microphone. Well, booze started going everywhere, and when the bouncers came to haul her off, she started to kick and scream, which caused quite a riot.

"I'm a star! I'm a star!" she screamed, clawing and fighting for one last glimpse of tabletop fame as the boys pulled her down. Andrea was a whirlwind of terror! A blond tornado! My God, there were so many screams and kicks coming out of her, I thought I was watching a cheap Kung Fu movie. And when one of those kicks happened to land in the ass of Miss Jackie Curtis, I knew we were in for a good time. Honey, I was standing right there and saw it all firsthand as Curtis threw down her cocktail, grabbed Andrea by her blond head, and smacked her in the face. Well, Andrea smacked back and both of them went at it like two cats with their tails tied.

Andrea grabbed Jackie by her cheap, Barbra Streisand look-alike wig and ripped it out by the bobby pins. We were all shocked that night, honey! There was Curtis, standing at the bar with her hair in Andrea's hands! Curtis didn't even have the chance to get her hair back when Andrea pulled out all of the punches, grabbed hold of Curtis's neckline, and ripped that ratty housedress entirely from her body.

Oh, *mon Deux*! The place was horrified, not because Curtis had been stripped of her dress, but because she was wearing a pair of men's

Fruit of the Looms with her stockings pinned to the sides! And to think she called herself a woman. The nerve!

But Miss Curtis or myself weren't the only ones whose noses were rubbed in humiliation. Miss Darling had a doozy herself once in the back room during the screening of some home movies. A contributing editor to Andy's *Interview* magazine who was freaking out on LSD stood up from his table and began to hurl insults at Miss Darling. "Like uh, Candy Man. Look man, you're a man, Candy man."

Candy stood up in the middle of the movie, the images of the film projected on her face. "I'm a serious actress!" she screamed, clutching a copy of Patrick Dennis's *Little Me* in her arms.

"But you're not art, man."

"I have an image. Image is art," Candy lashed back.

"Bullshit!" he shouted.

"Go back to Massepequa Park, where you belong!" shouted another tripped-out bystander. "You can take the drag queen out of Long Island, but you can't take Long Island out of the drag queen!"

"I'm a star! A star, do you hear me?" Candy cried, waving her arms in front of the screen. Everyone heard but no one could give a shit. She was ruining the movie.

In the late Sixties, Andy reigned over Manhattan's avant-garde café society from the back-room throne at Max's, which allowed the queens-to-be such as myself and Miss Curtis to hold court at the infamous round table. We ran amok in that place like floozies in a speakeasy, picking up men and dragging them home for a night of our charms. Sometimes we'd just drag them outside! There was an alley behind Max's that was quite convenient if the bathroom stalls were full. I indulged every now and then, forcing men to be my love slaves and then tossing their exhausted bodies to one side and crawling back inside for more wine and revelry.

It was always so demoralizing, because the door to the alley was located in the back of the room, and no matter how discreet you were, no matter how hard you tried to keep your sexcapades a secret, the door always gave it away because it opened and closed with a loud "Ba-boom!" Everyone would be yelling, screaming, drinking, and carrying on, but when they heard that "Ba-boom," the entire place stopped and all eyes turned to the back door to see what low-life tramp had just walked in from a quickie. Once, Curtis swaggered in from the back alley with her lipstick smeared up to her nose! It was a sight to behold.

But Curtis and I weren't the only two hussies carrying on in that dump. Upstairs on the second floor was a disco, which didn't open until later in the evening. Late one afternoon Eric Emerson and Elda, one of the backroom vamps, slipped away from their table, snuck off to the second floor, and proceeded to whoop it up in a phone booth. This was one of those old glass-enclosed phone booths, the kind with the long narrow door that folds in the middle and swings inside to open. Well, they managed to get in, but after this whim of passion had been exhausted, they soon found that they couldn't get out! They had crammed themselves in so that there was no room for the door to swing open.

We were all downstairs drinking and carrying on when all of a sudden this yelling and screaming could be heard from upstairs. It was so loud, at first we thought it was a Vietnam protest. Elda and Eric were causing such a riot—screaming, yelling, and rocking the booth—that Philip ran upstairs to investigate. Well, there was Elda, her dress was over her head and Eric against her, butt-naked with his pants around his knees. Both of them were panic-stricken and about ready to kill each other. Philip, mastermind that he was, untangled the two from their duress, which left them in quite a state of disarray. I'll never forget the moment they descended the stairs onto the first floor. Elda's hair was pushed to one side of her head and Eric looked as if he had been beaten. The two were exasperated and humiliated, but we thought it was a riot. It's funny how some of life's most embarrassing situations can be the most rewarding. It was during this harrowing experience that a son was conceived.

It was very common for the impresarios who came to New York to visit with Andy, first to be taken to the Factory, where they screened rushes, and then to Max's for dinner. Going to Max's was like walking into a movie or being in the center of a carousel while all this craziness floated around them. The regulars were never impressed with who was there; at least I wasn't. If someone turned to me and said, "Hey, Fellini's over there," I didn't care. It was only a big deal if he was going to buy me dinner, which of course he did!

Fellini in fact, *had* just been to the Factory, where Andy had shown him *Trash*. He was in town promoting his latest film, and was sitting in a banquette with Hiram Keller. I was sauntering through the place, dressed in my usual attire and carrying a silver tackle box as a purse when he invited me to join the table. Naturally, I was thrilled! Imagine, being invited to dinner by a legend such as Fellini. I loved *Juliet of the Spirits* and *La Dolce Vita*. We hit it off famously. I picked up the fork and he picked up the tab! It was divine.

So there I sat with Fellini telling me how fabulous I was in *Trash* when all of a sudden Andrea Whips Feldman came over, plopped her ass down in our banquette, took off her shoes, and put them on the table! I thought I was going to die, especially since she had been locked away in an institution for the last couple of months. Well, much to my surprise, Eric Emerson had signed her out for the weekend. Honey, LuLu was back in town and the Fruit Cocktail she had between her ears had ripened! We were all taken aback, particularly when she took Magic Markers out of her purse and proceeded to color her entire face!

"I'm Andy's wife and he loves me," she began, talking out of her mind while gazing around the room. It was terribly sad, darling. This girl was ruining my career! Fellini and Hiram didn't know what to think, although I sensed they were amused. I, on the other hand, was ready to grab a dagger! I was never so embarrassed in all my life.

Oh, yes I was! Whenever I think I have been humiliated to the point of no return, I always remind myself of the time I shot heroin at Max's. Philip told me that the only safe place to do it was in Mickey's private bathroom on the third floor, and since Mickey wasn't around, it seemed to be the best place to go. But I had to do it quick, because if Mickey found out, we'd all be skinned alive.

Philip and I snuck up the steep narrow steps to the third floor, where we were met by a large chicken-wire gate. Philip unlocked it and we entered onto the floor, where I made a beeline for the bathroom.

"Holly, will you calm down!" Philip laughed, amused by my eagerness.

"Hurry up!" I whispered as he handed me the syringe and the smack.

"I gotta get back downstairs. Come on down when you're finished." And he shut the door and was off. Well, darling, I went about my usual routine, but I gave myself a Texas-sized shot that could've wiped out a cow.

Forty-five minutes had passed before Philip noticed that I was nowhere to be found. He looked everywhere for me. By this time, I was so far gone, I couldn't even find myself. Well, the phone rang and Bob, the cashier, called over to Philip, "It's Mickey! He's on his way in!"

Philip's face went pale and he ran as fast as he could up the two flights, only to find me undressed and passed out on the toilet! My dress was on the floor and my stockings were around my ankles.

"Holly, come on!" His voice filled with panic as he tried to pick me up from the pot.

Somehow he managed to get me off the toilet, but I was in a semiconscious state of mind and I couldn't walk. I was clinging to him for dear life as we wobbled down those treacherous stairs. And while Philip had done his best to dress me, I came down looking like I had just come out of a world war.

When we finally made it down to the back room, Philip walked me over to a banquette where several of his friends were cocktailing, squeezed me in among them, and stuck a cigarette in my mouth. There I was, propped up like a stiff at an Irish wake with a feather boa hanging off my head, my pantyhose around my knees, and one arm lost in my dress. I looked worse than Jackie Curtis, a fate I dreaded more than death itself!

Later that night as I strayed outside to inhale the crisp night air, I stumbled off the sidewalk and landed face down in the gutter. Well, you know what they say—there's no place like home! But I was plucked nonetheless, and before I had the chance to gather my scattered self, I heard the sound of approaching footsteps and a somewhat amused voice:

"What are you doing down there?" asked Mario Rivoli, the fabulous artist who later was to become one of my best friends. I peered at him over the curb and replied, "I'm trying to get over this wall!"

CHAPTER
11

Sumptuous
Soirees

I hightailed it to Max's night after night and simply forgot to go home ... for nearly two years! Actually, I had no home. I had let the apartment I once shared with Johnny go, as I had no time for such frivolity. I was far too concerned with my celebrity! So with the flutter of my bejeweled hand I whooshed my worries of rent completely away and became a vagabond.

As strange as it may seem, it's true. Usually, I would start to hang out with friends, and before I knew it I was living with them. I drifted from one place to another, carrying with me a Gucci bag stuffed with makeup and the clothes on my back. Often, friends would give me clothes to wear, and I would wear them until they fell apart. And as

I moved from place to place, I acquired clothes here and there, but usually left them behind.

This wayward lifestyle began after *Trash* opened. Once Larry Rivers had sprung me from the coop, I returned eventually to George Mulligan's apartment, where I had been staying on the Lower East Side. Just my luck, George had fallen head over heels in love and had turned that rat hole into a love nest. It became quite apparent that I no longer had a place to run, hide, or hang my hose. So I immediately called my dear friend Sidney, a handsome young gentleman from a wealthy family in Kingston, Jamaica. He was studying to be an actor and we got along famously, especially since we became acquainted at Max's one eve while I was in one of my debauched pagan revelries worshipping the God Methedrine! Anyway, Sidney resided in a fashionable bachelor's flat on Twenty-third Street and Sixth Avenue. He invited me over for dinner one night and I stayed for six weeks.

Sidney and I were ravenous party-goers. And now that I was a star of the underground, we were hanging out at Max's every night. I had horned my way into the round table and was holding court with Mick Jagger, Jean Shrimpton, Roger Vadim, Alice Cooper, and other celebs. Often, Sidney and I would invite people back to his apartment and party ourselves into a drunken stupor, staying up all night until everybody either went home or passed out!

One such stuporous occasion was my twenty-fourth birthday party, which Sidney had thrown for me just a few weeks after *Trash* opened. It was the wildest party I have ever known. Cocktails were flying, pills were popping, and everyone was mesmerized by the loud music that pulsated so loudly that the soles of my feet vibrated. My dear friend Estelle was in a corner romancing a bottle of Stoli, Andrea Whips Feldman was talking to herself on the sofa, and across the loft was Andy, standing next to a young man with long hair, both of them amusing themselves with the hors d'oeuvres.

I had just popped several Quaaludes and was feeling quite the social butterfly, flapping around in my three-tiered red chiffon minidress— strapless, of course. Honey, it was so strapless, it was around my knees by two in the morning! I had no shame. There I was thinking that I was a glamourous goddess, but at the drop of a dime (and usually a pill or two) off came my dress! I was a ballsy broad—and I had the balls to prove it!

I breezed across the crowded room and kissed Andy on the cheek.

"Andy, I'm so glad you came," I said, hugging his frail body close to mine.

"Holly, I want you to meet a friend of mine. His name is Jim Morrison. He's with the Doors."

"Oh—hello." I smiled, extending my hand to his.

"Happy birthday," he said with a grin. I returned the smile with a wink. Well, it didn't take long for us to wind up necking in the corner. It was very innocent, really. Just a slip of the tongue and a few gropes. But as the party wore on, my friend Philip who worked at Max's had started talking about a gay S&M bar in the skanky part of town called Mineshaft. Jim was intrigued and asked if we would take him. I couldn't believe what I was hearing. Jim Morrison wanted to go to a gay bar? He was inquisitive, of course, and I was more than willing to satisfy his curiosity. Andy was tired and took a cab home while we three—Philip, Jim, and I—hailed a cab and sped off to witness the darker side of life.

And dark it was! The lighting was so bad in that place, I couldn't see to powder my nose. And to think I had spent the whole day making up my face. A glamourina like myself had no business being stuck in the darkness of a gay S&M bar with big, burly men flogging one another into a rapturous frenzy of delight. I, of course, made it my business, as Phillip and I took Jim on a whirlwind tour through the dump.

This was the pit of barbarous heathens that smelled of sweat and Amyl nitrate. To our left was a blindfolded man strung up from the ceiling in a harness with his mouth gagged with a chain while a group of men gangbanged him silly. And when that group was finished, another group came on. Meanwhile, over in the "leatherette lounge" there was one fat daddy spanking the hell out of a nasty little queen while he choked on another man's phallus. Oh, these boys were reckless.

Then we wandered into the chamber of horrors, where we found a beautiful young Adonis flung over a urinal while two men urinated on his back as he masturbated. Needless to say, we were all taken aback by these extremities, but in that setting they were commonplace. The gay culture in New York at this time was ravenous. Sex was a priority, it seemed. After all, gay society was founded on it. But there were so many extremes to gay sexuality, so many kinks! It seemed that gay men weren't just having one-on-one intimacy. They were gorging themselves with group sex, multiple partners, bondage, discipline, and fetishes galore. If only we knew the devastation that lay ahead.

I, fortunately, hadn't the time for such sexual shenanigans since my social calender was booked. I was being taken to gallery openings and upscale parties, and being introduced to people I never dreamed of meeting. I'll never forget meeting John Lennon and Yoko Ono for the first time. It was at an opening I had attended with Andy. John was very friendly, smiling often and being quite the conversationalist. Yoko, however, was quite the opposite, a very austere presence. She didn't know what to make of me, I suppose.

Once, not too long after we had met, Larry Rivers and I went to the Bowery where John and Yoko were making a movie. I haven't the faintest idea what the film was about, except that when we arrived and entered the loft, there was a nude girl stretched across the sofa. They were filming a fly crawling across her curvacious body. This was obviously *cinéma du avant-garde*. Well, when they took their break from filming, I casually approached this little gal and inquired as to how on earth she could stand lying there for so long while a bug, of all things, traipsed across her buttocks. She turned to me with an expressionless gaze and said she had shot heroin to prepare for the scene. Well, this picture wasn't as cheap as I thought. While I was making *Trash*, I was lucky to get a beer!

In 1971, I attended the Film Critics Awards with Andy Warhol, Paul Morrissey, and Jane Forth. Jane was the youngest Superstar in the menagerie, having achieved her status at only eighteen years of age. She was an exquisite creature with a beautiful porcelain face and big, dramatic eyes topped with a stitch of an eyebrow that survived a horrendous plucking!

At one point of the evening, I excused myself from our table and headed upstairs to the powder room. As I ascended the stairway, I saw coming toward me the legendary screen goddess herself, Bette Davis, smoking like a chimney as she came down the stairs.

"Miss Davis, is that really you?" I inquired as I briskly waved my hands to clear the cloud of cigarette smoke that had engulfed her tiny head.

"Yes, it is," she pronounced in that unmistakable choppy voice. I was stunned.

"Oh, my God. You talk just like her." I beamed, referring to her on-screen persona. I was so struck by her star magnetism that I nearly fell down the stairs. Davis took the cigarette into her mouth, gave it a swift puff, threw her head back, and blew smoke all over the place.

"I saw your movie," she stated, batting her big, luminous eyes behind her round glasses. "You did a good job. Congratulations." And then she turned on her heel and trod down the stairs, leaving a trail of smoke behind her. I was so overcome by her compliment that I nearly plotzed and fell over backward. And then I thought, "When the hell did she see *Trash*?" She probably never saw the movie, she was just at a loss for words. And darling, when you have nothing to say, a compliment is always the best way out of an awkward meeting. I should know.

One thing I learned to master while attending these social soirees was the art of successful party conversation. In pondering over this, I've concluded that there are three basic elements to the successful party conversation formula. One: a strong cocktail. Two: lots of flattery. And three: a fabulous laugh (just in case that last martini killed off your last brain cell and you can't think of a thing to say!).

But there have been those times when all of the above couldn't save me from the trenches of social despair. One such occasion (probably the most embarrassing situation I have ever endured) was during one of Salvador Dali's grand lunches at the St. Regis Hotel. Upon being introduced to Dali's wife, Gala, I leaned in to kiss her on the cheek. She pushed me away and screamed, "NO!" Her hands flew in the air like two flapping pigeons and she squealed at the top of her lungs, "I do not kiss nobody." I shriveled right there on the spot! I felt so humiliated and immediately proceeded to apologize.

"Oh, I'm terribly sorry. I didn't mean—"

"Nobody kisses Gala! Not even Dali," she ranted.

Well, hell, why would he kiss that old fishwife? He was having far too good a time with Ultra Violet—who, incidentally, was holding court across the way.

Ever since that afternoon, I've always had a strong distaste for Gala Dali, and looking back, I can't say I was ever really fond of Salvador himself. Dali was so caught up in being this bizarre artist, and I found them both to be terribly affected by his success. But the wine had a breathtaking bouquet and the food was easy to take, so I forgot about the Dalis and went about my merry way, stuffing my jowls with giblets and my bag with the silverware!

When the eats were on the house and the booze was flowing freely, you can bet I was there for the haul. Now, there were those occasions when the booze flowed too freely, but I never let that hamper my evening. Matter of fact, it usually made my night! Of course, one can get too inebriated during these social functions, which is why I've decided to dig deeply into my bag of wisdom and pull out this tip for the tipsy: The best way to remember everyone's name is to not even try! After all, imagine the embarrassment of realizing that Fred, to whom you just said hello moments before, was actually Louise! Those broads with flat tops—they throw me all the time! Therefore, I recommend calling everyone "darling" or "hon." It's simple, generic, and easy to remember! Half the time I didn't know who the hell I was talking to! I just stuck with "Darling, you look fabulous!" and hoped I didn't offend anyone.

Another little tip for the tipsy is to know the difference between an ashtray and a salt cellar. Once, at a luncheon hosted by Kenneth J. Lane, the famous *joaillière*, I asked the host to pass the salt and he told me I had put my cigarette out in it! Darling, I was so terribly mortified that I could only think of one way to redeem myself from the depths of humility.

"Well, here's to social graces," I flippantly laughed, toasting him with my finger bowl!

I attended many of these social functions with my friend Asha, a wealthy socialite who had achieved fame as a film actress in India. She had starred in numerous Ismail Merchant films there, but fled her native land to pursue a jazz-singing career in the Big Apple. We met spontaneously one night at Max's, when she appeared from out of the blue and exclaimed:

"Hello, darling! You're fabulous, I think you're wonderful. I love you madly!" She had recognized me from *Trash* and had just read a feature story about me in *The New York Times*. We hit it off immediately, and she introduced me to her friend Valli. Valli was very bold, with a distinct style stamped right on her face! You see, Valli was an uninhibited, avant-garde artist from Europe. Well, you know those Europeans—give 'em a foot and they'll take a leg! One day Valli went wildy mad with inspiration and tattooed her entire face with black, swirl-like designs! They were everywhere: around her eyes, extending from the corners of her mouth, circling her cheeks. She looked like an aborigine priestess! It was quite a sight, but she was a doll, a pure pleasure to be around, and I admired her daring style and her courage to flaunt it.

Asha was of the regal set; very high class and stunningly beautiful. One afternoon I arrived at her penthouse suite for cocktails, and within two rubs of a genie's lamp, I was moved in! Hers was a swank Park Avenue apartment, lavishly decorated with treasures from all over the world. I felt just like "Queen for a Day" as I looked over the terrace into the dazzling Manhattan skyline.

"Yoo-hoo!" I waved to the crowded street below. "It's me, Holly Woodlawn."

Asha, being who she was, moved in very high social circles. We were always going to parties and blowing kisses. It was fabulous. It certainly was a much-needed alternative to Max's Kansas City, which was becoming dry. Andy wasn't hanging out there any longer, Andrea

Whips Feldman was back in a nuthouse, the place was becoming overrun with rockers, and it just wasn't the same. So, I re-focused my interests and entered a new phase in my life called high society.

A few blocks away from Asha between Third and Lexington lived Gino and Marion Forbes. Marion was a wealthy heiress to a vast fortune, and she, Gino, Asha, and I would get together often. We became very close, and Marion decided that she wanted to make a film starring Asha and me at her house in Southhampton. It sounded like a wonderful idea, and we all took off to the manse to film *Bad Marion's Last Year*. It was some epic tale about two goddesses who rise out of the sea and terrorize a wealthy couple. Don't ask me why. It didn't have much of a plot. But then, some of us were so strung out on drugs that the only plot we could possibly encounter—if we weren't careful—was in a cemetery!

What I do remember of the film is Asha and me ascending from the chilled waters of the Atlantic stark-ass naked! Miraculously, we discovered two full-length fur coats lying on the sand, which we slipped into immediately. How the furs got there, I don't know. I suppose Zeus had something to do with it. Anyway, there we were, two wet, fur-wrapped divas of the gods who, for some strange reason, hitchhike our way into town! Now, I'm a great fan of mythology, but not once have I run across a goddess who had to thumb it. Hell, if we were going to ascend from the ocean and step into designer furs, you'd think someone would've at least called a limo!

The film ended with Marion, who played the lead role of the wealthy young snippet taunted by Asha and me, kicking up her heels from an overdose and catching a ride on the next wind to heaven. The film was screened at the Guggenheim Museum in New York and was forgotten soon after. Oh, well. They can't all be hits.

Then one day Bernie Ozer of *Women's Wear Daily* called and asked if I'd participate as a guest model in one of his fashion shows. Of course, I was delighted to be sashaying down his runway in a Chester Weinberg gown. As a matter of fact, I was so moved by the experience that I decided it was high time to be high paid! And with that notion in mind, Asha and I rolled into the Wilhelmina Modeling Agency, fully painted and dressed to kill. Why shouldn't I be a high-paid fashion model? I had been photographed by every shutterbug in town, including Skrebneski, Scavullo, Avedon, Annie Leibovitz, Ken Haak, and Bill King, and I had compiled quite a portfolio.

So there I was, looking more glamourous than a mole on a movie star as I strolled into the agent's office, portfolio case in hand. Well, what I had forgotten was that inside that case I had stashed a collection of my favorite all-male erotica! I had hidden it in there because I had no mattress of my own to stuff it under. And I certainly wasn't going to stuff it under Asha's. (Although I'm certain she wouldn't have minded in the least.)

Needless to say, when it came time for me to display my photos, I unzipped the case and it all spilled to the floor! The entire office gasped—some even panted, and one fainted! Imagine: graphic photos of young, beautiful men carrying on like savage beasts. Oh, the thought just makes me shiver! Those girls had never seen the likes of such shenanigans—and in full color, too! Oh, at first I was so mortified I felt my face blaze into a vibrant, Technicolor red! But then, after I fell to the floor and scrambled to gather up the mess, I thought, "What the hell?" And off to Eileen Ford we went!

We never did stir up any hot modeling jobs, but that was okay. Asha and I came to the conclusion that we didn't want to be "real" models—we wanted to be fabulous *celebrity* models! You know, the kind who dash off to Europe to have their hair done by Suga, and then to be shot by Scavullo over tea and crumpets.

The times Asha and I had together would be simply incomprehensible to any civil human being! We were "out there," living high on the hog—and everything else! I'll never forget the marvelous cocktail party George Plimpton threw for Valli at his house.

We were the hits of the party (which, incidentally, was a divine little affair that continued into the night as we partied over to Elaine's for dinner). We ate well, laughed a lot, and drank until we were senseless, and then as it came time to leave, Asha, Valli, and I thanked our host, blew our kisses, and approached the coat check to retrieve our furs. I, of course, was looking quite the serene highness in a dazzling Indian sari, dripping with jewels and about to be swathed in my legendary Jacque Kaplan gorilla fur that I had borrowed months before and never returned! That was one very cultured monkey by the time I got through with it.

Anyhow, there we were, painted and primped, feeling very fwa-fwa-fwa when this young, arrogant drunk began to slur some off-color remarks about Valli's tattooed face. Then he proceeded to verbally attack the three of us. "Freaks!" he yelled at the top of his lungs. "You're all a bunch of freaks." Darling, I had downed a few too many cocktails myself and I was in no mood for this creep. Suddenly, I was overcome by a whirlwind of raging fury. I was so appalled. Who was he to slander Valli? There she stood, of no harm to anyone, suddenly falling victim to this venomous abuse. It was more than abuse; it was an assault. And all I could think about were the times I had encountered the same prejudice. My anger began to churn deep inside my gut. Why was he so full of hate? Why?

Suddenly, I forgot all my lady-like savoir faire, turned on my heel, and decked him right across the chops. He sailed across the floor and landed in a potted fern. "You son of a bitch!" I screamed. "Go fuck yourself!" The entire restaurant—even Elaine—gasped. Asha and Valli were beside themselves. They had never seen me in such a state, and boy, was I in a tither! And after all, this was the era of women's lib. What did I look like—a wimp? A coward? No! I was woman (so I thought!) and I was revved to roar.

You see, this didn't just affect Valli. It affected the entire human race, as far as I was concerned. Blacks because they weren't white. Jews because they weren't Christians. Gays because they weren't straight. And me. Naturally, I was hated because I was the most beautiful. Of all the crust!

By this time, I had created quite a stir, as the entire place was watching. I snarled at the cowering scoundrel, spewed out a few more zesty expletives, flung that monkey suit over my shoulder, and stormed out of the restaurant in a thunderous rage. I hurried into the back of the waiting limo and collapsed in Asha's lap over the distress. "Don't you see? He's right. They don't care about us," I began. "They think we're freaks. That's all we are to them. A night of free entertainment," I blithered while black, mascara-stained tears began to streak my crumbling face.

Finally, I came to realize the ugly truth behind my popularity. These party people weren't interested in me as a person. Like Valli, I was a conversation piece; a curious bauble on display. I felt used by them because I really wanted to be accepted for myself as a person, not because I was a good laugh or something to talk about. I felt like a joke and it hurt. I didn't want people laughing; I didn't want to be demeaned. I wanted respect. I was a human being, whether a man or a woman. I wasn't a freak, I kept telling myself. I was Holly. Unfortunately, however, that was easier for me to say than it was for people to accept. And so I kept on crying, hoping that enough tears would be shed to wash away the stigma that blemished me. But that, my dear friends, would've taken the Johnstown flood! And so there I sat in the back of the limo with chapped cheeks, a runny nose, and the truth of where I fit into the scheme of it all. At least I had the truth. That was better than nothing. And nothing was what most of those people were about. They had no depth, they had no character. They had money and they had taste. But they were dismal really, lacking imagination, afraid to live beyond the norm, and coloring their own dreary lives with a rainbow of characters that were robust and charismatic.

A rainbow of freaks.

CHAPTER

12

Women in Revolt

*A*ndy was capti-
vated by Hollywood. He liked the glamour and status associated with
filmdom, but he was disappointed by the crumbling of the old Hollywood studio system. No longer were movie moguls like L. B. Mayer
or Jack Warner around to groom beautiful people for stardom. The
contract players were gone because Hollywood was becoming increas-
ingly independent.

Andy longed to be a part of the Hollywood scene, but I think he was
too wigged out. Not that they minded that white thing he had on his
head—it's just that his ideas were far too progressive for the conser-
vative movie ideals of the day. Entrepreneur that he was, Andy decided
to create his own studio system. So in 1963, he began to recruit what

was to become his own arena of stars. In Andy's mind, the Warhol stars were magnified far bigger than any other star in Hollywood history. We weren't just any movie stars. Warhol thought we were more glamourous, more fabulous, and more sensational than anything Hollywood could have hoped for—and, because our pedestals were hiked up so high, he decided to invent his own brand of movie icons: Superstars.

Among Andy's earliest creations were Ingrid Superstar, Viva, Ondine, Ultra Violet, Taylor Mead, and, of course, the ill-fated Edie Sedgewick. Edie had fallen to drugs and alcohol, which resulted in her untimely death at the age of twenty-eight. Edie was Andy's own Judy Garland of the underground, a woman whose star trip crossed into self-destruction and devastation. But to Andy, it was exciting to have such a parallel, as it seemed to draw him closer to old Hollywood, where lives were ravaged and destroyed by the star system.

Andy also felt that "girlettes" like me were "a living testimony to the way women used to be. Drags are ambulatory archives of ideal movie-star womanhood," he was quoted in a book (the book may have been his, but the words were Pat Hackett's). And in his new menagerie of Superstars he had three such testimonies: Candy Darling, Jackie Curtis, and me.

Trash had become Andy and Paul's most critically acclaimed film thus far, probably because it had plot and direction, unlike the earlier films Andy directed, which were stagnant and lacked imagination and a creative story structure. But *Trash* had everything. It had drama, sex, comedy, tragedy . . . it even had a musical number! George Cukor said it was the comedy/drama of the decade. It was, in my mind, a parody of the old Hollywood movies. In the early days of filmmaking, stars didn't swear, they didn't screw, they didn't even take a piss. What a bunch of Pollyannas! Paul broke those conventions and took his films to the opposite extreme, to the point that the characters were downright decadent. But no matter how low Paul's characters sank, you could empathize with them and care about them.

Paul had a good eye for story and direction, and Andy had an eye for cashing in on talent when he saw it. With the critical and monetary success of *Trash* at hand, I could just picture the two in the Factory discussing their latest vehicle as if they were Louis B. Mayer and George Cukor talking about *The Women*.

"We need to do a film with Holly. Something that she can sink her teeth into. But it's got to go along the lines of the current trends," says Paul as he paces the Factory floor. He scratches his head. Andy scratches his wig. Then Paul shoots up. "I know! We'll do a film on women's lib. That'll be perfect for Holly."

"Gee," replies Andy in his monotone voice. His eyes grow wider.

"Yeah, and we can call it *P.I.G.S.*"

"Pigs?" Andy asks, his voice still a monotone. "Golly."

"For Politically Involved Girls. But the real twist is that all the girls are drag queens. And we can get Jackie and Candy to be in it, too."

"Wow."

Paul was interested in making art that imitated life, and the idea of making a movie about the radical women's lib movement was very timely; bra burnings were at their peak. Paul called me at Asha's, where I had been staying that month, and asked if I'd be interested.

"Yes, I want to do it!" I screamed into the phone, my heart pounding with excitement.

"Well, what do you think about having Candy and Jackie in it as well?"

"That's fabulous!" I squealed. I thought it was a great idea, not only for the film's sake, but because I was thrilled that we three would all be working together again. At last there was a way for us to get back together and be girlfriends like we were before this Superstar crap got in the way.

We began shooting *Women in Revolt* in the spring of 1971 on the fashionable Upper East Side in a swank, upscale apartment. My first scene was with Martin Kove, who later became successful in his role on the TV series "Cagney and Lacey." He was gorgeous! Tall and dark, with a build that could make the most frigid of all girls flush with desire. He had a nice, big smile and the personality of a true charmer.

The scene started off with me telling my boyfriend (Martin) that I'm tired of being a kept woman. I wanted independence from male domination. Of course, I had no idea what I was talking about, because

I had indulged myself in a teensy bit of wine earlier in the day just to ease my frazzled little nerves. Well, one little glass hardly numbed the nerves in my toes. I was a tense, crazed woman on the verge of revolutionizing the female role in society . . . and I had the jitters! So I threw back another glass just to squelch those impetuous butterflies aflutter in my stomach.

Well, that wasn't enough, so I had another. And then I decided to make a toast in honor of Barbra Streisand. Of course, I had to have another. And finally, half a jug later, when I had toasted myself into a stupor and no longer knew who I was, I was aflutter, too!

Not only was I one sauced cookie, but I was also misinformed. Somehow I had gotten the idea that this picture was about lesbians. I didn't know this was a burn-your-brassiere movie. I just knew that my character had met Jackie's character at a women's lib meeting and had fallen madly in love with her. I had no idea what women's lib was—I was too engrossed in my own happy hour. And it seemed logical that this was a film about lesbianism, since, in my first scene, I tell Martin that I hate men and love pussy.

"I hate men and I love pussy!" Such a profound thought from the mind of one who was undeniably twisted. "I want to eat pussy!" I screamed, proclaiming my newfound sexuality. Darling, if this was women's lib, I wanted no part of it. On second thought, I would do anything for my career! Martin screamed that he loved me, and the next thing I knew, he was ripping his clothes off and climbing on top of me. The ship was docking and I wanted it out of my port. So I screamed, yelled, and carried on like some dizzy broad who had no idea what she was missing.

I later found out that Martin had no clue as to who or what I was. He had just come out of the service and was trying to break into acting when his uncle introduced him to Paul. Martin didn't have a clear idea as to what the Warhol crowd was about. Nor did he realize that I wasn't an authentic woman. Nobody bothered to tell him. And all through the scene he was trying to lift up my dress.

Once we had finished shooting, Martin and I hung out for a while and talked. He was such a nice guy, but after we parted I never saw him again. He went his way and I went to Asha's, and off we flew to Max's for a night of celebrating, where we met the famous model Verushka, who had arrived with her three sisters. I was surprised to learn that these sisters were all of high royalty. They had titles, you know, like Countess such-and-such and Baroness so-and-so.

Verushka was the supermodel of the Sixties. She was tall, with long blond hair and a very square face punctuated by high cheekbones and big, luminous eyes. Her long, spidery arms and legs gave her a most unusual look. She was the only model I knew who had a personal photographer.

The following morning we prepared to shoot my second scene, which featured Jackie Curtis and my friend Sydney in an apartment on Nineteenth Street in Chelsea. We were all loaded. Jackie and Sam, the guy playing her boyfriend, were flying on speed and wouldn't give us any. So Sydney and I began throwing back the cocktails.

This was Jackie's big introduction scene. She plays a schoolteacher from New Jersey who degrades Sam by throwing matches at him, spitting on him, ordering him around, and making him dance. The scene opens as Sam, wearing her panties, paints her toenails while she drinks a beer and puffs on a cigarette. I arrive carrying a plant with Sydney in tow, having hitched a ride with him on the turnpike. Sydney wants to have sex with me, but I can't stand the thought of making it with a man again, and Jackie and I toss him out into the street. Then I tell Jackie how much I love her. Well, Jackie starts talking about the women's movement, and I start talking about lesbianism. I *still* thought this movie was about lesbians!

Women in Revolt was filmed over a couple of months. It was a difficult film for me, particularly because I was so intimidated by Jackie and Candy. I had never worked in an improvizational situation with them before, and they always dominated the scenes. I was terrified they would outshine me, so once the scene got rolling, I would withdraw into myself. I didn't want to play their games. I didn't want to be like them. And most of all, I didn't feel like fighting to see who could get more screen time!

I was also drinking heavily. I didn't think I was an alcoholic, but

I was a helluva lush! I drank because it made life easier. It freed me of insecurities. It made me feel good. If I woke up feeling depressed, I could throw back a cocktail and suddenly my world seemed like a better place. The doubts or worries that I had were gone. And I felt flawless. A drink became my constant companion in the twisted charade that I had somehow deemed reality.

As fate would have it, the film that was supposed to be mine eventually belonged to Jackie and Candy. My big starring role had dwindled down to a supporting one. Jackie was so overpowering. I always wondered why her character wasn't giving me back any of the love I had been lavishing on her. But then, in reality, Jackie was so cold anyway. She was very straightforward and thought of no one but herself.

Candy was still blond as ever! She was aloof and arrogant and would show up on the set with her manager at her side constantly fussing over her. Miss Darling had caught a severe case of Norma Desmonditis. She actually believed she was this superior being and the rest of us were peasants. It made me sick to be around her. Ironically, her role was that of a rich bitch who aspires to be a Hollywood star.

The first time Jackie, Candy, and I were together on-screen was in Kenneth Lane's rococco apartment, where we had a big women's lib meeting. All the girls were there, including Baby Betty, Penny Arcade, and Rita Redd. Susan Chicklets, a former porn star, also showed up, and Patrick Higgins, who played Candy's grandmother, was there.

Candy's character was having a hard time making up her mind whether she was for women's lib or not, and someone screamed, "Candy, get off your trapeze and down in the sawdust with the rest of us!" It was a classic line because it was so true. Candy's pedestal was so high that her head was in the clouds twenty-four hours a day, seven days a week.

Miss Darling was so affected by her so-called stature that she became intolerable. And one day, her attitude just got out of hand. She was being very snotty and I had one too many Zinfandels and was in no mood for any of her prima donna crap. She said she was upset with my behavior, and I told her that I was upset with hers. And it wasn't a big deal, just a little tiff—until her manager waddled in and fanned the fire.

"What's going on here?" asked the manager indignantly.

"Who the fuck are you?" I snapped.

"I'm her manager, that's who I am. Now, quit harrassing my client."

No one was harrassing anybody until this moose hauled her chafed thighs into the picture. And because of her, what had started out as a little argument progressed into a loud, uproarious brouhaha. It seemed like the only way to end this banter was to slap the shit out of both of them. And that's exactly what I did. This resulted in a wild hair-pulling, face-slapping, gut-punching riot with cries of "I'm gonna kill you, bitch!"

Rita Redd and Jackie pulled us apart, and Candy stormed out of the room in a royal snit, snotty manager at her side. My insides were boiling with anger—so much so that it took another jug of wine to simmer me down. And even then I was still ready to carry on. It was one thing to have to put up with Miss Darling, but I was not going to be subjected to some fleabag housewife from Queens who thought she was Swifty Lazar!

Well, I had another thing coming. That night I went to Max's and I was blowing kisses and being my grand fabulous self when this big, stocky grease monkey approached and said, "Say, you's Holly Wood-lawn?" And just as I reached into my bag to pull out a plume to sign an autograph, he grabbed me by the neck, pushed me against the wall, and started to choke me! There I was, being choked to death with my eyes bulging, arms flailing, jewelry clanking, and throat retching! Oh, the horror, especially since a full carafe of wine I had barely touched was within eye's view. The nerve of this goon! I knew people were upset when I was shunned by the Academy and denied an Oscar, but this was taking it a bit far. He was messing up my entrance!

Well, just as my eyes were beginning to cross and my face was turning blue, Philip the manager pounced upon the scene and pulled this ape off my ravaged, nearly lifeless (but still fashionably clothed) body. "You touch my wife again and I'll kill you the next time!" he bellowed in a deep, gravelly voice. Oh, I was plucked. The brute wasn't a crazed fan at all, but the husband of that ruthless, havoc-wreaking hussy-turned-talent pusher! I was so devastated that I immediately took refuge in my carafe of wine. And then I moved on to yet another jug! Darling, by the end of the night, I had so much wine in me I was beginning to feel like a grape.

Filming *Women in Revolt* had turned into an insane folly of booze, drugs, and rigamarole. Just imagine Jackie, Candy, Rita, Estelle, Baby Betty, and me all piled into a bathroom, downing glasses of wine while painting our faces, primping our hair, and shooting up speed. It was drollery at its best, and when it came time to film our scene, we were all so hopped up that all hell broke loose. We all burst out into a riot, and were ranting and raving something fierce. It was a fiasco, and what made it even more ludicrous was that at one point I was upside down in a wheelchair getting banged by a man I had never seen before! This movie was definitely getting out of hand.

My animosity toward Candy had ripened and I pounced on every available opportunity to yell at her on film. I was always screaming at her because it was a way for me to let out my aggression, and soon I found myself on hiatus until further notice.

During the break, I went with Sidney to North Carolina to vacation with some of his wealthy friends on their private island retreat and arrived back in New York just in time to resume filming. We were going to do a big bar scene with the girls downtown in the East Village near Paul's house. Andy showed up to watch and it was the first time I had ever seen him on the set.

In the bar, we had to stage a fight. By this time we were all so high, you could look up and see our panties! It was a ball, all of us fighting, screaming, and carrying on. But, six months after we had begun filming this epic, I still thought we were making a movie about lesbians. While everyone else was screaming for equal rights, I was still screaming for pussy.

The movie ended with Jackie having a baby and running off to New Jersey with Mr. America, Candy fleeing to Hollywood to become a star, and moi, the gorgeous wannabee model, drinking myself into a stupor and hitting the skids. I was one pickled diva. The last shot was of me squatting in the slums of the Bowery in the rain with my panties around my ankles taking a piss against a delapidated building! Paul's art had imitated life indeed. Why the hell couldn't I have gone to heaven and had a big musical number, for Christ's sake?

Shortly after *Women in Revolt* had wrapped production, I was back riding the publicity wave of *Trash*, and it was a tsunami! I was making guest appearances at colleges and universities and had been invited to appear at the film's opening in Atlanta. Just before I was about to fly off to the land of cotton and Scarlet O'Hara, Ishmael Merchant rang me up on the phone and offered me a three-thousand-dollar role in his film *Tacky Women* (later retitled *Savages*), which also starred Martin Kove, Ultra Violet, and Asha. I was excited about the project, but while I was in Atlanta I received a telegram from another producer offering me a starring role in his film *Scarecrow in a Garden of Cucumbers*. He offered me sixty-five hundred dollars and I jumped on the opportunity, declining *Tacky Women* due to a conflict of schedules.

I enjoyed my stay in Atlanta, and upon checking into the Hyatt Regency, I immediately looked up my long lost love, Johnny. As I recalled, his body was as smooth as a Georgian peach and I was hungering for the succulent taste. Johnny was living in a commune and finishing high school. He was happy to hear from me and invited me to his parents' house for dinner.

Johnny's parents had achieved the American dream. They were lovely people with a lovely home in a lovely upper-middle-class neighborhood. And then I walked into their lives and created a commotion! They were kind, but they had no idea what I was, and the mere notion that I might have shown their son the other side of my midnight soured their dream entirely.

Needless to say, sparks flew between Johnny and me, sparks that kindled the flames of passion that melted our bodies into one. We carried on incessantly, torching one another with our rapturous delights. And when it came time for my departure, I packed up my petticoats and said, "Adieu!" Darlings, I hightailed it back to New York, leaving the boy in the cottonfields to ponder my return. If there's one thing I had learned about romance, it's to leave them begging for more!

CHAPTER 13

The Days of Cheap Wine and Paper Roses

*m*y next cinematic endeavor, *Scarecrow in a Garden of Cucumbers*, tells the whimsical tale of Eve Harrington (I couldn't believe it myself), a girl from Shaker Heights who comes to New York in search of fame and fortune and is bombarded with lunacy. It is a riotous romp of oddities and mishaps as she stumbles across a cab-driving nun, a pair of female twins on the rampage for women's rights, and a midget wrestler who falls in love with her, but in the end, Eve chucks New York and heads for Hollywood. Not only was Eve a funny role, but the show was a musical as well! And you know how I'd been dying to get in front of the cameras and belt out in song. Finally it happened. They gave me a big musical number with sequins, glitter, and chorus boys. I was thrilled, and signed the contracts immediately.

The producers moved me into the Chelsea Hotel and appointed a lawyer to oversee my finances. The Chelsea was a grand little hotel, and I cherish the torrid memories of living there. The profligacy was rampant then, as I spent many a sleepless night wallowing in the whims of Delilah. And Gomorrah. Not to mention Tallulah, darling!

I had my own balcony, located just beneath the grand Chelsea sign. I have always adored balconies, particularly the ones in theaters, which are excessively ornate and so heavy with gold leaf that you can't possibly look at them for more than a moment without going blind!

And right along with me was Estelle, that demented hoodlum and dear friend of mine. Estelle was continually drinking himself into a drunken stupor and having a blast. He was so full of booze he had pickled his brain and thought he actually was a woman. And I was not going to say anything to deter him from realizing the possibility.

I love gold more than King Midas, and one day in a manic rush of lunacy, Estelle and I bought some gold spray paint, threw back some cocktails, and gilded my balcony. We were going to glitter it too, but the landlord wouldn't allow us the pleasure. According to him, painting was decorating but glittering was defacing. Some people have no taste. But I was very flavorful and had more taste than a person should be allowed. Just ask any of the men who came up to my apartment.

Hanging off my newly gilded rococo terrace, I felt just like Rapunzel, my body draped in rich chiffon that flowed in a cool morning breeze carrying the faint scent of fresh-baked breads from the bakery down the street, fresh-cut flowers from a street vendor below, and fresh bus exhaust. Oh, the charms of living in the city! The street was bustling with people in a hurry, cab horns blaring, and tires screeching. Estelle and I would loll gracefully over the balcony's edge, just waiting for good-lookin' men to stride below us. And when they did, we hooted and hollered like hysterical hyenas, emotionally charged with passion and white wine. We popped our corks for every guy we saw!

Darling, I was always in the mood for love. I was a nymphet seething and sputtering with lascivious juices. Honey, my loins were so hot, I scorched my panties. My mind had been torched by vehement fantasies of men. Big men! Sweaty, gorgeous, muscular gods with bodies of steel I could devour voraciously and incessantly. I knew this urge had to be quelled, I would've thrown my hair down for the men to climb, but it wouldn't fall past my shoulder. So I threw down my room number instead.

Needless to say, my humble home was in an uproar with Estelle, Ondine, Jackie Curtis, and the rest of the gang whooping it up on my golden terrace. We were smoking pot, shooting speed, and dipping into all sorts of jollity. Wine, weed, booze, men . . . it was ancient Greece all over again.

I wasn't the only merrymaker in the Chelsea. This lively monstrosity housed other luminous personalities including Viva, the artist Richard Bernstein (known for his *Interview* magazine covers), and Jerome Ragni of *Hair* fame. Jerome used to invite me to *Hair* all the time, and during the finale, I'd run out of the audience and jump onstage with the rest of the cast to sing my heart out.

Also at the Chelsea lived a kid named Lance Loud, whose family was being filmed for the weekly TV series "American Family" on PBS. Cameras followed that poor family everywhere, baring their secrets for the world to see. One afternoon, Lance called me up and said he wanted to bring his mother by to meet me. I was dying to meet Mumsy Loud, and told him to drop in for crumpets. Luckily, I had fixed my hair and downed a cocktail, because when I answered the door, I was stunned to find lights and a film crew standing right in my face! And in the middle was Lance, introducing me to his mother. Mrs. Loud was just as overwhelmed by my celebrity as most fans, and she suddenly had an attack of the vapors and was rushed to the golden terrace for air.

Aside from such shenanigans at the Chelsea, I was also filming *Scarecrow in a Garden of Cucumbers*, which took three months to shoot. We worked twelve hours a day. It was a big to-do, with a big crew of big men. When we shot on location, there were large studio lights and dollies and reflectors and baracades and security guards blocking off the streets. They even had a clapboard marking the beginning of each scene. Gee, this was more professional than I ever dreamed. I even had my own trailer/dressing room, with an air conditioner that worked! I was feeling quite pampered.

The first scene we shot took place in a tavern. Naturally, I was the first to discover that the bar was fully stocked. And of course, since I am the nervous type, it behooved me to have a nip. And then I tossed back another for luck. And then another for health. Well, those cocktails are tricky, let me tell you. Every time I downed one, another popped up in my hand. Funny how that happens. And by the end of the day, my nerves were not only calmed, they were dead! So loaded was I, in fact, that while the producers were driving me home I simply lost my mind. I couldn't find it anywhere. I looked in my bag, I looked under the car seat, I looked and looked and looked and finally, in a fit of sheer anxiety, I jumped out into traffic and began to bawl hysterically. I was a touched woman. And the producers, dismayed and shocked by my distraught, erratic behavior, stopped the car and physically forced me back into the vehicle and hauled me off to the Chelsea.

The following morning I received a call from the director. He said that I either get my act together and lay off the booze or they were chucking the film entirely. I chose to give up the bottle (and the pagan revelries on my golden terrace), promptly checking out of the Chelsea and moving in with the film's screenwriter. She and her girlfriend were both recovering alcoholics, and it was felt that they would have a positive influence on my drinking habits. What did these people think—that I was a sloppy, loud-mouthed, bleary-eyed drunk? That was Estelle. I was not a drunk, darling. I was a cocktail connoisseur. And I had very positive drinking habits. I held a drink with elegance and style. I just held too many, that's all.

Now that I was off the bottle and drying out, everything was going smoothly. Filming was going well, and I was happy. Then I got a message from Johnny. He was in town with a friend and was staying at the Plaza Hotel. The message said he wanted to see me. I gave him a call and made arrangements to meet him after filming later in the day. As you might have expected, I fell head over heels in love, with my legs in the air like a dime-store floozy waiting to be ravished. And I was! Over and over again.

Johnny decided to stay with me in New York, and the producers hired him to be my assistant. He moved in with me at Sandra's and it was just like old times. I felt like a true woman again, now that I had a man. *And* a job!

Scarecrow was an independent film which involved the prolific talents of two people I had always admired and respected: Bette Midler and Lily Tomlin. They did not perform on screen, but perform they did. In one scene, for instance, I go to a movie theater, and while I'm watching the film, my mind drifts off into a fantasy and I become a little girl. The producers had cast a child who looked just like me; Bette Midler sang a lullabye on the soundtrack, called "Strawberries, Lilac, and Lime."

Later we filmed a scene in the apartment of Jane Wagner, a good friend of the screenwriter's. Jane, as you may know, is the comic genius and talented writer who later collaborated with Lily Tomlin on the Broadway hit *The Search for Signs of Intelligent Life in the Universe*. Anyway, the scene had me lying in Jane's bed covered with salamis (don't ask me what that symbolized). I pick up the phone, dial the operator, and—SNORT! On the other end was Ernestine! Lily Tomlin was a good friend of Jane's and the screenwriter's, and she made a cameo voice-over in the film as a favor to them.

I finally felt like a movie star, in the sense of the Hollywood definition, and I was eating it up. One afternoon as I sat outside in my professional director's chair while the cameraman was discussing the shot with the crew, I heard all this screaming, yelling, and carrying on behind me. I turned around to see what all the commotion was about and saw Estelle (my dear friend, you know) barreling down the street, bottle in hand, hollering my name. Security tried to apprehend Estelle, but he barged through the barricades and came running to my side.

"Who is this person?" I shouted in defense, trying to uphold my reputation.

"Holly, you'll never guess what happened!" Estelle barked, wild-eyed and on the verge of collapse.

"Honey, we're getting ready to film. You can't just burst in like this—"

"But it's Crazy Sylvia. She's dead!"

Dead? Crazy Sylvia, the legendary cross-eyed drag queen known for busting a bottle over a cop's head at the Stonewall riots? It couldn't be.

"It's true!" proclaimed Estelle. "She looked out her apartment window, saw a Tuinal in the gutter, and went for it. She fell fourteen floors!"

I was flabbergasted! Sylvia would've done anything for a "Tuiey," but this was taking it a bit too far.

We filmed the finale of *Scarecrow* at the Broadway Central, an old Deco hotel that collapsed a few years later. The scene has me taking an acting class when off I go into another dream sequence. This time I find myself on a Hollywood sound stage surrounded by handsome chorus boys dashingly attired in white tuxes and top hats. I felt just like a Ziegfeld girl! My costume included a Christmas tree garland I'd strung all over my body, along with a silver metalic waterfall headdress cascading from my head. Looking like a float out of the Macy's Thanksgiving Day Parade, I was flanked by gorgeous boys in white as I sang "I'm Lost in My Dreams of Heaven."

When filming finished and the movie went into postproduction, everyone went their separate ways. Johnny and I moved back into the Chelsea and stayed for a month until my funds started to dwindle. We went to the production company's lawyer every day to get twenty-five dollars, which was deducted from an account set up from my earnings. Fifteen dollars went for food and ten dollars went for a bag of heroin. Yes, I was back to my old ways.

Now that I was on hiatus, I had become very bargain-minded and tight with the dollar. But when Estelle came banging at my door like the town crier, I knew I'd have to loosen up. "Hear ye, hear ye! Hear this, honey!" she announced. "The Puerto Rican queens on Nineteenth Street are selling smack for ten bucks a bag."

"Ten bucks a bag!" I screamed.

I pulled on my panties, threw on my fur, stuffed ten dollars in my brassiere, and headed toward Chelsea. I figured why not? I was out of a job, I had no idea when I'd work again, and besides, I had some bucks and I wanted to spend 'em. *Scarecrow* had been the first movie I *really* got paid for and I worked hard. Now it was time to enjoy the fruits of my labor.

Eventually, the till ran dry. We left our comfortable surroundings at the Chelsea and moved into a hovel on Tenth and Hudson Streets. It was depressing, so I decorated the place with tinsel I had gotten from the movie's art department. People were usually shocked by the gaudy interior, but I explained that I wanted it to look like the inside of a Christmas tree. Unfortunately, that place looked like the inside of a Dumpster!

One night, Asha invited Johnny and me over for a screening of a little film she and I had made during one of our spasms of creativity. While we were watching it, I got drunk and wound up in a horrible fight with Johnny. Earlier in the day, someone had flirted with him, which always irritated me to no end. And what was worse was that he had flirted back! I was livid, and the episode had been eating at me all day. Finally, after I had had enough wine, I blurted out, "You don't love me anymore!" One thing led to another and before Asha knew it, she had a screaming match in the middle of her living room that ended with me running from her apartment in tears and Johnny screaming behind me.

I ran into traffic, banging on cars while screaming that a madman claiming to be my husband was trying to kill me! A cab pulled alongside the curb and I jumped in, leaving Johnny behind. When he came home later that night, he packed his bags and left the next morning. I'll never forget the moment he walked out the door. Rod Stewart's "Maggie Mae" was playing on the radio when I heard the door slam.

I was broke, there was no doubt about that. Rent was due and the only person to whom I could turn was Andy. I ran to the Factory, told him I was desperate and he bailed me out. Everyone talks about how cheap Andy was, and I've even said it myself. But when I was down and out, I could usually count on him to pick me up, dust me off, and send me on my way with a few bucks—if not the whole rent—in my pocket.

Meanwhile, Jackie Curtis was kicking up her heels in a play called *The Vicissitudes of the Damned* at the La Mama Theater in the East Village. Candy was in it, too, playing a mermaid in a wheelchair. I saw it and thought it was speed-freak lunacy. All my "girlfriends" were bombed on stage and having a good time. Even Estelle was carrying on.

I went backstage and Jackie introduced me to an actor named Silva Thin. He was an incredible, androgynous creature: a tall, skinny, stylized man/woman with flawless facial bones who looked just like Marlene Dietrich. He even talked like Marlene. As a matter of fact—just between you and me—he thought he *was* Marlene! He liked cocktails and I liked cocktails, so we became fast friends.

I was terribly devastated by Johnny's absence and once again I was playing the Greek tragedian to the hilt. I had plummeted into the bowels of depression and become a mess. I shed my glamourous frocks for house slippers, a shredded black dress, and my black gorilla fur.

Then Candy dropped out of the play and Jackie asked me to play the lead. Of course I accepted, and once again my self-esteem was boosted from the depths of misery to the lighted marquee of the theater! Estelle, Silva Thin, Curtis, and I would get bombed in our dressing rooms and then go out onstage and act like crazed banshees. One night I rolled out in the wheelchair for my entrance and rolled right off the stage! I landed in the front row on top of Miss Candy Darling, of all people! Candy had come to see the show that night, just to see how I was doing. She was horror-stricken.

Miss Curtis's plays were in a constant state of change, and she would often rewrite herself into a stupor. She came up with new lines every night, and the same audience kept coming back because they wanted to see what changes had taken place. One night I sprouted legs. And the next night I was back in the wheelchair. There was always something going on.

But, honey, the real show was in the dressing room. Estelle would be carrying on with a vodka bottle in her hand while Jackie and I shot up in the corner, rehearsing over a bottle of Southern Comfort while Silva Thin chattered.

Silva and I were seen everywhere together. He was impressed with

Andy and wanted to be a Superstar, so we used to stop by every now
and then on our way to Max's.

"Are there any invitations? Any parties?" I'd ask and then Andy
would think, rummage through some papers, and pull out an invite.
"Oh, Holly, you must go to this one," he'd insist. "It's being given by
a big producer. Maybe he'll put you in a movie."

Andy always got a pile of invitations, and if there was booze and
eats, I did my best to show up at these free-for-all soirees. That's how
I supported myself. I didn't work, I just drifted from party to party.
And since there was a party every night, I didn't have to worry about
starving.

One day during one of my invitation quests, Andy perked up and
said, "We just got an invitation for you today. Yoko is throwing a
birthday party for John at a museum in Syracuse. They're going to
charter a jet to take everybody up. It should be fun, you ought to
come."

Darling, I didn't care where the party was or how I was getting
there. I was going! So Silva and I met at the CBS building with the
rest of the crowd on Fifty-fourth and Sixth, where we boarded a
chartered bus to Kennedy Airport. It was insane. Every nut in town
was invited.

The poor stewardess was terrorized by us all and eventually abandoned her drink cart and told everyone to help themselves. That was
all I needed to hear. While she was having a nervous breakdown, I
hijacked the cart, mixed myself a drinky-poo, and then went sailing
down the aisle to share my good cheer, filling glasses to their brims.
I was a true party hostess—even when it wasn't my party!

The party was held inside the museum showcasing John and Yoko's
artworks. The work did not impress me nearly as much as the hors
d'oeuvres. It was a very fancy, heavily catered affair.

We were having a fabulous time! Cocktails were flying, laughter
was ringing, and Phil Spector kept jumping up and down on tables
toasting everybody in sight. He was being so obnoxious I told him to
shut up and sit down.

Too bad the hors d'oeuvres don't last forever. I could live a life just munching on those fancy little giblets, but once they ran out, I got bored. Hotel rooms had been reserved for us, but there was another flight back to New York for those who couldn't spend the night, and at the last minute, Silva and I hopped on the bus and flew back home, giving yet another stewardess a nervous breakdown.

That summer I began to hang out with Silva a lot. I even moved in with him for a while on Bedford Street, not far from Seventh Avenue. He had a boyfriend named Chris who was a writer, and they shared a small apartment filled with books, magazines, and a refrigerator that housed several jars of peanut butter, jelly, bread, vitamins, a big bar of cheese, and facial creams: the necessities of life!

Frank Kollegy did a wedding shoot of us, with Silva as my husband. Silva wore a gray morning suit and I wore a white gown and veil. The photo came out in *Interview* magazine, where Silva wrote a regular column. One day I squeezed some money out of Andy and Silva took some money from his *Interview* stories, and together we went to visit some friends of his in Athens, Georgia. They were a group of young kids who shared this little house filled with strange percussion instruments. The kids had formed a band and were playing the local clubs. They later became known as the B-52's.

Later in the fall, I went to some mad party and discovered that someone had put acid in the punch. At this point, I had stopped taking acid completely. After all, this was 1972 and dropping acid was so Sixties! Well, the next thing I know, I'm flying all over the room. This was one helluva galactic trip, and I couldn't tell my toe from my nose. I was so fucked up I couldn't stand up anymore and a friend of mine took me to his penthouse loft down by the Williamsburg Bridge. He had a huge fireplace and it was cold. So we built a fire and fell asleep. Well, we forgot to open the flue, and the next morning, we woke up looking like two pickaninnies.

That winter, Gino and Marion—who had taken a house in Aspen during the previous summer—decided to get married. They invited Asha, Sidney, Richie Berlin, and me to witness the blessed event. Richie and I had met at high tea over at Asha's. She was a cute little pixie with straight brown hair parted on the side, big smiling eyes, and a button nose. She looked as if she had just stepped out of prep school. Her father was the esteemed Richard Berlin, Pooh-Bah of the Hearst Corporation in New York, and her sister, Brigid, was one of Andy's first Superstars—the infamous Brigid Polk.

Asha couldn't make the trip to Aspen and Sidney was going to arrive at a later date, so Richie and I set out on our own. When we arrived at Kennedy Airport, Richie was loaded down with suitcase upon suitcase of Hermes luggage and a small Yorkshire terrier named Toto, and I was lugging along my gorilla fur, that cat box I carried for a purse, and three designer shopping bags filled with makeup.

We boarded the jet and flew to Denver and then took a small chartered plane to Aspen. I had never been in such a teensy plane before. Darling, it only had one propeller to keep it in the air, and since I was a little worried, I downed some Valiums and drank some wine to control my hysteria. But as we were flying along, I happened to look out of a window and caught a glimpse of the top of a tree. And then I craned my neck to the opposite window and saw a forty-thousand-foot drop. That, mixed with the staggering effect of the Valiums and wine, made me think we were on our way down. In actuality, we were flying over the side of a mountain, but my mind was in such a whirl I thought we were in a tailspin on our way to death! I suddenly lost all control of my emotions and began shouting, "We're gonna die! We're gonna die!"

Cliff Robertson, the actor, just happened to be one of the passengers, and he was so disturbed by my outburst that he went to the captain and requested a landing at the next available stop so he could get off! Richie was mortified that I had created such turmoil and asked that I remove my pantyhose immediately.

"My pantyhose?!" I blurted in my delirium. "This plane is going to crash and you want my pantyhose?"

"It's a life-saving technique I learned when I was a Girl Scout. Hurry up!" she demanded as she pulled up my dress and began to remove the stockings. I quickly rolled the stockings down my legs and handed them over, assuming that this genius I was traveling with was going to make a makeshift parachute out of my nylons. As it turned out, Miss Berlin had no such inclination, and when the plane landed safely and Mr. Robertson departed, I was ready to run out of there myself. Unfortunately, I couldn't because I had been confined to my chair—tied and gagged with my own pantyhose!

When we finally made it to Aspen, we were whisked off to the rustic mountaintop lodge Gino and Marian had rented for the month. It was a big, rambling place built right on the edge of a cliff, with an enormous window in the living room looking over a three-thousand-foot drop. Just looking out of it gave me the vapors. On the opposite side was a splendorous view of the forest and, way in the distance, what was left of an old Indian teepee presumed to have been haunted. Just what I'd been looking forward to—a holiday with the ghost of Chief Howangowwa! Darling, the only spirit I was in the mood for came in a bottle, and with that notion in mind, I mosied into the den, where I helped myself to a glass of sherry. It was a quaint setting, with a large stone fireplace in the middle of the room and animal trophies staring down at me from every direction. A big black bearskin rug lay dead as a doornail on the floor as the heads of a cougar, boar, tiger, several deer, and a moose stared at me with their mouths open. I felt about as comfortable as a lamb amongst a pack of lions.

Suddenly, I heard the doorbell ring.

Well, just our luck. Just as I was getting settled in, out of the blue arrived this homeless hippie couple. They said their bus had broken down on the mountain road. Since it was getting dark, Gino said they could spend the night.

At the close of the evening, we all took to our chambers. Richie and I bunked together in a delightful little nook on the second floor overlooking the haunted forest I was forever trying to erase from my mind. Naturally, I brought up a bottle of wine to ease my nerves, and as I uncorked the spirits and treated myself to a swig, I heard a faint "Boo!" I choked on the bottle and spit and sputtered in a frenzy of fear. Shuddering from head to toe, I grabbed onto Richie for dear life.

"What the hell's the matter with you?" she snapped. Her nightgown was over her head as she desperately struggled to find the appropriate hole for her head.

"A ghost, Richie!" I cried. "I heard a ghost! It's that Indian chief. He's out there, I know he is!"

"Oh, you're just imagining things, Holly," she reassured me as I ransacked my bags, looking for a pill.

"Where's the goddamned Valium, for Christ's sake? I'm telling you I heard it. It came from out there," I said, pointing to the darkness outside my window. Richie, by now completely disoriented in her nightgown, fell over a suitcase and stumbled into the bed. She lifted the gown from her head, staring at me through tired eyes.

"Ghosts don't live in teepees and haunt forests. They haunt houses."

"That's supposed to make me feel better?"

I could tell by the look in her eyes she was going to get me with the pantyhose, so I reasoned, "All right, let's both go to the window. If we don't see or hear anything, I'll go to bed and I won't say another word."

Richie smirked, babbling on about how silly this all was, and as we both approached the window and stared long and hard into the darkness of the wilderness below, the biggest ghost I had ever seen flashed before our eyes, evoking shrilling screams of terror from us both. Our faces were stretched into horrifying grimaces as we faced the monstrous demon that appeared before us with glowing eyes and fangs. In the height of all this commotion, everyone in the house came running into our room to see what had happened. Darling, I was so shaken, the only way I could have been calmed was to have poured an entire bottle of wine down my throat and then be beaten over the head with it afterward!

"What happened?" asked Gino in a panic.

"A ghost," I told him.

"Big, with fangs," cried Richie.

"Out there!" I pointed.

Gino ran to the window, pulled open the sash, and looked outside as we quivered in one another's arms. Then we all heard that faint, ghostlike voice cry out again.

"That's not a ghost," said Gino, motioning for us to come to the window. We gathered by his side, looked out into the trees below, and staring at us from a branch was the ghost we had seen. Only it wasn't a ghost at all, but a big white owl. Richie and I felt like complete fools, and quickly piled into the bed and buried ourselves under the covers to avoid further humiliation.

Later in the eve, while we were sleeping peacefully in our mountaintop hideaway, a gust of freezing wind came bursting from the heavens, forcing our window open and lifting the covers from our curled bodies. Richie shivered as she scrambled across the floor to lock the window in place.

"Oh, my God, Holly!" she cried. "Look at it."

If this was another owl, I was not in the mood. But I raised myself from my slumber and crawled to where she stood and looked out into the most beautiful sight I had ever seen. Snow was falling everywhere and the ground was covered in a blanket of white that sparkled from the full moon above. It was as if we were inside one of those snow globes that had been shaken into a blizzard.

"It's beautiful," said Richie, grabbing hold of my arm as I stood with her in awe of this magical, wintery wonder.

By morning, we were ass-deep in snow! This had been the worst blizzard to hit Aspen in fifty years. It was so bad that the mountain roads had been closed and the telephone lines were completely down. We were literally imprisoned on top of that mountain, cut off from the world. And to worsen matters, the hippies decided to pass the time by singing folk songs! I wanted to die.

Then, when the hippies finally got bored with singing, they told us the story about the Donner Party—the group of pioneers who were traveling through this very same mountain range on their way to California and got caught in a snowstorm. They were stranded on the mountain for so long they resorted to cannibalism to survive! We were terrified. Gino, Marion, Richie, and I would just look at one another and gulp. There we were, snowed in on a mountain with cannibal hippies! I was horror-stricken. Not that I was that concerned about running out of food. There was more wildlife in the den than on an African safari. And although munching on a stuffed boar's head wasn't entirely appetizing, it beat a hippie in my book! But what really had me up in arms was that not only were we running out of food, we were low on liquor and speed. Darling, I could never sustain myself without these vital provisions.

One day, in a state of panic, I rushed out to the carriage house to see if I could muster up some forgotten cases of wine, vodka—anything to ease my cabin fever. And as I rummaged through the musty shelves and dug through forgotten boxes, I uncovered a large bundle of fireworks. It wasn't what I was hoping for, but it was a temporary end to my doldrums.

I trudged back to the house with my newfound treasure and, during our nightly cocktail soiree, Gino and I decided to shoot the sky rockets off the balcony, watching as they soared into the black sky and burst into a blaze of color. Suddenly, feeling rather gay after that last swig of gin, Richie began to sing "The Star Spangled Banner." "Oh-h, say can you seeeee . . ."

We were a patriotic bunch of buffoons as we all joined in, serenading the trees while Gino started in on another handful of fire rockets. We were drunk and high, laughing and carrying on until we noticed that the rockets that Gino had just shot into the air had spun around and were heading back at us! Our eyes nearly popped out of our heads as the house was about to be bombed by our own fireworks display! We all ran inside to take cover. All of us, that is, except Richie, who, in the middle of this chaos, had her eyes closed and was singing her heart out, completely unaware of the panic! I ran back out onto the terrace and quickly yanked her inside to safety. It's a wonder we weren't all blown to smithereens.

After a week, the snow plows came, and it wasn't a moment too soon. Gino and Marion kicked out the hippies, said to hell with life on the mountain, and we all packed our bags and moved to town, taking up residence in the Hotel Jerome. We rented two suites, one for Gino and Marion and one for Richie and me. Sidney finally arrived and replenished our stock of speed—thank God! I immediately gave myself a big fabulous shot and then ran out to the nearby skating rink, where I took ice-skating lessons with the neighborhood children. I caught on quick, and whizzed around the rink so fast I was a blur in a gorilla fur! A dynamo on ice, I was! There were only three minor problems. One—I could only skate backward. Two—I couldn't see where the hell I was going, continually leaving a trail of maimed children behind me. And three—I didn't know how to stop. An even bigger concern was *when* I would stop. After that shot of speed, it's a wonder I didn't go into a ferocious spin and bore my way to China!

Meanwhile, back at the hotel, Marion decided to stir up some commotion on her own. She called the Factory and arranged to have *Trash* sent to Aspen, and then promptly set up a screening at the local theater. Naturally, there was a lot of hoopla with the press on the night of the screening, and suddenly everywhere I went, people pointed. Our party went from being nobodies to somebodies overnight, and it was fun being bathed in all that attention. I was even invited to participate in a rinky-dink fashion show sponsored by a local women's club. It was a minuscule little charity thing patronized by stuffy house-wives, but I would've killed to get up on that runway nevertheless (even if the fashions *were* off the rack). So I accepted the offer immediately.

Gino and Marion caught wind that the Spinners were coming into town to play at a local nightclub and they made arrangements for us to attend. We all filed into the club, sat at our table, and began to toss back the cocktails when someone announced over the loudspeaker that I was in the audience. Well, people clapped and I stood up, waved, and did the whole celebrity routine. Then the Spinners came on and launched into their show. Well, we were sitting at our table having a riotous time when Richie turned to me and said, "Holly, get up there and sing with them." I was floored at the suggestion. Then Gino said, "Yeah, Holly. Go on." Before I knew it, my entire table was trying to get me onstage. It seemed like a fun idea, so I threw back what was left of my wine and up I went! I got up onstage and started to sing, but before I had a chance to complete the first verse, I was promptly escorted off. Oh, the humiliation! I had made a complete asshole of myself, and it caused such a disturbance that the incident was featured in the local paper. "WARHOL STAR MAKES ASSHOLE OUT OF HERSELF ONSTAGE!" That was the jist of the headline. I was plucked beyond belief, and when the women's club got wind of my shenanigans, they politely asked me not to attend their fashion show. How's that for being humbled?!

True, I was devastated, but I was not about to let it ruin my fun. I simply decided to commit suicide on a ski slope! Actually, going skiing was more Gino and Marion's idea; the idea of suicide lent itself only because never in my entire life had I been on skis. Richie had never skied herself, so it turned out to be a milestone event for us both. We had run off together to a local boutique and gotten little ski outfits in which to take our private lessons. Finally, when we were ready for the slopes, Richie and I decided to get brave. We latched on to the tee-bar lift and up we went, making a pact to drop off at the same time and ski down together. But when she let go, I suddenly came down with the vapors. I couldn't just drop like that! What if I broke my leg? How glamourous can one be in a cast? And as I pondered the consequences of dropping, I kept getting higher and higher, and the lodge below kept getting smaller and smaller. Unfortunately, I could only ride the tee-bar so high, because eventually the cable swung around on a wheel and returned, to pick up other skiers. By this time a woman behind me was screaming, "Let go! Let go!" Gino, Marion, and Richie were below screaming, "Holly, let go! Let go!" And there I was, about ready to crash into a pole. Well, someone stopped the tee-bar and I had no choice but to fall off the thing. And plop I went into a drift.

Since riding the lift was so traumatic, we decided it was best for me to tackle a baby slope. Everyone took off down that slope as if it were nothing. Then it was my turn. I was so nervous, I had no choice but to take a nip out of the flask cleverly concealed inside my fur. And once my knees stopped knocking, I shouted "Geronimo!" and threw myself off the slope. The cold wind knocked me senseless, and I was so traumatized that I literally forgot how to stop. My mind just went blank, as I had forgotten everything I learned in my previous lesson. I was a helpless mad woman in a gorilla fur, racing toward the lodge with my poles in the air and screaming my head off. I'm sure people were shocked as I flew by the lodge, with my friends running after me screaming, yelling, and carrying on. I, of course, couldn't hear a thing, because the terror of my own screams was ringing in my ears. And just when I was hoping I could find a nice little shrub to crash into, I suddenly found myself heading straight for a school bus. I was stunned. I couldn't stop, I couldn't steer . . . I was helpless! And as I came closer, I could see the shocked children staring wide-eyed out the bus windows, fearing the inevitable SPLAT that was to come. And I, not fancying the idea of such a repulsive death, blurted out one last scream, tossed myself into the air, and gave myself to God!

FLOP! I was stunned. The wind had been sucked out of me, and when I came to, I found myself under a pile of snow with an irate bus driver standing over me, yelling that I could have killed the kids. Richie, Marion, Gino, and Sidney were running toward me in hysterics. I could just see the paper's headlines now: "WARHOL STAR MAKES ASSHOLE OUT OF HERSELF ON THE SLOPES!" When was this humiliation going to end?

For a while, I remained inside the lodge, drinking hot toddies by the fire and talking to the boys with their legs in casts. One afternoon during one of my fireside chats, I met a dashing young fellow named Bijon who offered me a ride on his snowmobile. It was a thrilling experience I shall never forget! Off we went on a fifty-mile-an-hour jaunt through the wilderness, and nearly drove off a cliff! Everywhere we drove was white, so everything lost its dimensionality. We had no idea that the great white space in front of us was actually two thousand feet *below* us! We thought we were on one great white plain. Luckily, as we came upon the cliff's edge, Bijon realized the disaster that lay ahead and steered us into a drift.

I staggered back to the Hotel Jerome, beaten and bruised. I had never had so many disasters inflicted upon me in one vacation! All I could do was flop into my bed, pull the covers over my head, and stay there until Marion and Gino's wedding—which happened to be just days away.

It was a precious ceremony, with Sidney as best man, Richie as maid of honor, and me as flower girl. I even made the papers back home; Suzy's column noted that I had participated in an Aspen wedding at the Hotel Jerome. Frank Kolleogy read the column and called me at the hotel.

"Hello, you divine boy," I sang into the phone while lying in bed, dining on a breakfast of bagels, cream cheese, and caviar. "Oh, we're having a fabulous time. It's a winter wonderland out here. So breathtakingly plush!"

"Well, it sounds like you're having such a good time and all. You wouldn't want to come back to New York to do a nude centerfold, would you?" he asked.

I was shocked! Never in my life had I posed in the buff, nor did I have any desire to now.

"For what magazine?" I inquired.

"*National Lampoon.* They're sold on the idea, and they'll fly you out just for the shoot. And," he enticed. ". . . they're paying a thousand dollars."

I nearly dropped the phone.

"A thousand dollars?! Where's that airline ticket?"

Darling, if Marilyn Monroe could do it, so could I! It surely didn't hurt her career. Of course, her tomatoes had ripened to the size of casabas, while mine were still blossoming on the vine. But I was still ripe for picking, and with that little thought tinkering through my mind, I ran out to the nearest store and invested in a push-up bra!

CHAPTER 14

My Chocha for the World to See

mmmmm, what a guy that Frank Kolleogy was; a slice right out of the empyreal pie of manhood I so desired to gobble! In fact, I wanted to stuff my face! But old-fashioned girl that I was, I held back. "Don't make a pig of yourself, Holly," I reminded myself in a state of futile lust.

Frank was a dark, handsome Italian with thick, black curly hair, deep-set eyes, a thick mustache, and a body that I swore had to have been chiseled by Michelangelo. He was just like a hero in a cheap romance novel. Naturally, I fancied myself as the fair young maiden from *The Canterbury Tales*, swigging a tankard of ale with my bosoms pushed up to my chin, just waiting to be ravaged in the shrubs. But whoa, it never came to be. *Quel dommage.* Frank didn't like maidens

—he liked men. Nonetheless, we made a striking couple: he the Hun and I the gorgessa, though there was nothing between us but a good friendship. And since I had moved in with him after I returned to New York, I had no choice but to tell everyone that he was my husband. We used the word "husband" loosely then, mainly because we were loose!

Frank lived in a cute bachelor apartment on Tenth Street and Sheridan Square in the West Village. It was decorated in a Spanish motif, with a bull's head and two matador's swords on the wall. He loved everything Spanish—including me!

Frank was a successful commercial/fashion photographer, and occupied a studio on Fifty-seventh Street next to Carnegie Hall. He had done a variety of commercial layouts for advertising agencies and clients such as Saks Fifth Avenue and Revson, the Revlon conglomerate. He photographed such models as Jennifer O'Neil and Lauren Hutton and also shot album covers for rock groups such as the Doors.

When the gods made Frank, they rolled him in virility and sprinkled him with charm. "Out of all the stars, they wanted you," he cajoled while prepping me for the *National Lampoon* layout. Darling, out of all the stars, I was the only one who would do it! But Frank was persuasive, knowing very well that I'd make an appetizer out of the flattery and a main course out of being in front of the camera. I find that flattery is the best food. There are no calories and it makes one feel fabulous!

"Mucho Macho," as the layout was called, featured me as a man, of all things! There were several shots of me engaged in various "manly" activities such as riding a horse, playing cards and drinking beer with the boys, jogging through Central Park—I was even pictured in bed with a woman! This was getting out of hand, I told Frank. I wanted to relish the maddening pleasures of being a woman, goddamn it! I wanted to shake my can and jiggle my jugs! I didn't want to ride a horse. But Frank persisted, and no matter how pretty I tried to look, no matter how long I kept a pose, no matter how wide I smiled, it was to no avail! No matter how much lip gloss I tried to smuggle in, Frank always caught me off guard, and whenever I objected, he always came back with, "The editors want the natural look, Holly."

"Natural?" I snapped. "Natural? You want natural?! Why don't you go photograph a chimpanzee beating its breast in the Bronx Zoo?"

I was born of a jar of Maybeline, and that's oil—petroleum! Isn't that natural enough? Why, the very fiber of America is dependent upon this natural resource. I begged, I pleaded, I even groveled for mercy!

"Please, how 'bout a smudge of blush? Or just a pinch of mascara? I need color!" But Frank refused, insistent that I appear with a naked face.

When the photos were published, the article began, "Latin-about-Manhattan Harold Santiago Rodrigues is one hombre who knows what women want ..." The photos of me as a man served to build momentum until the notorious centerfold was unfolded and BAM! Readers were knocked senseless by my glorious womanhood. There I was, consumed in falls and wiglets, stretched naked across a lynx fur, dripping with Kenneth Lane jewels. My arms were crossed to hide my nipples and my dubious "chocha" was masked by jewels. It was more tasteful than I had ever imagined!

When we went into the studio to shoot the centerfold, Frank had borrowed fifty thousand dollars' worth of fur from Ben Kahn Furriers, which included only a lynx bed spread and a full-length mink coat. The coat was the color of sable and was cut very straight and tailed with pelts at the bottom so that when it opened, the bottom flaired out like a little skirt. It was very *haute couture*, but with a price tag of twenty thousand dollars, you'd think they'd throw in a chinchilla snood. Instead, they threw in an armed guard!

After we finished shooting the nude layout, we started to play around, with me camping it up in front of the camera and the flashbulbs popping away. Frank was inspired and suggested that we shoot photos to submit to Blackgama Furriers for their "What Becomes a Legend Most" ad campaign. We had all the fur we needed and more jewelry than a person should be allowed to wear. And I was dying to be a fur-cloaked legend!

The photos were beautiful. Unfortunately, however, Blackgama's ad agency declined the concept on the grounds that I was too con-troversial for their image. Now, I am not bitter in the least, but PISS ON THEM! Besides, I had my own Jacque Kaplan gorilla I was dragging from here to eternity—which, incidentally, was a legend in itself. I took that coat everywhere! I even lived in it for a while. It was huge, it was black, it was fierce, and all I had to do was spray it with Black Flag once a week and it was ready to wear! Not to mention that by this time the only thing holding it together were several boxes of safety pins, the obvious influence of Miss Jackie Curtis. Little did I know that this would be fashionable when punk became glamourous. Jackie did have a positive effect on my life after all. Or at least on the longevity of my gorilla fur.

I tried to take the Blackgama decision in stride, but in all honesty, I was devastated. I took it personally. I also wanted to take that mink personally. I just assumed that they hated me and thought I was a freak. Oh, how I hate rejection. It's probably the biggest fear in my entire life—aside from the thought of a reorganized prohibition.

After the Blackgama idea had been shot down, there really wasn't much use for me to be hanging around Frank's place. The *National Lampoon* assignment was completed, and it was time to go on to bigger and better things. The only problem was that I didn't *have* anything bigger and better to do! Frank suggested that I take a holiday and fly off to Puerto Rico to visit our mutual friend, Robert Jones. It was a brilliant idea, since Robert lived in a lush villa and would love to see me, but there was one *problema*. No money. I told Frank I couldn't afford the ticket, but to my surprise he had it all arranged. Robert was expecting me and, later in the week over cooked papaya and wine, Frank gave me a round-trip ticket. I was so titilated that my nipplettes got hard. Cocktailing in Puerto Rico—what a divine way for Frank to get rid of me, instead of throwing me out into the gutter. What class, what a man!

Lewd thoughts and fanciful visions of the tropical beaches were frolicking through my mad little mind as I packed my bikini and heels in a suitcase, when suddenly the phone rang. It was a deep male voice, belonging to someone named Dallas. It wasn't Stella, nor was it Texas. It was a Peter Dallas, to be exact, and I had no idea who this person was—except that his voice sounded worth my while.

Upon introduction, Dallas began telling me how he loved me in *Trash* and that I reminded him of Anna Magnani, my favorite Italian actress, who had won the Best Actress Academy Award for her role in Tennessee Williams's *The Rose Tattoo*. I was beyond flattered. I was honored, not to mention a little skeptical as to why I was getting such compliments. At first, I thought he wanted money. I had none! Then he explained that he was a filmmaker and that he wanted to star me in a movie venture he was producing called *Superstar*. Then I thought he was going to give me money, until I found out he had none neither. A double negative for the both of us.

So I stayed on the line just to hear the rest of his monologue. He expounded on the film, telling me it was a story of love lost, a woman left broken-hearted amidst the Gothic concrete artistry of Central Park. He said it was the return of the silent film, and that I was the only woman who could play the role.

I told Dallas that the idea sounded intriguing and that I'd be thrilled to star in it, but that I was leaving for Puerto Rico the next morning and I wasn't coming back to New York for several weeks. He said he would wait for my return, and then asked if I'd come to dinner with him that night to discuss the project further. I heard free eats, dropped my suitcase, and said, "Let's go!" Not only did I want the grub, but I was also curious as to what kind of person was behind the handsome voice.

Dallas was a striking man. He was tall, with dark features, broad shoulders, and a very charming demeanor. And he was of Greek descent. I just love Greece, and Dallas was built just like a column. Big and strong with long, black curly hair, beautiful eyes, and luscious lips. Best of all, he had a personality that lit up like downtown. When he rang the bell, I opened the door and swooned. His smile was as bright as the Great White Way, and he was so eloquent and debonnaire. He was flaaaaawless.

We took a taxi to a little Italian café and sat outside, chomping on linguini and sipping wine under the moonlight. Afterward, we strolled to Bethesda Fountain in Central Park, which was the location he had chosen for the film. As the night wore on, our souls connected. We were artistes: He worshipped beauty, and I certainly needed some worshipping. He saw the Greek tragedian in me, and I did too. I was pretty tragic if I do say so myself. Besides, I love all that ancient insanity with the tormented woman suffering and wailing and beating her breasts.

Dallas told me that my vacation would give him time to raise money for the project and so, bright and early the next morning, I headed for JFK and boarded the plane with my bags, bottles, lotions, wiglets and falls, maracas and mules. And off I went to sunny San Juan! Back to that lush tropical paradise of my childhood! Oh, how I had loved the tropical frolics of my youth. Not to mention those deadly piña coladas, which I knew would be awaiting my arrival at Robert's villa.

Robert lived in old San Juan, which was very pretty with its polished cobblestone streets shining in the blinding Caribbean sun. The cobblestones were as blue as lapis lazuli. It was pure Meditteranean charm. The houses were built in the sixteenth century, adorned with tiles imported from Spain and everywhere I turned there were wrought-iron balconies with plants spilling over them in a cascade of greenery. If only I had had some gold spray paint, I could've really had a ball.

Robert lived in a small Spanish house built around a center courtyard. He worked evenings as a bartender at a local hotspot. One night at the bar, over Bacardi and Coke, I ran into Sam, the guy who had played Jackie Curtis's boyfriend in *Women in Revolt*. Of all people to run into! We played kissy, kissy poo-poo, gave each other hugs, and he introduced me to a tiny, curvacious blonde with lots of hair and lots of bosom. Her animated gestures and her soft voice reminded me of Marilyn Monroe. Her name was Suzanne.

Sam and Suzanne were in Puerto Rico for the summer and were living in the Condado area, which is the tourist section of San Juan, where all the casinos and hotels are located. I would go over to their apartment to hang out. Usually, we would smoke grass, do Quaaludes, or go to the beach. Well, one day after we popped the last Quaalude, we became bored and decided to go shopping. There was no purpose to it, really, because none of us had any money to spend, but never-theless we went. Well, as we walked past the store windows, Suzanne saw a pair of shoes that grabbed her attention and wouldn't let go. She insisted that we go in and let her try them on. I thought it was a silly idea because she couldn't buy them, but she was insistent, so Sam and I gave in and followed her inside.

The size-five shoes fit her perfectly. She strolled back and forth before the mirror, acting as if she were trying to decide, and finally declined. Suzanne and I walked out of the shop and slowly strolled down the walk, thinking that Sam was following behind. Suddenly, Sam walked briskly ahead of us, a tone of urgency in his voice as he said, "Come on. Come on. Hurry up." We didn't know what the hell he was talking about or why he was walking so fast, but when we caught up to him, we realized that he had those stupid shoes in his windbreaker.

"What are you doing with those?" asked Suzanne.

"I thought you wanted them," he said.

"No, put them back, you idiot!"

Suddenly, the old shop woman came screeching out of the shoe store, screaming in a heavy Spanish accent, "Teef! Teef! They stole my chooz!" Suzanne and I were aghast.

"Run, honey!" I yelped.

Sam took off like a bat out of hell and Suzanne and I followed, with this little woman chasing after us, screaming, "My chooz, my chooz! Teef! Teef!"

Unfortunately, Suzanne could only run so fast in her platforms and hot pants (not to mention those unrestrained Double D's that were beating her senseless).

"Dump the fucking shoes, Sam!" I yelled in a panic as we scurried like rats down a narrow brick alley.

"Get rid of them!" screamed Suzanne.

Sam tossed the shoes in the bushes and then he ran to the right as we ran to the left, and as we scrambled around a corner, we ran smack-dab into the cops, with the old shop woman at their side. "Dat's dem," she said, pointing at us, her face puckered in a grimace. "Dey're da ones. Dey stole 'em. Pillos! I saw dem." Before we knew it, we were frisked and whisked into a paddy wagon, where we came face-to-face with Sam, who had been nabbed by coppers on the other side.

"Well, fancy meeting you here," I quipped. "You son of a bitch."

I was a wreck. Off we were hauled in shackles and taken to the station, where we were booked and locked up in an old, dilapidated dungeon known as "La Princessa." It was right out of *The Count of Monte Cristo*—frightening, old, and looking as if it were built when Christopher Columbus discovered the goddamned island in 1492! We were tossed in with rapists, murderers, wife beaters, drunks, and vagrants. There was no getting out of that dump, since it was surrounded by a forty-foot wall topped with broken bottles and barbed wire. I just knew it was a place where people went in and never came out . . . just like Bloomingdale's.

I was terrified, positive that the next time anyone would ever see me would be after I had escaped through a tunnel I dug with a spoon. Like Miss Tubman, God bless her soul. But I was in no mood to start up an underground railroad.

I wasn't the only one consumed by the horrors. Suzanne was petrified, as she—this little blond boop-boop-be-doop—had been thrown in with the *lesbians*. And these weren't your everyday truck-driving, horn-blowing, plaid-shirted, blue-collared ladies. These were brazen broads bound for the roller derby. They were madder than mad! Meaner than mean! And Puerto Rican to boot, which meant they had tempers that flared hotter than a jalapeño. "I cut ju bad, bitch. Don't ju fuck wit me. I cut ju bad!" I heard them scream. Suzanne's being tossed in with these chili-chochas was about as bad as a Christian being thrown to the lions. After all, Suzanne was young, tender, and voluptuous—the perfect appetizer. The guards might as well have rolled her in a tortilla, stuffed her with beans, and brought her in on a platter!

Our bail was set at a hundred dollars each, and they might as well have said a million because we couldn't cough up ten cents. I pleaded and begged them to call Robert, and finally they allowed us that much. Robert called Frank in New York, who gave him the name of two good friends living in Puerto Rico who, despite not knowing us, put up the money to spring us from the clink the next day.

Our trial was set for two weeks later, and we were put in the custody of the friends who had bailed us out. After a couple of days, however, Sam flew the coop. He knew he was guilty, and he feared that he would be locked in "La Princessa" forever. One morning we woke up and he was gone. He had run off in the night and left Suzanne and me holding the mules, so to speak. And there we were, stranded, with these guys who turned out to be quite disturbed.

Next thing we knew, as part of the terms until our trial, we had to stay in their house. They had us doing the slave labor. I was mowing the lawn, Suzanne was doing the dishes. We weren't allowed any freedom whatsoever, except to go across the street to the beach.

One afternoon, we went to the beach and a pack of Puerto Rican boys attacked us. They were threatening to rape Suzanne, so I ran across the street to the house, grabbed a Kenneth Lane rhinestone belt, and came tearing out into the street, waving the belt in the air like a Mongolian Hun, screaming in Spanish, "You motherfuckers, get your hands off my woman! I'm gonna kill you!"

Meanwhile, they thought I was a woman, too, but I managed to cause such a commotion that they fled for their lives.

Ironically, *Trash* had just opened that very week at one of the local art theaters in San Juan. At last, maybe I could reap some fame and have some fun! Suzanne called one of the newspapers and told them I was in town to promote the movie. The paper wanted to do a feature story on me, and sent over a photographer and reporter immediately. In that Sunday's edition, my face was plastered across the page with screaming headlines: "Local Boy/Girl Makes Good." Little did they know. If they had, the headlines would have been emblazoned on the page: "Puta Susia Ase Buena!" Loosely translated, that means "Dirty Whore Makes Good." If Ma could see me now!

Back to reality, our trial was still nearly a week and a half away, and we were broke. We needed money to pay for lawyers and talked Frank's friends into letting us return to New York to raise funds.

Back in New York, I couldn't move in with Frank because he had taken on another roommate, so I moved in with Suzanne on Tenth Street between Fifth and Sixth Avenues in the West Village. It was a small place that Suzanne had been sharing with an Indian man from Bombay who sold jewelry on the street. The place looked like an earthquake had hit it! Clothes were in piles everywhere. On the bed, on the floor—everywhere I turned, there was a pile. And underneath it all lived a dirty little peach-colored poodle named Danté.

We were so emotionally distraught over the fiasco in Puerto Rico that we started popping Quaaludes to ease our stress. And one night, as we lay in her bed in our luded-out stupor, I began to pet the poodle. And then I realized that what I had been petting wasn't a poodle at all; it was Suzanne! Well, one thing led to another, and before I knew it, we were a heap of pulsating, gyrating, groaning flesh.

I had stopped taking female hormones and was quite virile! Every morning I would wake up, roll over, and stuff the muff, poke the poon, or pound the mound. Whatever you want to call it, she loved it. Her legs kicked high in the air and jiggled as her hips undulated, her breasts bounced, and the bed nearly collapsed. I'm surprised we didn't kill the poodle the way we carried on! Her body would go into convulsions, quivering all over that bed as if she were a strangled chicken.

During our week in New York together, I became her boyfriend, although inside I felt strange with the new feelings I was experiencing. Most people thought we made a cute couple. Estelle thought the whole setup was sick and unnatural. "Lesbianism!" Estelle would scream at me. "That's what this is. What's the matter with you? You're a star and she's, she's—she's a woman. This'll never work. Heed these words, she's going to start wearing your jewelry." But we carried on none-theless. All I knew was that I was confused.

I managed to wheedle some money from Andy. I was on the lam again, damn it! I lied and said the money was for rent. Suzanne squeezed some out of her parents and together, we flew back to Puerto Rico for our trial. Somehow, however, our reservations got mixed up at the last minute and we wound up on a different flight, which was scheduled to arrive five hours later than the one we had originally scheduled. We tried to call the boys, but we couldn't get through. And when they arrived at the airport to pick us up and we weren't there, they panicked and called the police, fearing that we were jumping bail.

When we finally landed, it was chaos. We were greeted by the authorities, shackled, and tossed in the back of a paddy wagon with our luggage and my precious portfolio, which I had learned to never travel without, thanks to Jackie Curtis.

Back to La Princessa we went, and this time it looked gloomier than ever. We were treated like hardened criminals and it was hell, far worse than my gig at the Tombs in New York because my cell turned out to be as big as a banquet hall and was filled with thirty other real hardened criminals. One morning while I was taking an early shower this dirty old slimebag, a perpetual vagrant, tossed in after a night of booze, grabbed my leg, and said, "Come here, sweetie" and began to hump me like a wild dog. I was not in the mood to be violated by this snaggle-toothed ne'er-do-well, so I reached for a broom that was lying on the floor and broke it over his head. He squealed, ran away, and never bothered me again. Neither did anyone else, for that matter, since this particular incident gained me some respect. And to survive in that dump, you couldn't let anyone push you around, because these were heavy-duty low-lifes who'd kill you for a dime and toss you over the wall into the moat.

After a few days, I resigned myself to my destiny. Actually, I've always tried to look on the glamourous side of things, and one day I persuaded the guard to bring down my precious portfolio from the front office so I could show the boys my pictures. I had become quite chummy with these guys. Everyone was amazed, and suddenly I became a jailhouse celebrity. All the men wanted to know what it was like to work in the movies and the theatre, and naturally they asked if I knew any of their favorite American stars. Of course, I said I knew them all. Cher, Diana Ross, and I always went shopping together, I professed.

Soon my days were filled telling tall tales of the time Clint Eastwood and I saved the Alamo, or how I lost Richard Burton to Liz Taylor.

It was all a pack of lies, but it kept everyone entertained—myself included.

Finally, the day of our trial arrived. We were found innocent, and since neither Suzanne nor I had committed a crime, we were served our walking papers. So we hailed a taxi, fled to the airport, and kissed Puerto Rico good-bye!

Once we landed in New York and had kissed the tarmac, I moved in with Suzanne and we became lovers once again. It was a strange relationship. I didn't really love her, I was just taken by her—literally! She started wearing my dresses, my jewelry, and my makeup while acting as if I were her boyfriend. It really made me feel uncomfortable because I didn't want to act like a man. I was Holly Woodlawn. But I stayed because I didn't have anywhere else to go.

One night the Kinks threw a party at Tavern on the Green and I was invited. Their hit song "Lola" was about a transvestite, so I immediately told everyone that I was its inspiration. It was a glitzy affair, and I was excited. I had planned to arrive as a Greek goddess draped in a white chiffon gown with lots of jewels. As I stepped into the bathroom to put on my face, Suzanne looked at me quizically and asked, "Why are you doing that? You don't need to wear makeup. You're my date." I was puzzled. What was she saying? I had to wear makeup with this dress!

Suzanne's influence was detrimental to my mental state. I was losing my identity and it not only affected me, but it really pissed off Estelle. I liked being glamourous. I didn't like being a man. As I said, I was Holly Woodlawn and I was in no mood to be outshined by this cheesy blonde. After all, there's only room for one star in a family. But I chucked the gown, the jewels, and the makeup, and arrived at the party in overalls, sneakers, and a long face. It was disappointing.

Estelle was a true devotee of the classical ballet, and Nureyev was coming to town to star in *Swan Lake* with Margot Fonteyn at the Metropolitan Opera in Lincoln Center. Now, I hate to say that Margo was getting old, but how many relevés can a girl do in her fifties? And in a tu-tu no less! Pretty soon she'd twirl herself into a stupor and be doing the "Dying Swan."

Estelle was Nureyev's biggest fan. He was a ballet groupie, so to speak, and followed Nureyev everywhere. Estelle went to great lengths to be near his idol, and after a while the two became acquainted. One time Estelle (whose real name was Douglas, but we hated that name, so we never called him by it) climbed a tree that overlooked the stage to watch Rudy rehearse. When Nureyev heard the rustling of the leaves, he looked up into the tree and spoke in that deep Russian voice: "Doglas? Eez dhat you?" The limb of the tree broke and Estelle plummeted to the stage in a heap.

Estelle was also friends with Nureyev's dresser Larry Ray, who had smuggled Nureyev's smelly old dance belt, toe shoes, and other costume remnants for Estelle to keep as his private treasures. Estelle learned that Nureyev was a fan of mine, so on the night of the ballet, Larry arranged for us to meet Rudy backstage after the show. I was so excited. This time I made up my mind to wear a white backless empire gown with all of my Kenneth Lane jewelry. I even had a diamond belt to wear beneath my bosom, and crystal bracelets to adorn my wrists. This was going to be my night of glamour at Lincoln Center.

Little did I know that Suzanne had the same notion in mind.

Estelle always amazed me whenever he got dressed for the ballet. He'd get all decked out in black thigh boots, a Victorian velvet jacket, and white trousers, and look stunning. It was a major transformation. He walked with his chest out and his shoulders back. Estelle was very regal. Of course, a pint of vodka always helped with the attitude.

Suzanne was putting on a white satin slip when I went into the bathroom to put on my makeup. She turned to Estelle and asked, "Why is he wearing makeup?" And Estelle, having bit his lip time and time before in an effort not to bite her head off, said, "Suzanne—why is 'he' wearing makeup? Because 'she's' Holly Woodlawn! What's your excuse?"

It was the tiff that caused my spirits to tumble. Suzanne was upset, Estelle was livid, and there I stood trying to straighten my eyelashes. I became so disgusted that I took off all the makeup and went to Lincoln Center in my overalls, because, aside from female frocks, I had nothing else to wear. Everyone was dressed in tuxedos, furs, and

diamonds. And there I was, surrounded by all this opulence and grandeur, looking like a peon while Suzanne was wearing my jewels. I was
très miserable. I had it in my mind to snatch that diamond necklace
from her neck and wrap it around my own, but I refrained. At least
I had the sense to bring along an autographed eleven-by-fourteen black-
and-white glossy of me the way Holly Woodlawn was meant to be
seen: glamourously swathed in gorilla fur and loaded down with jewels!

Swan Lake was one of the most brilliant ballets I had ever seen,
mainly because it was the only ballet I had ever seen, aside from that
all-male ballet troupe, "Trocadero De Monte Carlo," down in the East
Village. Margot Fonteyn and Rudolf Nureyev were magnificent. And
after the thirty-two million curtain calls, Larry Ray came up to us in
the audience and brought us backstage. We followed him to the dressing
room, where a line of socialites—headed by Jackie O—had gathered
to pay homage to the deities.

Larry knocked softly on the door and poked his head inside. I
waited, my heart pounding when I heard that unmistakable voice say,
"Vhere is Holly?" I nearly fainted. Estelle and Suzanne grabbed me by
my elbows to hold me up as we sailed into the dressing room to find
Nureyev covering his naked body with a silk robe. Larry brought me
forward. "Rudy," he said. "This is Holly Woodlawn."

"You were wonderful." I beamed. "I have never seen legs jump
higher or wider. Your *jetés* were absolutely *je ne sais quoi. Mon Dieu,
quel arabesque!*" I rattled on, trying to talk some ballet lingo when really
I didn't know what I was saying.

"Your French is refreshing." He smiled, and then I handed him
the envelope, to which he replied, "For me?" He opened it carefully
and pulled out my picture. There I was in black and white, stretched
across my gorilla fur, covered in jewels and nothing else.

"I love it!" he laughed.

"Listen, let's go drink some Stoli one night and carry on."

"Yes, my deear, ve must."

Well, at least the night ended well.

A few days later, I was invited to attend an elegant party Monique
Van Vooren—yet another glamourous blond who had been Rudy's

constant companion in New York and later starred in Andy's *Frankenstein*—was throwing in honor of Nureyev at a chic uptown restaurant. Again I took Suzanne as my date, and again she wore my jewelry while I was stuck in those dreadful overalls. You'd think I'd have learned by now. These overalls were by far the most unglamourous, unflattering piece of attire I had ever owned, and I was wearing them every time I went out. These people were going to think that I had traded my movie-star image for that of a farmer. I was dressed for slopping hogs, not for an elegant affair. If I was a movie star, why was this bleached-out blonde wearing my jewels? Something had to be done.

CHAPTER 15

The Broken Goddess of Bethesda Fountain

*B*roken Goddess began filming in Central Park on a cold April morning in 1974. The trees hadn't even budded and there we were, a crew of four trudging to Bethesda Fountain at four in the morning with the camera, a tripod, and a cheap bottle of Almaden. We were artists out to prove ourselves, and instead of shooting speed, we were shooting film. It was grand.

The film was originally named for the song "Superstar," which Bette Midler always sang in her act at the Continental Baths. Dallas, who ran the lights for Bette's show, had the idea of making a short film based on the song and starring Bette as the damsel in distress, envisioning that the film could be projected behind her as she sang the lyrics on stage.

Dallas wanted to be the next D. W. Griffith, and his heart was dead set on producing *Superstar*, but Bette became so busy with her now-soaring career that she didn't have time to appear in the film and Dallas turned to me.

"There is no pay," he said, "but we'll feed you all the wine you want! Not to mention that you'll have your hair done by the acclaimed Michael of Vidal Sasoon and your makeup designed by the fabulous Vincent Nasso of Bendel's. You know, Holly, rumor has it that Vincent's going to give Way Bandy a run for his money."

Well, I was happier than a cochon in merde! Dallas painted a fabulous picture: hair by God, face by Michelangelo, and a starring role to boot! How could I possibly think of money after learning that I was going to be primped, pampered, and prinked by two very handsome and talented young men? I'd have a flawless face, beautiful hair, and a jug of wine. For the moment, my life seemed complete.

But what was I to wear? Marion Forbes came to the rescue and reached into one of her steamer trunks and pulled out a black crepe Balenciega off-the-shoulder gown. The dress was one of those long, flowing things that dragged on the floors of the poshest Park Avenue parties, and I was honored by Marion's generosity; however, the dress was much too glamourous and refined for the role. I was playing a destitute woman on the brink of despair, not a debutante. I couldn't look as if I stepped out of the society pages; I had to look like I had been through hell.

Well, one night while sipping wine and smoking weed—a notorious combination if I do say so myself—I became possessed by the spirit and was struck by the muse! In a sheer fit of gay inspiration, I grabbed a pair of scissors and shredded my way into a fainting delirium. That dress looked as if it had been put through a Vegematic. It was magnificent, for not only had I created a sensational costume, but another reason for my character's despair. What woman wouldn't beat her breast and teeter on the edge of insanity after her five-thousand-dollar gown had been shredded beyond recognition?

The night before shooting began, I slept over at Dallas's because I had to get up so early in the morning for makeup. Michael arrived before I went to bed and set my hair in hundreds of pin curls, a marcelled style fashionable for a 1920s screen siren. Once the pin curls had been pinned, pushed, and prodded into my head, we had a big party to celebrate our excitement and drank, smoked, and sang ourselves to sleep.

Vincent woke us up at three the next morning to do my makeup. I was awake long enough to get out of bed and make it to the kitchen chair, but once I sat down, I fell back asleep and stayed that way until Vincent had finished his wizardry. It was just like the way George Masters used to paint Marilyn Monroe. He would make up her face while she slept, and pop a pill in her mouth to wake her up. What woman wouldn't go nuts after that?

We arrived in Central Park at daybreak to set up, began shooting at five and finished at eight, when the fountain became crowded with the morning's rush of people.

After we screened the footage, we were shocked at the artistry of the film. It was rich with brooding blacks and stark whites, with a composition much like that in a Maxfield Parrish painting. We were so excited that Dallas decided to expand the original concept, and our little super-8mm film snowballed into a much bigger project than any of us had ever imagined. Dallas decided to make *Superstar* into a thirty-minute film and retitled our labor of love *Broken Goddess*.

"It'll be the return of the silent film," I remember him saying. "And Holly will be the first silent screen star of the Seventies."

Money was a major setback since we didn't have any, but Dallas had the determination of a thunderstorm and formed his own production company: Immortal Films. He hocked his furniture and some jewelry and even took on a night job in order to be able to afford film stock. His enthusiasm was infectious, and soon he had earned the support of several of his friends, including Eric Boer, a top model at the time; Bill Corely, a publishing house editor; and Laura Nyro, the singer/songwriter for whom Dallas worked as a personal assistant.

Making *Broken Goddess* wasn't easy, but it was fun nonetheless and took seven weeks to shoot. Every now and then I would have trouble with my motivation and I'd carry on like some cheap diva: "Dallas, I can't do this without inspiration. I need direction. I need music. I need wine!" So I took a swig and the crew took to singing, all of them joining in a chorus of the song "Superstar" while Dallas directed me down the steep stairs into the square. These men were singing, "Long ago and not so far away, I fell in love with you," while I staggered from one side of the stairs to the other and then stumbled and nearly fell down the entire flight!

"Cut!" shouted Dallas.

"Cut? Cut?!" I yelled back. "Fuck you, cut! I haven't finished yet. That was my best take ever!"

Then I'd have yet another nip of inspiration and we'd all gear up to do it again.

I sat on top of the stairs and came down again, still sitting. I wasn't a broken goddess—I was a bombed goddess, and it was beginning to show.

"Cut!" screamed Dallas again.

Once we completed filming, it was as if a carousel I had been riding suddenly stopped and I had to get off. It was sad, not only because it was over but because I was back to doing nothing. I looked forward to the premiere, but Dallas had been robbed of his cameras and his film-editing equipment. All that was left were cannisters of raw footage. It would take yet another year to raise the additional funds necessary to get the picture in the can.

So there was Dallas in a desperate search for money while I sat in the back of Max's raising a ruckus, with Bill Corely trying to hold us together.

"Don't dump Holly," Bill said to Dallas one eve in a spasm of marijuana-fueled inspiration. "Everyone takes her, uses her, and then dumps her. Do something with her!"

It was a scene straight out of the musical Gypsy. Dallas was skeptical, but Corely was like Mama Rose—he had a dream. Take the trollop, dry her out, stick her in a gown, and throw her on the stage. Of course, there was always the question of what I would do once I got on the stage. I wasn't quite sure myself. After all, go-go dancing can only get a girl so far in life.

Dallas lived three blocks from the Continental Baths in Bette's old apartment. Or perhaps I should say Dallas lived at the Continental Baths and kept Bette's old apartment three blocks away?! Bathhouses were a big to-do in those early days of the swinging, drug-induced Seventies, and the Continental Baths was the hottest spot on the map. Back then, it was very popular to take baths five, six, twelve times a day, because the sexual revolution was at its peak and it was very important to be clean. All the boys hightailed it to the baths every chance they could get just to scrub down. And down they went, again and again.

It was very social to congregate at the baths, and since it was open twenty-four hours a day, it was bustling from dusk till dawn seven nights a week. There were lockers and rooms for rent, and it was equipped with all the amenities: a pool, jacuzzi, showers, sauna, lounge, and men. Loads of men: naked, sweaty, and wrapped in towels. It was like ancient Greece, an erotic feast laid out before my hungry little eyes. I indulged heartily and made a pig of myself, gobbling in a trough of bulging, throbbing, heart-pounding flesh.

Gay men weren't the only patrons of the Continental Baths. Since the place boasted well-known divas of cabaret, women were admitted into the stage area to catch the shows. It was quite an eclectic mix, with these women in their furs amid the towel-clad men. Believe it or not, the Continental Baths had become a respectable place for live entertainment.

I was constantly going to the baths, and since I had been touched by the wand of celebrity, I was blessed with my very own complimentary room, where I could carry on like a true tramp! Not that I, Holly Woodlawn, star of stage, screen, and Max's Kansas City, would ever resort to such shenanigans. I would have to get severely bombed to participate in such sexual revelry. And since I was drunk half of the time, I felt quite at home! I frolicked and fluttered through that joint like a cheap carnal-crazed kewpie, and when I wasn't quelling the fires of my passion, I was hiding in the shadows, living vicariously through the whims of others. I was quite a voyeur and it was very exciting seeing all this hot, volcanic lust being flaunted right in front of my wide-eyed face.

The attitude among gays was "Live today because you could die tomorrow." Little did we know that tomorrow was on the horizon. Sexuality was rampant and everyone carried on incessantly. Which brings me to me, of course, and my first nightclub appearance, which took place at these infamous Continental Baths.

At this time in New York, there were two Continental Baths, a small one that had been built in the 1950s and the larger, more progressive one where Bette Midler had appeared. I started out at the smaller one after Dallas had arranged a booking for me to stage my own drug-rehab benefit for Phoenix House in New York.

I thought it to be a fabulous publicity stunt, really. Holly Woodlawn, well-known drunk, jailbird, and drug user mustering up all the brain cells left in her pretty little head to perform her own benefit for the addicts. I, of course, immediately held my very own press conference and, fancying myself as the next Evita, proclaimed to the world: "I have to help my people."

I had a simple act which began with my telling glib tales from a large, oversized book—tales about myself, of course. I blathered on as to how I came to hitchhike from Miami, get hit by lightning, and turn into the voluptuous beauty that stood before them, supercoiffed and painted to death. After my glib ad lib, I closed with the song "Lost in My Dreams of Heaven" from my stellar hit film *Scarecrow in a Garden of Cucumbers*.

When it was over, I was paid a hundred and fifty dollars and donated half to the cause. Naturally I had to make a presentation speech. "For all they have done for all of my husbands lying in the gutter on Avenue D," I said from the bottom of my heart. "And of course for the help they gave my late ex-husband, Manny the Cheese, who used me, abused me, and forced me to do things that I have long since perfected, I present this check for seventy-five dollars to Phoenix House." I handed the pillars of charity a huge cardboard check for seventy-five dollars, making a big production of the presentation, as if the check were for a million bucks. I could've just handed them a sack of quarters, but I was determined to make the most of the moment.

The boys at the baths loved me. Of course, they were all drunk and high and would've loved a French poodle barking out "Jingle Bells"! But I made them laugh, and I didn't try to be anything bigger than what I was; I was genuinely Holly, pure and simple. Well, at least simple. My close friend Mario Rivoli, the artist who I'd met while I was face down in the gutter, once recalled, "Holly was very human onstage. She was very glamourous and entertaining, but she wasn't out of touch with her audience. You could scratch through the glitter and she'd bleed."

Meanwhile, by this time, Suzanne had clawed off nearly all of my glitter and I was bleeding to death. Suzanne never quite grasped the fact that I was an up-and-coming Aphrodite, and her desire to tone down my glamour hindered my image. She was raining on my parade and it pissed me off! So I packed up my Kenneth Lane jewelry and hightailed it to my friend Elda's place on Tenth Street and Avenue A.

Elda lived in a small brownstone with her small son, who, if you'll remember, was conceived with Eric Emerson one lust-filled afternoon in a telephone booth at Max's. Elda was a nice woman of a strong will and a heart of gold. She was a real New York Italian, raised in a house full of brothers, so she knew how to fight for what she wanted. She gave birth to the son illegitimately, against her parents' wishes, and raised him on her own and didn't ask for help from anyone. Eric would traipse in and out of her life every now and then, but his priorities were in the fast lane, not in the home. Although he loved Elda and the boy, he was useless as a father because he was too busy taking drugs and fucking everything in sight.

Elda needed a babysitter and I needed a place to live, so I moved in and took care of the kid in exchange for room, board, and wine. Wine was definitely in the contract, as was my dear friend Estelle, who visited often to help me educate this little child on the fabulosities of life. We took him on a whirlwind tour of the city and visited the Factory, the park, the museums—we even took him to Tiffany's so he could develop a sense of taste. Every day was an adventure as we delighted in the prolific fruits from the cultural cornucopia that had spilled before his eager little heart.

Elda worked in an office during the day, and as a seamstress on the side. She was going with Sylvain Sylvain, one of the guitarists from the New York Dolls, and she made all of their costumes and was a major influence on their style.

"Us girls are tired of this mucho, macho bullshit," she advised. "You should dress up like women and wear lots of makeup. The girls will love it."

And the girls did. The Dolls began to appear regularly at Max's, and the girls went crazy. They screamed, they yelled, some even threw their panties on the stage.

By 1973, Max's had gone heavy metal. Gone was the mad glamour I had relished. The Superstars had left the scene, the round table had disbanded, and the place was overrun with rock and roll groupies. I had no time for blasting guitars and screaming synthesizers, and had left the scene entirely, until one day Elda (bored with sewing for everyone else) decided she could sing. She wanted to wear her own costumes for a change, decided to form her own rock band, and asked if I'd be interested in singing along. I was hesitant at first, but she said, "Oh, come on. If the boys can do it, so can we. Who needs talent? All you have to do is scream and yell."

I always wanted to be a backup girl. As a matter of fact, I could just see myself on "American Bandstand" shoo-wop, do-wopping, hey-lah-lahing, and do-lang, do-langing my way into the hearts of millions. Visions of bouffants, mascara, pink Day-glo lipstick, and tight sequin dresses pranced through my dazed little head. Maybe we'd even sing a song about a boy named Johnny. And as my mind filled with dreams of glitterati, paparazzi, and having our photos in the bedroom of every teenage boy across America, I just knew we were going to be the biggest craze since the Ronettes.

That is, until I learned what we were to be called.

Elda billed the group Pure Garbage and it was true: We were pure. She had recruited another singer, a black girl named Jamaica Kincaid who had platinum-blond hair shaved within an inch of her head. Our repertoire was a mélange of Broadway show tunes, familiar classics, and a few original songs Elda had written (such as "Dracula, What Did You Do to My Mother?"). We sang rock versions of "Hit the Road Jack" and "All of Me," not to mention "Boston Beguine" and vocal selections from "Brigadoon." As much as I hate to say it, we weren't too good.

We would rent a rehearsal studio for ten bucks an hour in the West Village, smoke some weed, drink some wine, and sing ourselves into a stupor. The first song we rehearsed was "Hit the Road Jack." Elda beat the klaves while Jamaica banged a tamborine and I, being truly ambidextrous and double-jointed, jiggled my jugs, wiggled my hips, shook my maracas, and played the cymbals between my knees, a rare talent that I had picked up from a battery-operated monkey at F.A.O. Schwarz.

Monday night was talent night over at Reno Sweeney, the new cabaret in town. I was way too embarrassed to go onstage, but Elda had no shame and signed us up anyway. I was scared to death, afraid we would flop. To ease my heebie-jeebies, Vincent Nasso cajoled a black spandex dress out of his friend Norma Kamali, who had just opened a small boutique on Madison Avenue. I thought if I was going to ride the Titanic, I might as well go down in style.

When we all plodded onstage, heavily drugged on substances that shall forever haunt my body and soul, Elda took the mike and sang "Rouge" from the Broadway show *New Faces of 1953*. Then I followed with "Boston Beguine," another show tune from *New Faces of 1953*, which was sung by the once-new face of Alice Ghostly.

My hair was piled under a fruit-covered turban, and I looked like a demented Carmen Miranda. Running around the stage like a chicken with my head cut off, I rolled my eyes, shimmied my shoulders, knocked my knees, and carried a tune, all at the same time. The audience ate it up, and what I feared to be a most humiliating experience turned out to be a good time for all.

Lewis Friedman, the small yet muscular man with a gruff demeanor who owned the joint, approached me after the show. He wasn't one to beat around the bush. He took me aside and said, "I want to be perfectly honest with you. You suck."

"Well, I know, darling, but how was I onstage?"

"To tell you the truth, I don't see anything in hiring the three of you together. But I'd like to work with you alone."

"Oh," I purred with my hands on my hips, having obviously seen too many Mae West movies. "A rendezvous?"

"No! A nightclub act."

I was surprised, not to mention elated by the possibility.

"You can appear on Monday nights," he continued. "And we'll see how it works out. That is, if you're interested."

Of course I was interested, but what was I going to tell the girls? I couldn't just toss them aside as if they were cut-rate trinkets cluttering up my soon-to-be rhinestone-studded career. So I went to Elda, told her the news, and explained that I was hesitant because I thought we should stick together. She looked at me as if I was a fool and said, "No, go on. Take it! I can always get another girl."

I took Lewis up on his offer, and to replace me, Elda enlisted the help of a pretty brunette from New Jersey named Debbie. Debbie was working at Max's as a waitress, and the two met one night when the Dolls were doing a show. Elda decided to revamp the band's style and head more in the direction of original material, instead of butchering Broadway show tunes with synthesizers and strained vocal chords. The group changed its name from Pure Garbage to the Stilettos and landed gigs in the local saloons. I worked the light show for them once, standing on a stool in front of a naked bulb and turning it on and off before and after each song. Estelle was at my side, holding colored gels in front of the bulb for dramatic effect. Well, what are friends for, right?

The band was playing around town at some of the better hot spots, but they just didn't catch on. Debbie eventually left the group to form another band headed by her boyfriend, Chris Stein. Elda found yet another replacement, but nothing much seemed to happen for the Stilettos. Debbie, on the other hand, was making waves with the new group and was hurled from her heels as a waitress at Max's into fame and fortune. No more dishing up Surf and Turf for her. She was the star of the nation's hottest new musical group, Blondie.

Meanwhile, on my side of the wilderness, the New York cabaret circuit was sizzling and Reno's had become the hottest spot in town. The thought of developing my own nightclub act had occasionally entered my pretty little head, but now the ball was rolling. Lewis, who was an excellent pianist, worked with me during the afternoons to develop my vocal range.

Meanwhile, on the other side of town, Dallas had landed another booking for me this time at the big Continental Baths. I will never forget the night (although I have tried many times). I was opening for Miss Tally Brown, who had developed quite a following, and the place was packed to the rafters.

"Whatever you do, don't give Holly anything to drink," Dallas warned Vincent before he left his apartment. Dallas had to arrive at the Baths early to set up while I stayed behind with Vincent, undergoing a major cosmetic overhaul. This mad queen named Alberto tossed my hair like a Caesar salad, and when it was over, I had a pile of curls that shot up so high it looked like I had a poodle perched on my head. I felt just like a Puerto Rican Betty Grable!

I had just slipped into a silver lurex dress that had a gaping slit in the front with ruffles up to my "cooze," when the zipper snagged on the fabric. As I fussed with the zipper, I completely broke down and went bananas! There I was, ruffled to death with a snagged zipper and going through the horrors of stage fright. I hated to perform, I just did it because I couldn't afford a TV. I was a nervous wreck.

Alberto took me aside and in an effort to unravel my nerves said, "Here, hon, this'll calm you down," and threw half a Quaalude into my mouth. That little pill did more than calm my nerves—it wiped out my entire central nervous system and I arrived at the Baths sideways!

Dallas met me backstage and saw immediately that something was wrong, but there was no time to back out because I had just been introduced for my opening number. I staggered out onto the stage and began to blow kisses to the cheering crowd. My accompanist had started to play the intro to my opening number, "Aye Yi Yi Yi Yi" (made famous by Carmen Miranda), but I was higher than a kite and couldn't hear a thing. I kept blowing kisses to the audience with Dallas in the wings waving at me, trying to get me to start singing. The pianist kept stopping in the middle of the intro and going back to the beginning.

Finally, I noticed Dallas's hysteria. I shot him a confused look and shouted, "What's wrong with you? Are you okay?" I looked into the audience, befuddled by my surroundings. "Where am I?"

"Sing, Holly! Sing!" Dallas shouted as the audience broke into laughter. I had completely forgotten where I was or what I was supposed to do. And having no wits about me whatsoever, I planted myself in the middle of the stage and started to sing whatever came to mind. The pianist tried to follow as I belted out the lyrics—those that I remembered. Most of them I had forgotten and made up as I went along.

Needless to say, the entire performance was a fiasco. Not only did I forget what the hell I was doing, but when lurex gets near moisture, it shrinks. And there I was, in a steamy bathhouse wearing a lurex dress that was too short in the front to begin with. When the steam from the Baths wafted my way, those ruffles shriveled and climbed up my slinky hips like a curtain in a peep show. And I was in no mood to be peeped!

While the dress was rising, my fabulous Betty Grable "do" was falling. It, too, was affected by the steam, and it wasn't long before the whole mess of towering curls toppled over into my mascara-stained face!

It was a sight to behold, this bombed bimbo staggering across the stage, tugging at her dress to keep it below her crotch and tripping over the microphone wire because she was blinded by a wad of curls. Who wouldn't forget their lyrics after enduring such trauma?

By now I was completely tangled in the microphone cord and the audience was laughing hysterically. I was getting irritated by this humiliation and chucked the song I was singing entirely and began to sing another, although I didn't get very far, as I had forgotten those lyrics as well. "Fuck this shit," I cursed. "How dare they charge seven-fifty to get into this dump anyway?"

Meanwhile, as I ranted and raved, Tally Brown was backstage gluing her eyelashes on as fast as she could because Steve Ostrow, the owner of the joint, was screaming, "Tally, you gotta go on. You gotta go on!"

Eventually, Ostrow came on stage clapping his hands and said, "Isn't she great? Let's give her a big round of applause." Then he grabbed me by the throat and promptly escorted me backstage as I yelled, "Thank you for coming! I'll be doing an encore in the orgy room."

The crowd was wonderful. They didn't boo or hiss, they just laughed and carried on.

As I staggered backstage, I ran into Miss Tally as she was coming up to the wings. "Go get 'em, girl!" I screamed enthusiastically. "I got 'em all warmed up for ya!"

I had no shame! And in a fit of sheer gaiety, consumed by effervescence, I shed my lurex dress (which by now was a halter top!) and in my delirium ran haphazardly through the halls wearing only pantyhose and heels. I headed straight for the pool, into which I threw myself and proceeded to stage my own water ballet in honor of the late, great Anna Pavlova.

My water acrobatics succeeded in creating waves, but not of the catastrophic dimensions demonstrated by my onstage antics. The entire fiasco sent Dallas into a tirade. He was madder than a wet hen!

"Where's Holly? Where did she go?" he screeched at the top of his lungs in an irate tizzy.

"She's in the pool," said Corely.

"In the pool?! I can't deal with this! What is she doing in the pool?"

"What do you mean, what's she doing in the pool? She's playing Jubilee on a French horn, you asshole!"

I was quite a horn-blower in those days, darling, and at the Continental Baths there were plenty of horns to blow. The French horn, the German flute, the Irish bugle, the Italian piccolo, the African

238 A LOW LIFE IN HIGH HEELS

bassoon (now, that's a horn!), and let's not forget the good ol' down-home all-American tuba. I've blown them all to smithereens and back, banging out tunes like a trained seal in a circus of debauchery.

Dallas was not impressed in the least with these escapades and jumped ship immediately, telling Bill Corely that he couldn't deal with my madness any longer. Well, toot-toot-tootsie, good-bye. And kiss my ass! I loved Dallas dearly, but he was a social butterfly, and as my manager, his interests lay in the free drinks at the bar—not my career. Dallas was far more concerned with his own ego—an ego too easily bruised by my unprofessionalism. All right, so I fucked up. I apologized! We parted amicably and he directed his energies into finishing *Broken Goddess*, while I invested mine into rehearsal time with Lewis Freedman.

CHAPTER 16

Life Is a Cabaret at Reno Sweeney

*R*eno Sweeney had class with a capital "K." It was the first gay club for straight people, meaning that it was staffed by gays and patronized by both gays and straights. A very mainstream club, it showcased top-notch entertainment and was originally opened so Bette Midler could have a classy place to perform. Bette never did appear at Reno's, however, because she wound up on the road, but it was nice of Lewis to think of her nonetheless.

Reno's was housed in the basement of a building among a row of brownstones on Thirteenth Street in the Village just off Sixth Avenue. It had an intimate atmosphere with a big, black baby-grand piano on the stage and bright fuchsia neon spelling out "Paradise Room" on the wall behind it. The Paradise Room was a very disciplined room and first-rate all the way. I rehearsed with Lewis every day until he had the confidence to book me as an opening act for Betty Rhodes, a big cabaret star in town known for doing Jacques Brel.

My act was a far cry from any other "drag" act in town because I didn't rely on lip-synching to perform. I didn't wear padded bras, wigs—I didn't even wear shoes! I came onstage barefoot (no one was ever allowed to do that but me) wearing a slinky black gown and Joan Crawford hairdo topped with a fruit headdress, and I sang Carmen Miranda's "Aye Yi Yi Yi Yi," followed by a trail of comedic patter. I pulled items out of a shopping bag I had brought onstage and performed various characters, satirized television commercials, and had a good time. I was still on the sauce, but I rehearsed my act and I knew the material, so wetting my whistle only enhanced my farcical revue.

One of my characters was Principessa Lucianna Mortadella Balonne, an Italian beauty who endorsed facial products with a heavy Italian accent. My script went like this:

> Halo, my name iza Principessa Lucianna Mortadella Bal-
> onne. [Holding up bar of soap] And I wasn't always this
> beautiful. No, I used to be a real dog, until I used this
> soap. Which is ninety-nine hundredths percent pure. Pure
> shit. If you really want to be beautiful, do what I did and
> marry a plastic surgeon!

My opening night at Reno's was a hit, and the applause nearly brought the roof down. Betty Rhodes had a tough act to follow, and when she went onstage, she admitted it! After my show, a lot of the crowd was leaving, so Betty decided to switch our appearance order so she could open for me! This was unheard of in cabaret. Betty was the headliner and she had the pull, so she could have easily thrown a fit and had me booted off the bill, but instead she was wonderful about the whole situation. After she had reversed our order, she joked to the audience, "Listen, I know you're all here to see Holly, but please try to put up with me first."

Lewis was thrilled with my success and booked me as a headliner. Dallas stepped back into the picture as my manager and oversaw the paperwork. I got a three-deal contract, starting at five hundred dollars for the first stint, seven hundred and fifty for the second, and a thousand for the third.

My success at Reno's was a triumph. Until that opening night, audiences didn't take me seriously. I had gotten some bad press and I was a man in drag, so people didn't expect to be moved by me. But they were. Suddenly, the audience had this heart-wrenching social comment going on right in front of them, and they were touched. Barriers were falling. Was I a boy? Was I a girl? Did it really matter?

It never occurred to people that they might like a drag queen, although I've never considered myself one because drag queens are such dehumanized creatures. Well, suddenly here was this man/woman-person in the spotlight who was very connected with the audience. People were surprised just how good I could be, and it wasn't that I was a great singer, because I wasn't although I could carry a tune. It was my personality. I was entertaining and it wasn't because I was a bitchy queen. I was real when I got on that stage. I wasn't a fake, I was being myself. And it worked.

My Reno Sweeney debut made waves around the cabaret circuit. According to *Variety*, "Holly Woodlawn . . . is an absolute delight in an ultra-camp, totally outrageous way. At Reno Sweeney, where backing is provided by Tom Vogt on piano, Woodlawn romps through some excellent special material to big applause. . . . While the singing is more talk than pure vocalizing, it isn't bad, and if Woodlawn had a real singing voice, there would be no limit to how far he (she?) could go."

I was finally getting the respect I deserved, and within a few days, I was contracted for a week's engagement at another up-and-coming hotspot called Trude Hellers. Trude herself was a tough-talking, cigarette-smoking broad who really knew how to "deal the deck" when it came to booking talent. Corely used to say that the only way to deal with her was to lay all the cards on the table with a .45 and a bottle of gin. My run at Trude Heller's was a success. I was getting more rave reviews and the people who had previously dismissed me as a low-life joke really began to turn their heads and take notice.

One night during my run, I was in the middle of singing about cooking breakfast for the man I love, wailing about baking him biscuits, when I looked out of my frying pan and into the audience and was struck by this beautiful white figure glowing in the front row. It was Candy, and although I managed to keep up with the tempo, I kept thinking, "What's she doing here?"

It was strange to see her at my show because we hadn't spoken for months. As a matter of fact, Candy, Jackie, and I were completely estranged. After *Women in Revolt* we had nothing in common except for the press, which was forever linking us together as Warhol's transvestite trio and comparing us to the stars of the Forties. Candy was always compared to Lana Turner because she was the seductive, glamourous blonde! Jackie was the hardened, take-it-on-the-chin Joan Crawford type; and I was the loose, full-lipped *chiquita* comedienne, which somehow earned me a combined comparison to Phil Silvers and Marlene Dietrich! Ain't that a pisser? As far as I was concerned, I was the next Hedy Lamar and no one could tell me any different!

In the eyes of outsiders, we were the Andrews Sisters of the Underground. I would have loved it if it were true, but the fact is after we each attained our Superstardom, we became competitive rivals and couldn't stand one another most of the time. Candy was always off on another planet, and she had become a facade—a Norma Desmond-like caricature who had lost touch with herself and was drowning in a sea of celluloid and movie magazines.

Jackie was the complete opposite of "Miss D." Curtis was an acid-tongued cookie who came from the pit hole of hell on the Lower East Side. She was born John Holden and was raised by a grandma named Slugger Ann.

Curtis was pushy, had the personality of a bulldozer, and wouldn't let anyone or anything stand in her way. She also felt that her real-life gender was a deterrent in her quest for superstardom. She never wanted to be a woman, but there was no way she could achieve the same amount of attention as a man. Curtis knew that Andy was fascinated by transvestites, and this was a way to get discovered.

Jackie was a slob, often spraying herself with Glade air freshener to hide her manly body odor, while Candy reeked of Chanel. Candy was so convincing she even carried tampons in her purse, playing the part of a vulnerable lady to a "T."

Anyway, there Miss Darling sat in all her glamourous vulnerability, glowing in full regalia. I was taken aback by her aura, and after the show she came to my dressing room and greeted me warmly.

"Oh, Holly, you were so wonderful," she said in that voice borrowed from Kim Novak. "I had such a good time."

Yeah, right. What was she trying to pull, I thought. Candy was always catty and aloof, so I was a bit leery as to what brought on this sudden surge of charm and graciousness, since she and Miss Curtis were always on the defensive. Those two were armed with wicked tongues that could rip a person to shreds.

In our early years, whenever we were in social situations together, I was usually bombed out of my mind and screaming "Free pussy!" to anyone who'd listen. Candy was always proper and couldn't deal with my blatant, carefree, I-don't-give-a-shit attitude.

"Holly, I can't believe you're behaving like this," she'd scold. "You know, you really should control yourself. You're in the public's eye now and you have a responsibility to uphold your image. Remember ... keep your stomach in, your shoulders back, and your head held high. You're not just a star—you're a Superstar."

I wanted to puke. Who was she to quote me some half-baked lines she stole from a Lana Turner movie?

"What's the matter with ya, huh?" I'd snap back. "Can't a girl have a good time?"

It's no wonder that Jackie and Candy ran the other way when they saw me coming. I knew they were ashamed, and I always felt that I needed their forgiveness for being such a rowdy, loud drunk, not to mention the fact that I was screwing everything I got my paws on. So when Candy expressed this warmth toward me, I was shocked, but when I realized that she was being genuine, I was touched. Perhaps we could be friends again.

The next afternoon the phone rang and it was Corely.

"Holly," he said. "I have something to tell you."

I didn't like the tone in his voice. He sounded much too serious and I sensed that something was wrong.

"Oh, what is it?"

"Candy's dying."

I felt my head go numb with shock and tried to continue listening as my mouth dropped open. And then came tears.

"She's got cancer," Corely continued. "She's got six months to live." He told me she was hospitalized at Mother Cabrini and that she had gone against her doctor's orders to come and see my show. I broke down into sobs. I felt so bad for her. Even if she was bleached-out, snot-nosed, and self-centered, she was still my sister. We were always there for each other . . . particularly when she needed something, the bitch. All right, so I hated her guts. I was still concerned, however, and once I got off the phone with Corely, I called Curtis immediately with the tragic news.

Candy was released from the hospital a short time later, and it looked like she was getting better because she was back to her old haughty self. Occasionally, I'd run into her at a party while she sat in a corner being fawned over by her fans. I always greeted her cheerfully, but she always gave me this condescending attitude as if to say, "How did you get invited?" Miss Darling was still used to my wallowing in a trough of booze, and couldn't quite grasp the fact that I was out of the gutter and on an upswing with my career.

It was Curtis who was on the downswing. She was strung out on speed and back in the welfare trenches, desperate to make a comeback.

I, on the other hand, felt just like Cinderella, especially after all of my creative friends pitched in to resurrect the former broken goddess who was now aspiring to become a chantootsie!

"You just can't go up onstage barefoot," Bill Corely instructed one day in an attempt to revamp my style.

"Why not? The pagans did."

"The pagans were thrown to the lions!"

"These people come to see me perform. They don't care if I wear shoes or not," I reasoned.

"If you're wearing a three-thousand-dollar gown and a million-dollar face, you've got to have shoes to match!"

And that was that.

It was like Old Hollywood all over again. I was a starlet being seasoned for stardom. Although my act was funny, Corely pointed out that it lacked focus. I always drank heavily before a performance because I thought it was fabulous to get up onstage drunk, pull out junk from my shopping bag, and ramble on. But as I got more bookings, I had to become more professional, more serious. I was a diamond in the rough, but if I was ever to shine as a true cabaret artist, it would take a serious commitment and hard work to polish that rock.

Corely stepped in and polished away. His idea was that I should be flawless, like a mannequin in a Bendel's window. The mannequins at Bendel's were so perfect, so poised, with an air of hauteur, they inspired Corely to write the song "I Want to Be Airbrushed."

In my new act, I opened the show posed like a mannequin as I rotated on a tiny turntable no bigger than a record, with a bubble machine behind me. The bubbles were bubbling as I rotated, frozen in a pose right out of a Bendel's window while looking in a hand mirror and singing "I Want to Be Airbrushed." There was no way I could throw back a cocktail and do that! I was on my way to becoming a seasoned professional, darling. Not a soused one!

And as Robert Palmer of *The New York Times* confirmed: "Holly Woodlawn, who is in the second week of a three-week engagement at Reno Sweeney, brings a new dimension to the conundrum of putative sexual indentity. But Miss Woodlawn . . . is not just another ambitious ambiguity; she is talented."

Womens Wear Daily noted: "Holly Woodlawn is a genius talent . . . [she] unveiled a totally new act this month at Reno Sweeney and it is a stunner. Holly sings with faultless timing and verve, a surprising and satisfying range of material. In between the songs, Holly delivers some beautifully written [by Lenny Dean] material which is the hippest of the hip and killingly funny."

Word spread that I was gettin' pretty good, and soon I was getting booked in Philadelphia, Chicago, and Boston. But I must admit, out of all the clubs I have performed in, none of them compared to Reno's. It was magic.

People from all walks of life came to Reno's. It had a highfalutin attitude and a dress code was strictly enforced. It didn't matter who a person was; if he or she wasn't dressed to the nines, they weren't getting in. Also, paparazzi weren't allowed, so celebrities could come in and enjoy themselves without the bother of the press hounds. It was a very appreciated luxury, and Reno's was always abuzz with personalities. Lou Reed used to come to my early shows when I closed my act with his song "Perfect Day." Andy used to come with Candy and Bob Colacello. Jackie used to come with Rita Redd. Barry Manilow came with Bette Midler. David Bowie showed up with Mick Jagger. Other celebs included Jackie Onassis, Roberta Flack, Faye Dunaway, Lauren Bacall, Ethel Merman, Rock Hudson—honey, with names like these in the audience, I *had* to be good.

There was always something exciting going on at Reno's. I'll never forget the night when the place was robbed. It was after the late show and Bill Corely, Robert Richards (the sensational fashion illustrator), Baby Jane Dexter (a divine singer), Judith Cohen (a fabulous entertainer), Peter Allen (the brilliant performer), and I (all of the above) had just finished our cocktails, and as we opened the door to leave, we were pushed back inside at gunpoint by a pack of ruthless robbers.

There were three of them all together; a man, a moll, and a lesbian midget named Stubby.

"All right, in the kitchen with yahs all. In the kitchen, see," demanded Stubby, poking us with the back of her .45 while chewing on the nub of her cigar. She was obviously the head hoodlum, ordering her sidekicks to tie us up.

"Don't shoot! Don't shoot!" cried out Judith as she chivalrously announced, "If you have to kill anybody, kill me because these people are artists."

"Judith, shut the fuck up," snapped Robert Richards under his breath. "They probably haven't even thought of killing us. They're probably too stupid."

And stupid they were, since the money had been safely carted away in an armored truck just hours before they had arrived. We tried to tell them, but Stubby wouldn't listen and persisted in her quest, searching high and low for nearly an hour trying to snoop out some hidden cash.

Luckily, Eliot Hubbard, the club's publicity agent, heard what was going on from the back room and managed to escape. It wasn't long after the crooks' departure when he arrived with the police.

Usually during these late-night get-togethers, the waiters would spill all the dirt on who was in the audience, what they were like, who they were with, and what they were doing. One night Mick Jagger and David Bowie came in and sat at the round table all the way in the back. They were so cute together. They were very polite and courteous, and ordered two bottles of Dom Perignon—which, incidentally, cost a hundred and ten bucks a bottle—and sent one to the waiter's station! They were adorable.

Every now and then, Liza Minelli would pop in with Ben Vereen. Once Liza, who was starring in *The Act* on Broadway at the time, stopped in to see the late show. After the show, all the paying customers left and all of us who busted our asses would hang out, have a cocktail, and wind down. Miss Liza was very gracious, and when Lewis invited her to get up onstage to sing a few, she got under that spotlight and belted out an entire show! She sang one song after another, and it was beyond fabulous, sitting with intimate friends and having Liza Minelli carrying on with us just like an old friend.

Then there was "The Merm." Ethel Merman arrived for the late show one night with two young white-tuxedoed men in tow, and as she paraded her can over to her table, her chauffeur approached my friend Philip, who had left Max's to work as the maitre d' at Reno's.

"Miss Merman's wine is in the trunk of the limousine," said the chauffeur. "May I bring it in?"

Whoever heard of anyone bringing his own wine to a bar? Philip assumed that the wine she had brought was rare and very expensive, so he took the question to Lewis Friedman. Lewis figured that since the place was named after her role in *Anything Goes*, she could do whatever she wanted, so the chauffeur was given the okay to lug up the bottles.

There sat Ethel at a table in front of the stage, slurping her gaspacho soup and gabbing away, when her driver comes in with a cheap jug of Almaden that sold for five bucks a half-gallon down at Cousin Charlie's Bargain Barn in Soho! Ethel got tanked on the wine, and in the middle of her conversation she raised her spoon, shook it in the direction of one of her white-tuxedoed studs, and splattered his suit with gaspacho! See what cheap booze does to a person?

During performances, there could be no noise. If there was a noisy table, Philip would stop the show! Which reminds me of the time Eartha Kitt almost got thrown out of the joint. I'm not sure, but I think she had gotten into the rest of that jug Ethel had left behind, because she was carrying on so loud that Lewis Friedman got on the loudspeaker and announced, "Ladies and gentlemen, we're just going to hold it up here for a moment because Eartha Kitt's table manners are so intolerable that we can't go on with the show!"

Eartha and Ethel weren't the only ones to cause a scene. Richard Chamberlain came in once and became disgruntled because he had to wait at the bar to be seated. When he finally grew impatient and demanded to know when his table was going to be ready, Philip cooly replied, "It'll be ready when it's ready."

"Hey, do you know who I am?" snapped Chamberlain.

"I know who you used to be," replied Philip.

In later years after Jim Maxey had bought Reno's from Lewis Friedman, Rock Hudson would stop in on Saturday nights with his young male friends, and they always wound up in a fight. Rock always brought in these boys and they would sit ringside after having indulged in cocaine upstairs. Something terrible would always happen to upset their evening, and they'd wind up causing a ruckus.

It didn't matter who a person was or how much money he or she had, it all boiled down to class. Some have it, some don't. It can't be bought, borrowed, or stolen. There was one incident when a man and his date tried to get into a show that had been overbooked. Philip politely declined to seat the couple, explaining that there were no tables available. The man, thinking he could toss his monetary weight around, pulled out a twenty-dollar bill, waved it under Philip's nose, and asked, "What'll this get me?" Philip quickly snatched the bill from his fingers, pocketed it, and replied, "Attitude."

CHAPTER

17

Candy Darling's
Last Bow

*I*f it is true that Andy had set out to recreate and magnify the grandeur of Hollywood's past, he was also plagued by the undesirable burden of having mirrored Tinseltown's legendary tragedies. Fallen stars, wayward starlets, lost souls desperate to find acceptance—perhaps even themselves—all flocked to the Factory in the quest for Superstardom. Edie Sedgewick was one of Andy's first casualties. Although she was one of Andy's most celebrated Superstars and became the toast of Manhattan at the age of twenty-two, Edie's tits got caught in a pill-popping, speed-shooting twirl. Like Judy Garland, who blamed the studios for her drug addiction, Edie blamed Andy. She died tragically of an overdose in 1971.

Andrea Whips Feldman's hair-raising suicide in 1972 was another faint echo from the sordid side of Hollywood. In the 1930s, a blond starlet by the name of Peg Entwistle, who had been ridden by high hopes and shattered dreams, climbed to the top of the Hollywood sign and dove to her death. Andrea, who had recently starred in the film *Heat* with Sylvia Miles, leapt out of the fourteenth-floor window of her Fifth Avenue apartment, clutching a Coca-Cola in one hand and a rosary in the other.

Rumor had it that Andrea left behind a malicious suicide letter condemning Andy and the Factory, blaming them for her despair. Others have said that the only note left behind was a scrawled message which read, "I'm going for the bigtime, I hit the jackpot!"

After all she did to maintain her Superstar status, all the times she screeched out, "It's showtime," all the disasters when she was dragged bodily out of Max's, kicking and screaming that she was Mrs. Andy Warhol, Andrea Whips Feldman had finally whipped up a topper to end all show-stoppers. And like any truly distraught woman who wants to make the world pay for her woes, she called all of her former boyfriends on the telephone and arranged for them to meet her outside of her apartment on the afternoon of her so-called "arrival." Little did the boys know that they were going to meet with a splat.

Poor Andrea. She had reached the pinnacle of her Superstardom, realized the nothingness it embodied, and simply fell over the edge. The curtain had fallen and the show was over.

Andy wasn't the only one out to emulate old Hollywood. When *Scarecrow in a Garden of Cucumbers* opened at the Waverly Theater in March 1972, everyone tried to outdo one another to see who could be more fabulous. It was a small but festive gathering, and I arrived, Tally Brown at my side, in a white Rolls Royce, my body draped in a black crepe gown created for me by Getty Miller, one of New York's top designers, with two trained doves perched on each wrist. Frank Kolleogy had given me the doves as a good-luck token for the premiere, and I named them Frankie Poo Poo and Holly Poo Poo. It was such an extravagance, wearing trained doves on my wrists, but to us it was flamboyant glamour that hadn't been seen since the days of silent film, when Clara Bow tooled up and down Sunset Boulevard in her red Kissel convertible, her chow dogs dyed red to match.

All the girls saved their welfare checks for weeks just waiting for a gala like this, so we could get all decked out and arrive in style. Naturally, I couldn't let anyone down by making a normal entrance. I had to be flamboyant, eye-catching, and worth reading about in the next day's paper. I was going to milk this for all the glitz it was worth!

Little did I know, however, that those little symbols of peace, love and, tranquility riding on my wrists had caca-boomed right on my lap moments before my arrival. They might have been trained to look pretty, but they weren't trained to go potty! And if that wasn't humiliating enough, the lovely and unforgiveable Candy Darling arrived with a bag of tomatoes.

"Just in case I need them," she quipped behind her dark sunglasses, clutching the brown sack against her tightly drawn trench coat with the sneaky turned-up collar.

The nerve!

Sylvia Miles, who arrived head to toe in furs and jewels and looking more like Gloria Swanson at the premiere for *Zaza*, schmoozed for the paparazzi in the lobby while Jackie Curtis ran amok, whispering, "Pay no attention to that woman in the corner in the dark glasses." Miss Curtis was forever trying to rival Miss Darling and showed up with bananas! Well, at least she ate them.

Estelle arrived dressed up in his black thigh boots, white pants, and a white shirt with a dark blazer. Andy was there making chitchat with Mario Rivoli. Silva Thin had sauntered in looking like Marlene Dietrich in *Morocco*, and Taylor Mead fluttered among them all like a little amphetamined fairy, playfully prancing from one figure to the next, sprinkling them with his whimsical charm.

I sat in the back row of the theater with Tally at my side, nervous as hell. Not only was I concerned about how the audience would react, but I was a little worried that those little dumplings who were still perched on my wrists would get the runs!

The film ran in New York, Los Angeles, and at various art houses in between, but it didn't receive the same hoopla as *Trash* or *Women in Revolt.* My career in film seemed to be stagnating, and I wasn't getting anywhere. I wanted to work badly, but producers and directors just didn't know what to do with me. I was branded a drag queen (a stigma which has haunted me throughout my life) and America wasn't ready for that. So I figured, to hell with the cinema, darling. At least for the moment. Why should I knock myself up against a brick wall and have all this rejection bullshit dumped in my lap, when I could work in cabaret and get great reviews?

So I took my act all over Manhattan and had gained a following. I was feted in Liz Smith's column, and once again I felt like the toast of New York. Holly Woodlawn was back on the rise, and that fall, for my twenty-sixth birthday, Mario Rivoli threw an uproarious party. He, Dallas, Estelle, and I, along with a few festive friends, gathered in his apartment for wine and revelry. I had always been fascinated with smoke bombs, ever since I saw Liz Taylor's entrance into Rome in *Cleopatra*, and Mario, aware of my fascination, bought two for the occasion. I was thrilled, and immediately we lit one up, imagining a little poof of gold smoke to titillate our fancies. Well, we lit that little bomb and smoke started to spew out all over the place! Within a moment, the apartment was so clouded, we couldn't see, and we all ran to every available window and threw open the sash, coughing our heads off as the smoke rolled out into the street.

A neighbor across the way saw us hanging over the sills and panicked. Suddenly, sirens were blaring, red lights were flashing, and three fire trucks pulled up below us. We all began screaming to the firemen that it was a false alarm, that it was only a smoke bomb, but they couldn't understand a word we were saying and came rushing upstairs with their axes in hand to save us. We were all so embarrassed, but the clincher of this fiasco was that one of the firemen, a tall, strapping blond who clutched me into his arms to save me from doom, looked into my eyes and said, "Hey, aren't you Holly Woodlawn?"

"Well, as a matter of fact I am. Now kiss me, you fool, before the smoke clears."

I winked. He laughed and then he asked, "Can I have your autograph?"

"After you put out the fire. Now, where's the hose?"

I winked again and he laughed again. This relationship was getting on my nerves. The fool obviously thought I was kidding, but I was ready for marriage. Much to my surprise, he never popped the question, so I never popped my cork, and instead I scrawled a thank-you note on a piece of paper and with that he was off, out of my life forever, leaving me in the smoke with a broken heart, an inflamed libido, and the thrill of knowing that even in the most chaotic situations, my fame prevailed!

By the summer of 1973, my career was well-grounded in cabaret, and I was spending most of my weekends with Corely, who had rented a house on Fire Island. Halston had a house there as well, and we became good chums. Corely was always looking for ways to boost my image and one day he said to me, "Holly, you gotta call up Halston and get yourself a gown."

"Oh, I couldn't. What would I even say?"

"Just tell him you're doing a new show and ask him if he has anything you can wear."

Well, I just didn't have it in me at the time to be so brazen. Funny how I could get up enough gall to impersonate a French diplomat's wife, but couldn't seem to muster enough courage to ask for a dress. But I couldn't. Unless, of course, I could be clever about it. And then I began to wonder how someone clever would approach such a situation. Like Dorothy Parker, for instance. How would dear Dot snag such a treasure from such a high and mighty artisan as the great Halston? I wondered.

And then I wondered some more. I was stumped for about a week or so, with Corely constantly pestering, "Did you call him? Did you call him?" And whenever I said I didn't, his spirit seemed to sink and he'd shrivel up. And then finally one afternoon, I picked up the receiver of my gold-glittered French Provincial phone, tacky thing that it was, and proceeded to dial the great emperor of fashion.

Pat Ast, who was working as his assistant, answered the phone and

I told her I needed Halston immediately. If I didn't speak soon, I might lose the little dabble of spunk that had come over me. I held the line for what seemed like an eternity when suddenly the deep, elegant voice came on the phone.

"Hello, Holly."

"Halston, darling, I really hate to trouble you like this, but I'm putting together a new show at Reno's and there's something that's been befuddling me for the longest time and, well, you're the only person I could turn to for the truth."

His voice seemed concerned.

"Oh?"

"How do you spell sequin?"

The darling man broke up into laughter.

"Sequin?" he asked. "S-E-Q-U-I-N."

"Do you think I could borrow a few?"

Halston was a doll; so elegant, so tailored, and very stylish, just like Fred Hughes from the Factory. I loved being around Halston. He was spellbinding, literally. The way he moved was very graceful, much like the way a long black cat slinks along the ledge of a roof. Very careful, very surefooted, but sophisticated and elegant. He was wonderful.

And generous, too!

When I arrived at his studio, he invited me in and treated me to two holographic sequin gowns, one silver and one gold. He also tossed in a pair of Liza Minelli's black spandex gloves, adding, "Oh, Liza left these here last week. Go on, you take 'em. She'll never miss them."

And take them I did, thinking that just maybe they'd bring me luck on my opening night. But perhaps I should've lent them to Candy Darling, who was opening her own nightclub act that same summer at the club Le Jardin. And to think she had the nerve to bring a bag of tomatoes to the screening of *Scarecrow*. I should've brought a bazooka!

Candy had a lot going for her: She was beautiful, she was blond, she had wit and nerve. And boy, did she ever need a lot of nerve to get away with this. She couldn't sing to save her life. And when she tried, her voice was still a soft whisper. Now, how many songs can a person tolerate in that style? The only redeeming quality that night was that she looked stunning, all decked out in white, with her platinum-blond hair and white gown, sitting at a white baby-grand piano.

Lainie Kazan, Lenny Dean, Estelle, and I greeted Miss Darling in her private cabana after the show and we were kind. Of course we told her the show was magnificent, but the truth eventually hit home when she was fired a few days later.

When *Broken Goddess* was finally completed, it was screened on my twenty-seventh birthday in 1973 with the 1929 silent classic *Salome*, which starred silent-screen siren Nazimova and was followed by a private bash at Reno's. It was the silent era of films all over again as I arrived with Corely and Dallas in a 1928 Rolls Royce wearing a black gown, sparkling rhinestones, and a mess of feathers in another Getty Miller original.

The film was a hit among the critics. "*Broken Goddess* has triumphantly broken new ground by breaking old ground and . . . conveys a haunting sense of style," wrote Norma McLain Stoop of *After Dark* magazine.

"*Broken Goddess* is a rare and remarkable film," wrote Freeman Gunter for *Michael's Thing* magazine. "Holly Woodlawn's enormous and spontaneous talent is given free reign. This actor, who uses a timeless female image as his instrument for communication, achieves a pathos which approaches genuine tragedy. It is astonishing that silent-film acting could communicate so profoundly in 1973."

"Holly moves with the grace of Nazimova," wrote *Women's Wear Daily*. "[The film] is suffused with a certain grandeur that is hard to come by these days."

Even Rona Barrett threw in her two cents. "Holly Woodlawn, one of Andy Warhol's former Superstars, who was the sensation of his film *Trash*, has just completed her solo starring role in the new silent film, *Broken Goddess*. Holly has been telling friends, 'It's my best dramatic role as an actress.' There must be something to it. Rumor has it that the film goes to next year's Cannes Film Festival . . ."

And a rumor it was. I was dying to go to Cannes like a real star, but it never happened. Even when *Trash* went to Cannes, Paul and Andy took Joe Dallesandro and Jane Forth but left me behind. They thought I would embarrass them.

A few months after *Broken Goddess* had premiered, the phone rang. It was Curtis.

"Miss D's back in the hospital again, and she's only got two minutes so you better hurry."

Nobody had a bigger heart than Curtis. And nobody had bigger sabers! I, being the uncontrollable, emotional one, broke down in blubbering fit of sobs.

"Shut up, Holly!" Curtis snapped. "We gotta go visit her. Photographers and the press are gonna be there."

"Jackie, how can you think of the press at a time like this?"

"Shut up, Holly. You know Candy, she don't miss a thing. She's dying this time. She'll milk it for all it's worth. There'll be lots of press, I just know it."

I met Curtis and Rita Redd in the Village, and on our way to the hospital, we passed a flower market. Curtis, chomping on a cigarette, uttered, "Hey, Rita, shove one of them roses in your bag. We gotta bring her something." Rita nodded and snagged a rose when no one was looking while Jackie rambled on. "Nobody's visiting her, Holly. It's sad. She's our sister, we gotta go see her."

Curtis said nobody, but what she meant was Andy. I don't think he could deal with death, having been so close to it himself after the Valerie Solanis shooting.

So off we marched to Mother Cabrini's, Jackie leading the way with Rita in tow carrying her shopping bags full of clippings, magazines, and a single red rose.

Candy was lying in bed all coiffed, painted, and posed, looking as if she'd just arrived from Liz Arden. She gazed through her sleepy eyes and whispered to me, "Hi, Holly. How are you doing? I'm so glad you came."

Jackie sauntered up to the bed, plopped down on the side with her elbows on her knees, and shouted, "Hey, girl, how ya feeling? Ya don't look too good. I'd give ya three months!" That was Curtis's style—loud, bawdy, and uncouth. Then she reached into one of the bags Rita had carried, pulled out a magazine, shoved it under Candy's nose, and said, "Here, I brought this." Then she flipped through the magazine until she came to the marked page and then she shoved it back into Candy's face.

"That's me in *Photoplay*. Hey, Rita, give me back that bag." And Curtis rummaged some more and pulled out another hidden treasure. "This is me in *Vogue*. Oh, you're both in there, too. Somewhere."

Curtis dug further into the bag.

"Oh, here's a rose we got for ya, and hey, here's some chocolates. You like chocolates?"

"Well, thank you, but I really shouldn't—" began Candy.

"Fine, I'll eat 'em. Rita, put these away."

"Jackie, the doctor said I should only have juices today."

"Juices?" Jackie snarled. "Oh, okay. Rita, where's the vodka?"

Jackie, Rita, and I would get so bombed while visiting Candy that I'm surprised we weren't hauled out of there on a gurney. But we always made it out on our own, staggering down the block with Curtis leaning into my face with a raised finger, ranting and raving, "Do you believe her? I don't. Not for one second. Honey, she's pulling one over. This is a stunt! She wants something out of Andy. Do you believe her, Rita?"

As usual, before Rita had a chance to answer, Curtis had already decided Rita's response. "No, I don't either. Look at her up there, acting like she's dying. Does she look like she's dying, Rita? No, I didn't think so either."

Jackie knew Candy was dying, but she didn't want to believe it. None of us did. Candy was too fabulous. She couldn't get sick and die. She was a star. She had so much ahead of her. We all did. It was different when Andrea died because she killed herself. It was her choice. But Candy didn't have that prerogative. Finally, we all began to realize just how mortal we were, how fragile our lives were, and how we took it for granted.

Jackie, Rita, and I were visiting Candy on a regular basis and always arrived half-crocked, causing quite a commotion with our afternoon cocktail soirees. After a while, the entire ward got to know us, as we were stopping by every day, usually around lunchtime. These daily luncheons rekindled the warmth in our friendship. I looked forward to the rowdy escapades that took Candy's mind off her illness, although most of the time she was far too concerned with trying to keep Jackie and me in line. Finally, I felt that Candy had accepted me for who I was and that we were friends again.

Jackie was a big con artist who was forever swindling whatever she could out of the nurses, whether it be drugs, cheap conversation, or a free lunch. She was a smooth operator, always appearing concerned about Candy when what she really had on her mind was a freebie. Often she'd snag one of the nurses from the floor and approach them with that cheap used-car salesman demeanor she had so perfected.

"Hey, you—come here," she'd utter from the side of her mouth as she reeled in the unsuspecting prey. "What's your name? Ellen? Listen, Ellen, Candy won't tell you, but, uh, she can't sleep that well. She's really having a hard time and you know how she hates to complain. Why don't you bring her some Demerol. Matter of fact, she'd like some now. You got any on ya?"

Naturally, the nurse would comply and Miss Curtis would take the pills herself! Meanwhile, I was on the other side of the room, rooting through the small bedside refrigerator, trying to scrounge up some eats.

"What time's dinner?" I'd bellow, popping my head up for air.

Then Jackie would poke her head out into the hall and holler, "Could I have a menu?" Miss Curtis didn't quite get it through her head that this was a hospital and not a supper club. We were both hungry regardless, and since Candy was on a liquid diet, it was a shame not to take advantage of the grub she wasn't allowed to eat. So we told the nurse to bring it in anyway.

"Listen—" Curtis would begin after having lured another unsuspecting nurse into her clutches. "Ya got anything left over from lunch? You do! Bring it over, we're starved!"

We ate like pigs; gibbling, gobbling, stuffing, and gorging, only to pause for a quick swig of vodka from a shopping bag. We laughed and carried on like true medieval peasants, and although the nurses knew exactly what we were up to, they looked on our antics with a sense of humor.

Every now and then, we'd splurge and bring Candy a box of chocolates which we knew she wouldn't eat, but it was a thoughtful gesture, and we were the ones who eventually invaded the box. Curtis reasoned that candy was a far better gift than flowers.

"If we bring flowers, we gotta leave 'em," Curtis said. Curtis was right, so we only brought Candy a flower every now and then. We gave them to her one at a time since it was much easier to steal one flower than it was to steal a bunch. Beside, eventually there would be enough to make a bouquet.

"That bitch," Curtis once said in jest as we walked to the hospital. "She's got these people waiting on her hand and foot. She's got something up her sleeve, I just know it!"

And when Candy went into remission and was being released from Mother Cabrini, Curtis ranted and raved all the way home. "I told you! I told you, Rita! Didn't I tell you? See, I knew Miss D. was pulling a number."

Miss D. went home to her mother's on Long Island to recuperate, I went back to Reno's to a packed house, and Jackie started writing a play. Everything was fine and everyone was happy again.

And then the phone rang.

It was Dallas. The curtain was finally coming down and Candy was taking a final bow in New York's Columbus Hospital. I didn't want to see Candy because I was frightened. I knew this was it. "You call her," I told Dallas. "And ask her if it's okay if I stop by."

The day was overcast and gray. We had bought her a big bouquet of spider mums and one red rose at a Korean fruit stand right outside the hospital.

When we walked toward her room, I was overcome with nerves. It was very somber, hardly like the days when Curtis and I would come charging in with Rita Redd. Famous people were trailing in and out of her room. We stood there and watched for a moment and then I took a deep breath. I had never seen a person on the brink of death before, and I was expecting the worst: an emaciated face with sunken eyes and a wheezing chest struggling for breath.

Well, I should have known better! As always, Candy was coiffed, painted, plucked, and looking as if she had stepped out of a Bergdorf Goodman window!

"Oh, hello, Holly. Hello, Dallas." She spoke in a weakened tongue. "It's so nice to see both of you."

"Here, hon," I said, handing her the rose. Dallas placed the spider mums near the window and sat down before her, placing his hand on top of hers.

"You look great," I said uncomfortably.

"Oh, thank you. A photographer is coming to do a portrait. A girl's gotta look her best for the camera."

The photographer was Peter Hujar, and the portrait was Candy's last. She called it "a farewell to my fans," and it was shot the day before she underwent exploratory cancer surgery.

Two weeks later I came back to the hospital with my friend Mitchell St. John, and as we walked down the long corridor to Candy's room, we ran into one of her young doctors in the hallway. I asked how she was doing and his eyes welled with tears. He said it was a matter of days. I wiped the tear from my own eye and then turned to Mitchell, commenting on how nice it was of Andy to have taken care of Candy's hospital bills. Mitchel shot me a look and said, "Andy who?" That's when I learned that Fred Martini, a wealthy entrepreneur and fan of Candy's had picked up the tab. I was stunned that Andy hadn't been more generous to the one Superstar who seemed to idolize him the most.

Mitchell and I entered the darkened room and saw the still figure lying in the bed. I crept over to her side and gazed into those piercing dark eyes, which were now clouded with morphine. Her once-painted, picture-perfect face had now faded to a dull, lifeless gray with the exception of her lips, which were painted a bright crimson red.

"Holly," she managed to say, enfeebled by the cancer and horribly thin, weighing only eighty pounds. She could barely muster the strength to speak.

"It's okay, hon," I reassured her. "You don't have to talk. I know you're tired."

"Yeah. Putting on lipstick . . . it really takes it out of me."

"What you need is some blush," I said, reaching into my purse and pulling out a compact. I swept her cheeks with color and the left side of her face smiled. The right side had been paralyzed from Bell's palsy.

"There, that's better." I smiled back and then pulled out my mascara. "Of course, a face isn't a face without fabulous eyes. Take it from one who knows."

The following afternoon I arrived at Reno's to rehearse with Lewis. Lenny Dean, my writer/director, was there trying to pick up the bartender when I sailed over to fix a bourbon and Coke, my favorite new drink since Estelle told me it was the last thing Tallulah Bankhead bellowed for on her death bed. Then Lewis approached. "Holly, I have to talk to you," he said seriously.

"This is the first drink I've had all week, I promise!"

He looked at me with concern and then put his hand on my shoulder.

"Candy's dead."

I held the bottle of bourbon in my hand and set it down softly. "Is there anything I can help you with?" he asked.

"No."

I stood motionless. I didn't cry. I didn't walk out. I didn't have any reaction whatsoever. I didn't want to hear it and I let it fly right over my head.

"Show's gotta go on, right?" I said to myself, opening the bottle and pouring a shot. To hell with the Coke, I thought, and tossed it back with the rest of my sorrows.

That night Curtis called me on the phone.

"Well, goddamnit, it took her long enough! Shit, I've been waiting all year," she snapped. And then we sat on the phone and bawled.

When we hung up, I was bombarded by a barrage of calls from all the phonies, all of them wanting to know who was taking me to the funeral.

Candy was laid out at Campbell's funeral parlor in the same room Judy Garland had occupied a few years earlier. It was a circus, the to-do of to-dos for that month. Everyone was there. The Superstars, the socialites, the relatives, and the press were all packed together. It was just like a premiere, and the guest list included the likes of Taylor Mead, Julie Newmar, Pat Ast, Paul Ambrose, Maxine de la Falaise, Kenneth Jay Lane, Victor Hugo, Baby Jane Holzer, Paul Morrissey, Peter Allen, John Phillips, Genevieve Waite, Jackie Curtis, Tally Brown, Eric Emerson, and Sylvia Miles. The only friend who didn't show was Andy.

I went with Dallas and wore a tasteful blue suit with no makeup. I felt so out of line going to a funeral in full paint and a gown, although Miss Darling had no qualms. She was decked out in a white chiffon beaded gown with a humongous topaz slung around her neck. That rock was so big, I'm surprised people didn't bring in their loupe to have a closer look at it.

Her hair was platinum and her skin was milk, so clear and white that she looked as if she'd been carved out of alabaster. Her hands were folded with a single red rose nestled in her breast.

The casket was white and gold and surrounded with flowers. A large portrait of Candy with blond hair in a madcap swirl had been placed near the casket. Her father and mother and the rest of the family were on one side, and all the lunatics from her past haunts were on the other. Julie Newmar stood up and delivered a eulogy, as did Eugene of Cinandre and R. Couri Hay. We all knelt and said prayers, and not once did the minister mention Candy's real gender or refer to her by her real name, James.

When it was all over, I stepped to the side of the casket and gave her one last look. She looked so peaceful, so content. I just assumed she was up at the Pearly Gates trying to get past St. Peter with a sack of tomatoes, "Just in case I need 'em."

I leaned over, kissed her forehead gently, and whispered, "You're free now, honey. Happy trails to ya." She had suffered so much pain, but she never let anyone see it. She was such a strong little wren. Now she was free and I was happy.

After the service, everyone gathered outside on the walk to pose for the paparazzi, but I said to Dallas, "Please, let's just get out of here." We fled the scene and wound up walking home through the park, reminiscing about Candy and the hopes Dallas had had for starring her in his film *Blonde Passion*, which was never made. We walked by the Metropolitan Museum with its great Grecian columns and massive concrete steps, a location Dallas had planned to use for the film, and we imagined Candy slowly descending these steps draped in white chiffon in all her blond glory.

The day after Candy's burial, Peter Hujar's photograph ran in the *New York Post* with the headline "Candy's Farewell." She was lying on her side in her hospital bed with her left arm resting against the side of her head and her right arm extended beneath the pillow on which her head rested. At her side was the long-stemmed rose I had given her hours before, her body halfway covered by the rumpled sheets. Her blond tresses were tousled and coiffed. Her luminous eyes were big and sultry, topped by her perfectly arched pencil-lined brows. Her full sensuous mouth was painted a deep crimson. And the bones. Those beautifully sculptured bones and the shadows that gracefully swept across them, outlining her jaw, highlighting her cheeks and closing in on that haunting gaze staring desperately into the camera's eye, the eye that reaffirmed everything James believed about himself, and captured the illusion of a glamourous blond movie queen who in reality was just a dying young man lost in a world of celluloid dreams and Hollywood glamour.

My stare burned into the page and as she stared back, I recalled that soft voice echoing from our earlier years in the Village, surfacing from my sea of thoughts like driftwood from a sunken ship. And I listened.

"Remember, keep your stomach in, your shoulders back, and your head high. You're not just a star—you're a Superstar."

CHAPTER

18

Bombs Away

*D*uring the summer of 1974, I performed at a benefit for the Pines on Fire Island, organized by Laura Eastman, niece of President Franklin D. Roosevelt. It was a gay affair! I wore a cream-colored, silk crepe strapless gown designed by Edith Head for Lana Turner in *The Prodigal*. Lana portrayed the high priestess of Asarte who, just before she was tossed into flames, proclaimed, "When my people see me, they'll stop this madness!" I saw the film when I was ten and it changed my life. I just knew that I, too, would one day put on a dress and belt out the same. Little did I know that it was my people who encouraged the madness!

The dress was fabulous, with a jeweled girdle, belted waist and an over-the-shoulder train of chiffon that trailed past a very shapely caboose with pads in the hips and a built-in girdle that I shimmied, pushed, squeezed and struggled to get in. My stomach was in, my ass was out, my shoulders were back, and my head was held high. I felt just like a Ziegfeld girl!

During that sweltering summer, Corely rented a two-story house on Fire Island. The boardwalk was continuously crawling with fashion photographers, art directors, makeup artists, and models, not to mention a handful of stars sprinkled here and there like shimmering sequins sporadically placed across a sheer fabric. Two such colorful personalities were Liza Minnelli and Pat Ast, who both were hanging out at Halston's.

Pat Ast was always offering free entertainment on the beach. There she was, her stout legs planted firmly in the sand, her face painted brighter than the neon in Times Square, her dazzling eyes big and alive as she sang arias to the two muscle boys flanking her sides. She swayed back and forth, her fabulous Halston chiffon muu-muu rippling in the brisk sea wind, belting out operas to anyone who'd listen.

Pat was—and still is—a beautiful singer, and I was always joining her on the beach for vocal lessons. She could belt out notes so powerful, you could actually feel her voice vibrate.

I would generally spend my weekdays in Manhattan and the weekends on Fire Island with Corely. I was living near Sutton Place in a swank little neighborhood near the Fifty-ninth Street Bridge. Greta Garbo lived just down the block, and around the corner was a Rolls-Royce showroom and a taco stand! Movie stars, opulence, and refried beans—what more could a girl want?

Down the block and around another corner was a little gin joint called Gypsy's, which is where I used to hang out on my nights off. It was a nice, intimate nightclub that attracted a lot of Hollywood and Broadway impressarios. Gypsy was a mad queen who would get up in a tuxedo and high heels and rattle off these dishy, witty lines and have the house in stitches. He was brilliant. Eventually Gypsy and I were introduced by Craig Russell, the famous female impersonator.

While I was yucking it up at Gypsy's and cocktailing on the Island, Miss Curtis had finally come to her senses and gone back to being a man. We saw each other infrequently after Candy's death because it seemed we had nothing more in common, although we did get together for one last stint at the Cultural Center (the former Huntington Hartford Museum) on Columbus Circle and performed a show called *Cabaret in the Sky*. Jackie never looked better. She was off the drugs, on cue, and very good. It was shortly after then that she chucked womanhood entirely. Gone were Curtis's days of living in drag, as he had now entered his James Dean phase. Curtis looked cute dressed in jeans and T-shirts with a cigarette hanging off one lip and his hair combed back like the legendary icon. It was an extreme image change and it did Curtis justice.

It was also around this time in 1975 when Bill Corely had a similar idea for moi. I was twenty-nine years old and getting tired of singing in the crook of a piano, so Corely decided it was time to go "mainstream." "We've got to go mainstream!" he would declare. "If you're ever going to make it big, you got to go beyond cabaret."

Going mainstream meant appealing to Middle America and landing a recording contract. Disco was hot, and with a fast beat, the right mixer, and some makeshift lyrics, anybody could become a disco queen—so it seemed. Since Sylvester had just hit it big on the scene, Corely thought that I could follow in his footsteps. Corely, however, tapered down my glamourous image and we strived for a funky androgynous look, thinking I'd have a better chance at success. Personally, I thought I'd have a better chance of getting arrested, and Corely and I were forever debating the issue of high drag versus low drag.

"Sylvester's a queen!" I screamed.

"But he wears pants!"

"Well, so did Marlene Dietrich! What difference does it make?"

The parachute jumpsuit look was in for women, and they came in all sorts of wild colors—hot pink, neon green, lavenders, and blues. So I stepped out of a gown and into a jumpsuit, toned down my face, and cut my hair. The result? I looked like a queer Martian and it didn't sell.

Instead of going mainstream, we went downstream. Corely wanted me to do disco, so he started writing me songs, but I sang them with a piano. When did Sylvester ever sing to a piano? The man sang to soundtracks that were created by a musical wizard. I didn't have tracks to sing with and it didn't make sense for me to be singing these so-called disco songs in a cabaret room.

Corely and I both wanted to ride the disco wave that was sweeping the country, but I couldn't surf, so to speak, and we both plummeted into what seemed like a bottomless pit of frustration. In 1976 we split. He had tried countless times to get me a record deal, but the American public just wasn't ready for a man who sang in a dress. Little did we know that in eight years, Boy George would change all that. We parted amicably, but being without him was like being Marlene Dietrich without von Sternberg. I never heard from him again.

I floundered around for a while until May 1976, when I landed a week-long engagement in Ft. Lauderdale and stayed with my parents and with my friend Richard Banks, who had a house in Palm Beach. Richard was heavily grounded in Palm Beach society and I was soon caught up in a whirlwind of parties where I hobnobbed with divas of society, such as Lilli Pulitzer and Foxy Gillette.

My father came to see my show and loved it. My mother couldn't make it; she had to take care of the dogs. The dogs?! My parents had known about me living as a woman since my days with Jack, and although they weren't pleased, what could they say? My mother cried and my father was supportive, but it wasn't until after I became famous and was photographed with Rock Hudson that they really came around and accepted the idea. Also, by this time, my parents had moved into a new house, so it was okay for me to come home as a woman since the new neighbors didn't know the difference.

Shortly after my show in Ft. Lauderdale, I received an offer from a producer in San Francisco who was putting together a show in a nightclub called Bimbos. He offered me fifteen hundred dollars to play one week and I pounced on it. It was a big show with expensive sets and handsome chorus boys, but instead of performing in full regalia, I decided to do the show as a man in the parachute jumpsuit—and bombed hideously! And to make matters worse, the producer had gotten into trouble with the Chinese mafia and skipped town without paying me. I was plucked, not to mention stranded with no money, no place to go, and not one decent review!

Fortunately, I was taken in by some kind-hearted fans who used to hang out at the bar. They were young kids who had a nice little apartment on Sacramento Avenue. I had planned to stay with them until I could get enough money together to get back to New York, so I landed a job at an answering service on Castro Street. I worked during the graveyard shift and took calls for a prostitute named Sunshine, as well as the Suicide Hotline. I answered Sunshine's line seductively, purring into the phone, and men loved it. Sunshine loved it, too, as it boosted her business! Guys always tried to pick me up on the phone, but I declined, saying "I'm sorry, but this is an aswering service."

I answered the Suicide Hotline with an upbeat voice and talked to these poor lonesome souls for hours on end, telling them how gorgeous and fabulous they were and how miserable the world would be without them. One guy asked me out for coffee, but I had to decline. If he asked me out for a cocktail, I might have reconsidered. After talking to suicidal cases all night, a stiff drink never hurts, and every now and then I'd pull all the plugs on the switchboard, run downstairs to the liquor store, and drag up a bottle!

Finally, everything was coming together. I had a place to stay, I had a job, and by the end of the summer I planned to have enough money to get back to Manhattan. Then the bottom really fell out of my boat. Mitchell St. John, who had been subletting my apartment in New York, called to tell me that our apartment had been gutted by a fire. Everything I owned—the Halston gowns, my furs and memorabilia—had been incinerated into a puff of smoke. To this day, I don't believe in owning anything—except a pack of cigarettes and a pair of heels!

And if that weren't enough, the kids with whom I had been living were being evicted because they hadn't paid their rent in two months. I felt completely helpless, called my parents, and pleaded for an airline ticket back to the Big Apple.

My mother and father are wonderful people, and they have supported me throughout the ups and downs in my tumultuous life. So many parents have abandoned their children because they have chosen alternative lifestyles. My parents, however, just threw their arms in the air, screamed, and pulled out their hair. I suppose they thought I'd eventually snap out of it. Like all parents, they thought I was going through a phase. But for twenty years?

Still, no matter how much heartache I had caused in my youth, no matter how I was living my life, they never condemned or shunned me. They didn't understand my lifestyle; they just accepted it. Even in the highest of heels and a feather boa, I was still their son.

Mom and Dad sent me a one-way ticket to New York, and I called Lenny Dean and told him I needed a place to stay. Lenny called Richard Banks, who was back in New York, and arranged for me to stay with him and his friend Shawn in their artist digs—a plush townhouse on Fifth Avenue and Tenth Street.

I came back to New York a broken goddess indeed. I had flopped miserably in San Francisco, my gorilla fur had been cremated (a funeral which was long overdue), and my self-esteem had been stomped in the gutter. If anyone needed to call the Suicide Hotline, it was me. And I couldn't even remember the number.

Meanwhile, on the other side of town, Ron Link was directing Tom Eyen's play *Women Behind Bars*, starring Divine, at the Truck and Warehouse Theater in the East Village. It was right across from La Mama, one of my old haunts from my theater days with Jackie Curtis. The show had been running for three years and it was near to closing, but at the last minute they needed an understudy for Divine, who was starring as the bull-dyke matron of an all-women's prison. Ron Link had offered me a role in the show three years earlier, but the salary didn't even come close to the bacon I was bringing home from Reno Sweeney, and so Corley had declined the offer.

Ron heard that I was in town and called me. He wanted to know if I'd consider working as Divine's understudy. Then he sweetened the proposition by telling me that Billy Edgar, the actor who played Divine's sidekick Louise, was planning to leave the show. If I jumped onboard now, I could have the part. I had nothing else to do, so I accepted. Besides, it was a juicy role.

I had first met Divine years before, when I was in Philadelphia doing my nightclub act at a small club. Divine—or "Divvie," as I called him in later years—made a special appearance at the club since he was on a promotional tour for his latest film, *Female Trouble*. We met at a party after the show, and I was extremely intimidated by this huge, fat, semi-bald beast with exagerated Vampira eye makeup, a leopard-print mini dress and matching Springalator shoes, and a big red purse. He looked fierce. I had just seen *Female Trouble* and told him I loved the Christmas scene where his character attacks her parents because she didn't find cha-cha heels under the tree. Divine said "Thank you" with an air of hauteur and turned away. He could be such a cold bitch at times.

Women Behind Bars was about crazy women in jail, and was inspired by the movie *Caged*. I saw it when it first opened in D.C., and it was hysterical.

Every day I would show up at the Truck and Warehouse Theater to rehearse Divine's role with the girls, but Divine was never there. It's difficult to walk into a cast that's been together for three years, but I learned the script in a week, and wound up filling in for Divine after he had sprained his ankle and couldn't walk.

Then, when Billy Edgar did leave, I rehearsed the role of Louise with Divine for one day, and then was tossed on the stage to fend for myself.

Women Behind Bars was on its last legs going down, and the producers were doing anything they could to keep it going—which meant getting the show written up in as many gossip columns as possible. Divine eventually left the show, and it had been announced that I was going to replace her. Then, toward the end of the run, the producers held out on two weeks of my salary. One night I approached them just before showtime and refused to go on unless they cut a check. Well, they called every columnist in town and proceeded to tell them that I was drunk, I had refused to go onstage, and that I was being fired!

I went onstage that night, and the next morning I made a quick call to the late Arthur Bell of *The Village Voice* so at least someone could set the record straight. He wrote:

> A frantic early-morning phone call came from Holly Wood-lawn to explain why she has not replaced Divine in *Women Behind Bars*, as previously announced. Holly, who was Divine's understudy, claimed that the show's producers hadn't paid her salary for two weeks. (Ron Link, the show's director, acknowledges this to be true.) She said they threatened to break her kneecaps when she requested payment. "I'm taking them to court," said Holly, who is usually misunderstood by the masses. "All the women in the cast will testify on my behalf. They'll wear thrift-shop black crepe dresses and lots of pillbox hats with veils, and carry white hankies for dabbing at the eyes when they take the witness stand."
>
> Link claims that Holly was sacked because she got drunk during a performance in which she replaced Divine. "Holly crushed beer cans onstage," says Ron. "She ripped an earring off one of the girls and punched her. It was Jeanne Eagles time." (Holly admits she missed a few calls, but denies she was abusive or drunk.)
>
> Ellie Schmidt has replaced Divine instead, and it all makes you want to cry.

Not too long after, when I got a booking at Scene One, another cabaret around town, I took out an ad in *Variety*. It was a simple classified that read: "HOLLY WOODLAWN . . . NOW BACK FROM THE COAST—IS AVAILABLE FOR BOOKINGS IN TV, FILM, STAGE, AND CABARET."

I thought if Bette Davis could take out an ad and get the starring role in *Whatever Happened to Baby Jane?* I could at least land a cameo in something. No one called, and with my career in the slump, the big question I was facing was, "Whatever happened to Holly Wood-lawn?"

Fred Martini put me up in an apartment with Mitchell St. John on Seventy-second Street and First Avenue. It was a quaint little place with a garden in the back, and it only cost three hundred and fifty dollars a month.

Mitchell worked as a chorus boy in a French cabaret called The Blue Angel. He was blond, blue-eyed, and gorgeous. One night I went to the Blue Angel to see the show. I was gowned in chiffon, as usual, with my hair in Grecian ringlets, when the master of ceremonies announced from the stage in a very thick, French accent: "Ladies and gentlemen, in zee audience this evening iz zee one, zee only, zee infamous star of cabaret and Andy Warhol's *Twash* [why he said "Twash," I'll never know, because the French can roll their "r"s]— Mizz Olly Woodlawn."

A spotlight shone on me and I stood and waved. Then I sat back down as the overture began and this tall, gorgeous figure stepped onto the stage. I watched, and as the spotlight settled I saw the figure step into the light. It was Little Chrysis, who had by now changed her name to International Chrysis and was the star of the show! She was draped in feathers and sequins and glittery fabrics, and scintillated in the white light. She was hardly the fat little thing I remembered from years before, when she was wearing lipstick as eyeshadow in the Village. She had bloomed into quite a showgirl and she was so beautiful that she had a line of men waiting outside her dressing room door after the show. And these were highfalutin men of distinction—diplomats, Senators, and a sheik, to boot!

That night after the show one of the girls came up to me and said, "Hey, there's a man over there who wants to meet you and he's filthy rich."

"I'm sorry," I said, "but I'm not a prostitute. I don't sell myself, I'm an *artiste*." What an asshole I was.

Not long after, I was in my living room and I turned on the six o'clock news, and there was the Blue Angel being devoured by flames. It burnt to the ground, killing several people. It was very tragic, but I was fortunate in that Mitchell and Chrysis weren't there.

Now that Mitchell was out of a job, he decided he wanted to

become a hairdresser, so Freddy opened a salon for him. Then Mitchell got bored and said, "We have to open a club for Holly." And so they closed the salon and opened a club called Freddy's. Fred wanted to name it Mitchell's, but Mitchell didn't want the responsibility. I wanted them to call it Holly's, but they never got the hint.

Freddy's became a popular cabaret, a hot spot that attracted stars from both Broadway and Hollywood. Oddly enough, I didn't perform there until three years later. I was too busy going to parties.

Parties were a big thing in the mid-1970s. Cocaine was the rage everywhere I went. Once I arrived at a sumptuous penthouse party on Park Avenue and found everyone coming and going from the coffee table, where a mound of coke was piled on a silver tray with two mint leaves poking out of the top. Lined around the tray were tiny gold spoons so the guests could help themselves to as much as they pleased.

Cocaine was a very chic, elegant party favor in those days, particularly because it was so expensive. Everyone was doing it, young and old alike. The young people did it to secure their status and the older ones did it to feel young. It was a quick pick-me-up. Little did we know just how much damage it could do.

I had gone to a party at the Continental Baths, which by this time was quite a hot spot in itself, as far as social soirees and entertainment were concerned. Mitchell was there with this mad South American girl named Carmen d'Alessio, who was quite flamboyant with her big expressive eyes and inviting smile. She was a true social butterfly and knew everyone who was anyone. She would also play matchmaker and fix up rich men with the top fashion models, whether they were gay or straight.

"Darling," said Carmen in her thick Spanish accent, "I'm the new George Paul Rozzel [George was a big party thrower in town] and I have two very rich friends of mine who are opening up a discotheque at the Ed Sullivan Theater and you must come. We're gonna have lights, music, food, and we need some fabulous people like yourself to be there. I'm handling the PR, so just call any time and I'll put your name on the guest list."

Studio 54 was the social pinnacle of New York during the disco heyday. The Ed Sullivan Theater had been gutted and transformed into an enormous club, and hundreds of thousands of dollars were spent to make it one of the hottest clubs ever to appear on the planet.

In from the bars on Fire Island were brought DJ's who mixed their own dance tapes, and the bartenders were gorgeous muscle boys in tight shorts. Cocaine use was flaunted and encouraged, and occasionally during the night, a large illuminated crescent moon with a smiling face would slowly descend from the ceiling. Then a big silver spoon would come down and go up the moon's nose.

Everyone was snorting cocaine and amyl nitrate (a.k.a. "poppers") and carrying on.

Disco lights were literally invented for Studio 54. Long tubular poles would go up and come down from the ceiling and light up with chaser lights. Once I spun around and ran into one with my head! Huge strips of mylar would dangle from the ceiling, and people would throw glitter and confetti from the catwalks above. It was euphoria!

As the club became more popular, the doorman started to turn people away in droves. Some would bribe the doorman just to get in, but it soon became so that even a generous tip couldn't guarantee an entrance. Only social prominence and fame could pave the way. The place boasted snob appeal and people were turned away on their looks alone. It was so superficial, yet the bridge-and-tunnel crowd from Queens and New Jersey ate it up, and would flock to New York for the weekend and line up around the corner in their sheer polyester disco dresses and white John Travolta disco suits in hopes of getting in.

The famous people were the ones responsible for what Studio 54 had become. The Liz Taylors, the Liza Minellis, the Halstons, and the Bianca Jaggers were there as well as the artists, the infamous, and the rich—the very, very rich.

Cabs and limos would congest the block, inching their way to the white square canopy that was crowded with people, all waving their arms in hopes of getting in. "Let me in! Let me in!" they would shout to David, the doorman, who was a big straight guy with a lot of attitude. He would pick and choose among the beggars like a yenta fussing over tomatoes for her bisque.

Whenever someone notable arrived, the crowd would part just to see who was stepping out of the limo and the paparazzi would go wild. Making the entrance was half the fun, and Asha and I waited for hours in the traffic for that flimsy moment in the limelight. The chauffeur opened our door and we stepped out of the car, swathed in furs, dripping in jewels, and everyone would turn to look as we were surrounded by a barrage of flashing cameras.

The mass would part and Steve Rubell, one of the owners, greeted us as we slithered inside. On occasion, I would pick an entourage of handsome men out of the waiting line just for kicks. "Oh, he's with me and he's with me, and him and him . . ." I'd go along, picking and choosing, as my gang and I filed inside, and there was always one who would try to sneak in, saying to the doorman, "I'm with her."

"No, no! He's not with me! I don't know this person. He's not with me!" I'd retaliate, and then scurry off inside to the pulsating disco madness.

Whenever Studio 54 had special parties, invitations were always hand-delivered by a messenger dressed in the party's theme. Once Steve Rubell threw a jungle party and rented a giraffe, monkeys, and various other animals to climb among the jungle setting. It was quite elaborate—large trees with moss that dangled from the branches and real vines hanging from the rafters. Even the muscle-bound bartenders were dressed up like little Tarzans!

The basement was where Steve Rubell invited all the famous people to snort coke. Bianca was always down there acting every bit the spoiled brat that she had become. I always thought she should've been smacked, particularly since she was always hounding Halston for something to wear. It really bugged me, since there were far needier stars such as myself who could have gotten good use out of those gowns!

Studio 54 was quite risqué, as people were snorting, blowing, and carrying on in the basement, on the catwalks, in the bathrooms, and behind the bar! It was insane. Every time I walked into the bathroom, someone was having sex on the toilet!

Sex in the bathroom was a given, and everyone was doing it with everybody. Men were with men, women were with women, and no one seemed to notice the difference, or even care. Once Asha and I peeked under a stall and saw a young blond woman with her legs in the air while her boyfriend ate to his heart's content! Her dress was pushed up over her well-rounded breasts, and he rubbed her rosy nipples as she held on to the stall walls with both arms. We didn't say anything because we were too sophisticated, although I was dying to know where she got her dress.

One morning after a night of too much coke and way too much champagne, I received a call from a producer asking if I'd be interested in appearing on a talk show hosted by Geraldo Rivera. My mind was a little bleary, so I didn't quite understand what they wanted from me, but when I heard that it paid three hundred and fifty dollars, I said yes. Later in the week, I visited with the producer, who wanted to interview me before the show. I told him all about myself, babbling on about my life of unabashed glamour.

The following day, I arrived for the taping and I had no idea what was going on. I didn't even know what the show was about. All I knew was that I was going to be on TV, I had spent five hours putting on my makeup, and I looked fabulous.

Well, I was seated in the green room and I waited and waited and waited, nibbling on cheese and eyeing the bottle of wine across from me. Finally, I learned that the program was about sexuality, and that the other guests were Christine Jorgenson (the famous sex change), a bisexual, and various porn stars! I thought, "What am I doing here?" I thought they were going to talk about me and my beauty secrets, which were neatly penned down on a wine receipt and tucked safely inside my bra.

When it finally came time for me to go on, I was feeling rather festive, as I had had a generous portion of wine and very little cheese. I was escorted onstage, prepared only to talk about beauty, fashion, and stardom and was hurled the strangest questions I had ever been asked.

"Holly," he began, "when you were four years old and you wanted to be a woman—"

I shrank in my seat. I thought, "What's he talking about?" I never wanted to be a woman when I was four.

"Holly," he said, "when you put on a woman's dress, do you get sexually excited?"

I was stunned. He was asking me these below-the-belt questions, and one thing I had learned from Bill Corely was that whenever a journalist starts to go for the jugular, the best defense is to become a blithering dimwit. Geraldo tossed me wacked-out questions, and I tossed him answers that went right over his head and into left field. One would have thought I was possessed by Gracie Allen.

"Holly, what's it like be a woman trapped in a man's body?"

"I'm not trapped in a man's body, I'm trapped in New York City!" I quipped.

"But what are you? Are you a man, are you a woman—"

"Honey," I shot back. "What difference does it make, just so long as you're fabulous!"

And with that, they cut to a commerical!

CHAPTER 19

On the Lam

*T*he response from the Geraldo show was overwhelming: I was flooded with phone calls from people wanting to know where I was going to be appearing. So, as I had been out of circulation for some time, I decided to revive my nightclub act. I needed a manager, and called Lewis Freedman and asked if he'd be interested. He declined because he didn't have enough time, but suggested that I contact his friend Gerald Duvall. Lewis said that Gerald would be good for me since he had worked with Bette Midler and had been an influential spark for her career.

Thinking that I could reap some of the influences myself, I got on the horn and called the esteemed Mr. Duvall, who was quite a gentleman and had numerous show-biz contacts. He also had money and could afford to back me. Having been molded into a goddess by Corely, I was not about to go back to banging cymbals between my knees. Unless, of course, I was in a ten-thousand-dollar gown.

Gerald took me under his gilded wing, and we set about finding an appropriate accompanist. He introduced me to a pianist named Mark and tried to make us work together, but we didn't click.

Eventually, Gerald arranged a new contract for me at Reno's. I started doing shows with my friend Lenny Dean, who was writing my dialogue. We decided to create a different motif and built shows around a variety of personas. One week I was a woman standing under the lamppost singing the blues, the next week I was a pagan fire goddess, and the next I was a cheap Spanish fruit vendor.

Jackie Curtis would occasionally catch one of my shows and scream from the audience, "Oh, yeah! Gay gown! Gay gown!" Curtis wasn't together at this time. He was high on speed and drunk on vodka, and he'd whistle and carry on like some cheap hoodlum from Queens.

"Oh, ladies and gentleman," I'd say to the crowd. "In the audience this evening is my sister, Jackie Curtis." Curtis would stand, clap his hands, and yell, "Gay gown!" And I'd scream, "Gay voice! Now, shut up, it's my show!"

Curtis was a heckler from way back who could heckle his way out of a thunderstorm.

Disco, which had started in The Fire Island Pines, had spread to Manhattan and was taking the city by storm. Suddenly, everyone was taken by this fast-paced, pulsating beat that had so long been associated with the gay dance bars in the Pines, *the* getaway for the crowned heads of fashion.

Chic, Gloria Gaynor, Donna Summer, and a very strange, androgynous figure known as Grace Jones—this tall, Amazonian black woman who looked like a big butch drag queen—began to dominate the sounds of the club scene, and *After Dark* magazine rivaled *Interview* as the big arts publication of New York.

During this time I was living with a gorgeous blond chef named Charlie in an apartment on Fifth Avenue and Thirteenth Street. Charlie lived across from the Parsons School of Design, and my dear friend

Estelle and I used to hang out the window with binoculars and peer into the school's windows in search of nude models.

Lenny Dean used to come in on the PATH train from New Jersey wearing his pride and joy—a beaver coat that he named Beverly. In a way, Lenny took the place of Estelle, who was getting farther away from me. Estelle's life was revolving around the bottle, and he'd sink into a drunken stupor and disappear, only to surface after a few weeks looking like he had slept in a gutter. Finally, Estelle just disappeared altogether, and I never heard from him again.

One afternoon, Lenny and I arrived at Reno's and had just walked into the foyer when two handsome, finely dressed gentlemen approached. One asked, "Are you Holly Woodlawn?"

"Well, of course, darling," I said with a smile and reached into my bag for pen and paper. I was certain they were going to ask for my autograph, but to my chagrin, one of them reached out and handcuffed me! I was shocked.

"What is this all about? What did I do? I'm a clean woman! I wasn't around when Bugsy got rubbed," I joked, trying to break the tension.

As it turned out, this was no joking matter. I was arrested for avoiding my probation officer since my grand larceny stint seven years ago. I hadn't seen my probation officer in years! I just figured that since my face was in the papers every week, what was the point of schlepping all the way downtown for someone to ask me how I've been? All they had to do was drop twenty-five cents at the newsstand and read my reviews.

So, back to the Tombs I went, only to be sprung by Ethan Geto, a prominent gay political figure at the time, who got me out on recognizance and a promise that I would pay back the money that I had embezzled from the embassy. Gee, I forgot all about that two thousand dollars!

Lewis got the idea to stage a benefit at Reno's to raise money for the cause. The place was packed with talent—Tally Brown, Betty Rhodes, Jackie Curtis, Alexis Del Lago, Judith Cohen, Blossom Deary, Martha Shlamme, Anita O'Day, Bruce Roberts, Ellen Green, and Geraldine Fitzgerald all crowded together and lent their virtuosity to keep me out of the hoosegow. I even got up and sang a few myself, and Bette Midler sent a check for five hundred dollars.

Thanks to all of my friends, the debt was paid. Although I had been freed from that burden, I soon discovered that I was still haunted by the deed, for one evening while I attended a swank soiree at the Museum of Modern Art with Asha, I had the most gut-wrenching experience. I was standing among all these social dignitaries feeling quite resplendent, as I was bejeweled, bedecked, and bedazzled in A Halston Gown, blowing kisses and luxuriating in praise, when this finely tailored woman came out of nowhere, stared me in the face, and said amusingly, "Hello, I'm Madame Chardonet. Remember? You stole two thousand dollars from me once."

She was trying to be funny about the whole thing, but I was not amused. I did not want my scandalous past flaunted before me in the least, and I was plucked.

"Well, darling, listen," I said in a whisper. "I paid you back." And I turned and walked away. When will the nightmare end?

Every now and then I'd escape to Newport, Rhode Island, with my friend Richard Banks. Richard was an artist, and had been good friends with Andy in the early Fifties. They lived next door to each other in the same apartment building, and Andy was forever saying, "Oh, Richard, I wish I could draw like you. I wish I could paint like you." Richard always had naked men lying around the house because he used them as models, and Andy was always coming over for a peek.

Richard kept an apartment in New York off Fifth Avenue and a house in Palm Beach, but his house in Newport (which was a refurbished church) was where all the excitement happened. He was always having parties with Gloria Swanson, Eileen Pringle, and Doris Duke.

I would often attend Richard's ritzy teas and socialize with these rich dowagers, who had no idea I was a floozy on the make.

"Oh, she is such a lovely girl," they would later remark to Richard. Meanwhile, later that night Richard and I would be found at the sleaziest disco in Newport screaming, yelling, and carrying on.

*   *   *

In 1978, Gerald made a deal with a London producer named Bernard Jay to have me appear at a nightclub called Country Cousins. I packed my trunks and off I went to London, where I arrived two days before my engagement began, just in time to see Lorna Luft, who was ending her run at the same club.

I played for three weeks at Country Cousins, and I became the toast of the town. The club drew large crowds and I had the pleasure of meeting such celebrities as Danny La Rue, Shirley Bassey, Sarah Churchill (Winston's niece), the Prince of Jaipur, and Quentin Crisp, whom I had never heard of before. Just weeks before, Gerald had seen him on PBS in the film *Naked Civil Servant* (based on his autobiography), so he filled me in. Quentin was and is a beautiful little man with an exquisite pink face and lavender hair carefully arranged in a swirl around his head. He was elegantly coiffed, and looked dashingly smart in a black velvet evening jacket, white shirt, and silk scarf. We were introduced after the show, and he told me I wasn't like any other drag act he had seen before.

"You're such a pleasure onstage," he said fondly.

I enjoyed my stay in England, although I never quite got used to calling my cigarette a fag. Nor could I quite differentiate pounds from dollars and to me, flats were shoes, not apartments. I visited the Tower of London and ogled over the Crown Jewels. The royal crown had a diamond the size of a lemon, and on the scepter was an even bigger diamond. It was fabulous.

Not long after I had drooled over the jewels, a public-relations person arranged for me to meet the Queen Mama at the Old Vic Theatre, which had been refurbished and was having a big opening. The theatre was a big Elizabethan monstrosity that looked as if it had been around since the sixteenth century. The Queen Mum looked as if she had been around for some time herself, and was tastefully dressed in a little yellow dress with matching purse, hat, and shoes. She looked like a fat little canary, and beside her stood yet another queen who was of no royal standing whatsoever, but you could tell that underneath his prissy exterior, he was dying to put on a tiara. His purpose was to stand beside the royal highness and introduce her to whomever stood before her. I had no idea what to say to the old bag, although I was certain that "Hello, your queeness!" was out of the question.

I had heard that she kept a little bottle of gin tucked inside her purse and that she was quite a nipper. Well, I just loved those fun kinda gals, and entertained the possibility of the two of us getting on a good toot later in the eve. Just maybe I could wheedle a brooch or two out of her.

"And may I present Miss Holly Woodlawn," said the skinny queen to the fat Queen as I stepped forward and knelt before her.

"Oh, I'm so happy to meet you," she said in a little high voice, her cherubic cheeks pink with color. She was teetering on those little yellow heels, and I was shaking in mine. I was nervous as hell.

"Thank you, your majesty—" And just as I was about to say, "Hey, listen, doll, how about me and you getting together later for a drinkie-poo down at the pub," I was hauled off to the Oxford University Film Festival.

I was caught up in a social whirlwind, going here, appearing there, and one day found myself at Wimbleton with the famous Japanese fashion designer Yuki. I got dressed up in a lavender chiffon Zandra Rhodes tea gown with dangling sequins and a little bandau hat, Grecian curls framing my face. I was dressed up as if I was going to the Ascot races while everyone else wore raincoats and pants! I was the only one in a gown, eating escargot, prawns, and caviar while sipping champagne.

During my nocturnal jaunts, I occasionaly went to the Ritz, an incredible disco in London that was equivalent to Studio 54 in social prestige. One night as I was passing the coat check, I happened to notice Andy, Halston, Bianca, and Steve Rubell trying to get in. The doormen didn't know who they were, and Steve Rubell was throwing a fit, Andy was looking very bewildered, Bianca looked like Bianca, and Halston was standing there above it all, calmly smoking a cigarette. I stepped forward and approached the door.

"Oh, I know them," I told the doorman.

"Holly, what are you doing here?" asked Andy.

"I'm doing a show in town, what are you doing here?"

They would have gotten in eventually, but it just so happened that I was walking by and there they were, standing in the door with Steve Rubell screaming, yelling, and carrying on. These divas! Rubel was creating animosity, so I stepped forward in his defense and the doorman (since he knew who I was) let them in as my friends.

"Oh, darling, they're with me," I explained and he let them pass.

It felt so good. Finally, after all those years, the tables were turned.

chapter 20

Wrap It.
It's a Take

I returned to New York from my sojourn abroad in the middle of a snowstorm. The city was buried in snow so deep people were actually skiing down Fifth Avenue. It was hideously cold, but I remained cozily snug with friends, delighting in the joyous season. Chestnuts were roasting on an open fire, Jack Frost was nipping at my nose, and I was nipping at the gin! I just love holiday cheer and always stock up on a case or two.

This holiday season, I was overcome with that fabulous white powder infamously known as cocaine. I had a blizzard of my own carrying on in my nostrils while I partied at Studio 54, which by now was at its peak. Since I was hobnobbing with the Rich and the Famous,

I was always being invited to the disco's "inner sanctum," otherwise know as the cellar.

It was a gray concrete room with a mattress lying on top of crates and a chain-link fence covering one wall. There we sat amid the cartons of wine, all decked out in our Yves St. Laurents, furs, and our Calvins, thinking we were the *crème de la crème*.

A winter wonderland of cocaine, champagne, and limos fogged my memory until the summer of 1979. And by this time, Tom Eyen's latest play, entitled *Neon Woman* (loosely based on *The G-String Murders* by Gypsy Rose Lee), was the summer's off-Broadway hit. The show starred Divine as Flash Storm, with Billie Edgar as her sidekick, Kitty La Rue. Billie was leaving the show to move to Los Angeles, and once again I was called to replace him for the summer run in Provincetown.

Kitty La Rue was my favorite theatrical role. Kitty was a lesbian stripper who at one point in the play professes her love for lesbianism while dancing around the stage in the heat of passion: "Lesbian love, lesbian love, ooooohh, I love lesbian love."

In the play, Divine was supposed to cut me off in the middle of this emotional outburst, but there were times when he chose to wait and let me ramble, dance, and carry on until I was near the brink of collapse. I approached him about it backstage and said, "Listen, Rotunda! You're supposed to cut me off, not let me go on until I nearly die of exhaustion."

"Oh, Holly, you were having such a good time and they loved you."

I paid him back for it in the next performance when, at the end of the play, he shot me dead and I took fifteen minutes to die!

All our shenanigans aside, *Neon Woman* became the hit of the summer, and the lines were so funny that people were actually saying them in town. Divine was great to work with and a true professional, but living with him was an entirely different story. We shared a little white cottage built on stilts so the tide could roll in right under the house as we slept. There was even a little trapdoor in the hallway, and we could lift it and see the water underneath.

Divine was a severe pot smoker and I was always finding him snoring on the toilet with a joint in his mouth. It wasn't until later that I learned he actually suffered from narcolepsy, and would have instant attacks of deep sleep. He would be sitting at the kitchen table talking to me while eating a chicken leg and suddenly fall asleep with a bite of food in his mouth, snoring louder than a commune of frogs. It scared the hell out of me because all he had to do was choke on the chicken and it was all over—no show!

When Divine wasn't causing a ruckus, he was eating. And even that caused a commotion. Since he was the quintessential pot smoker, he had a ravenous appetite. I was afraid if we didn't keep the fridge full he'd start gnawing on the furniture. We would go to the market three times a week just to stock up, buying eighteen pork chops, five chickens, ten pounds of potatoes, twenty-four ears of corn, two gallons of milk, three cartons of ice cream, a box of Ho-Ho's, two dozen Ding-Dongs, one dozen chocolate-coated donuts, three boxes of Twinkies, and one Scooter pie for the road. Not to mention a box of diet breakfast bars, which I suppose was to keep the luscious Divine from ballooning into a Divoon!

I think Divine ate a lot because he was insecure. Although Cookie Mueller, Mink Stole, and John Waters would come to visit, Divine was basically a lonely person. I don't think Divine had any real friends. He was surrounded by a lot of people, but most of them sucked up to him because he was famous and because he always had grass. Usually, after these so-called friends came over, ate the food, and smoked the pot, they'd leave and Divine would be left alone to cry on my shoulder, blubbering about that infamous scene at the end of John Waters's film *Pink Flamingos*, where he walked up to a squatting dog and devoured the excrement. I think that was Div's biggest regret in his life, because that's how he was remembered—and he hated it, although his venture into theater helped erase the image.

Also, Divine wanted to be glamourous and look like his idol, Liz Taylor. He didn't want to be a beast, but he couldn't be accepted any other way. It was an image he had locked himself into until the making of *Hairspray*, where he plays a downtrodden housewife. And even then he wasn't glamourous. Well, at least he was perfectly proportioned. His hair was big because his body was big, and his eyes were painted to be enormous because his head was so large. Divine was a huge person. He looked like a giant beach ball being held up by these teeny-tiny spiked heels. The sight was both frightening and hysterical, although Divvie truly believed he was gorgeous. And he was, in a Lana-Turner-gone-berserk kind of way.

That fall, *Neon Woman* was brought to Chicago for two weeks. We piled into a fleabag hotel and opened to rocky reviews. I was left unscathed and actually received some praise, but the critics were not favorable toward Divine. Larry Kart of the *Chicago Tribune* had this to say:

> Divine is awful. Not awful for what he presents or represents, but awful because he pretty much fails to do anything. . . . None of this would be particularly bothersome if there were not standards of comparison. For example, among female impersonators (although Divine for some reason does not regard himself as one) there are several performers, such as Craig Russell, who present an image of and a commentary on grotesqueness in addition to the thing itself. And unfortunately for Divine, one of those performers is in the cast, former Andy Warhol protégé Holly Woodlawn.
>
> . . . Woodlawn possesses an innate, large-scale theatricality that makes his every movement purposeful and expressive . . .

I knew our relationship was going to be strained, but when I read the writer's closing statement—"But I imagine, or hope that some in the audience who have come to wallow in Divine's wake will leave with the memory of Woodlawn's skewed humanity"—I knew Divine would hate me forever. And I was right.

After the reviews, Divine stomped around his room like a bull in a china closet, screaming and yelling that the Midwest was fucked and no one understood the true artist that lay beneath his extremely demented facade.

The show closed early and I returned to New York to stay with a friend and soon discovered I was faced with a faltering career. I wasn't getting any work anywhere; cabaret was on its way out and, to heighten my depression, I was down to nothing, with nowhere to go to except the welfare line. So one night in a drunken stupor I called up my parents and said I was coming home. It was the call I had wanted to make so badly after I ran away, and it took nearly sixteen years to make. Well, finally it was done and Harold Ajzenberg was going home.

I cut off my hair, packed a bag, and boarded a plane to Miami. My parents were so happy to see me! I landed a busboy job at Benihana of Tokyo in Miami, and even resorted to lifting weights, trying my best to be a man.

Then I thought to myself, "What the hell am I doing? Who am I? Am I happy?" No, I wasn't. I had seen too much. And I wanted so much more! I didn't want to bus tables! So, by the fall of the following year I was back on a plane for New York. I was destined to be a woman again.

Back in New York, I moved in with Lewis Freedman, who had by now opened a little club called S.N.A.F.U. (which, I was told, was army lingo meaning "situation normal: all fouled up"). He gave me a job as a coat-check girl. I stayed with Lewis a few weeks, then moved in with Vincent Nasso on Sixteenth Street. Vincent was working with Way Bandy at the time, and by now he had reached the pinnacle of his success, having designed faces for such celebs as Gloria Vanderbilt and Liz Taylor.

By now, the Factory had moved to Thirty-third and Lexington, and I dropped in to see Andy. Brigid was at her desk looking better than I had ever seen her, and she was so pleasant and kind, a far cry from the mean-faced Brigid Polk I had first encountered in the 1970s. Fred Hughes, looking as dapper as ever, was tucked inside his office, and the rest of the gang must have been out to lunch because there was no one around.

I wanted to be kind to Andy because I felt bad about all the times I had terrorized him in the early Seventies.

When Andy first set eyes on me, he was stunned because I had just returned from Florida and had not gone back into my full dragoon. I was wearing no makeup whatsoever, my hair was short, and I was sporting a T-shirt, jeans, and Top-siders. I looked like a kid out of prep school, and it was the first time Andy had ever seen me looking like a man.

"Oh, Holly," he said with a glint in his eye, circling me as he eyed my frame like a hawk circling in for the kill. "You make such a good-looking man. You're so handsome."

Andy honed in on my crotch, released a soft gasp, and put his hand up to his mouth. "It looks so big, Holly. How big is it?"

"Andy!" I snapped back in embarrassment. "Please stop it. I'm a woman."

"Can I take pictures of it?"

"What?!"

"You don't have to take off your clothes. I just want to photograph it, Holly, just like it is now."

"Andy, you're just a dirty old man!"

"Come in the back," he invited, and led the way as I followed. Sure enough, Andy dragged out the Polaroid and snapped away at my crotch. I didn't mind, though I made him promise not to tell anyone whose crotch it was.

A few weeks later, I had gotten back together with Lenny Dean and we put together a show for S.N.A.F.U. I was back in the saddle again, and this time I was wearing a white Fabrice minidress and a blond Jayne Mansfield wig.

Vincent had just finished painting my face at the apartment, it was ten minutes before showtime, and we were standing outside trying to hail a cab with no luck. I was on the verge of panic when from nowhere came a white pickup truck, and it was rolling my way. I hoisted my thumb in the air and stuck out my leg, and the truck came to a screeching halt. The passenger door swung open and this gorgeous guy asked if I needed a ride. Vincent started to decline, but I cut him off and said, "Yes!"

"Climb in," said the driver. Vincent looked at me, befuddled.

"You get up front," I told him. "I'm riding in back on the bed." So Vincent got in the front of the truck and I got in the back, and as we neared the club, I could see a line of people filing into the place. Our arrival could not have been more timely. When the truck pulled up in front of the place, I was greeted by much applause as I waved and carried on to the crowd. I then hopped out of the bed, thanked the driver, and breezed into the club. Lewis was playing the overture and I walked right onstage and into a song.

Lulu was definitely back in town!

Nineteen eighty-one had brought another sweltering, humid summer to New York. I was living with Mitchell St. John in a quaint little apartment in the West Village and I was having trouble landing steady work. It was back to the hand-to-mouth routine. I had starred as Geraldine in Joe Orton's *What the Butler Saw*, opposite porn star Harry Reems, but the show flopped miserably. Reems was trying to go mainstream and make it as a legit actor. He was horrible! Not only was he awful onstage, but he was a major prima donna! He refused to do interviews with me, he kept my name from appearing on the bill, and he had the director fired! The whole production was a catastrophe and the show was so disastrous it closed after a week.

Not long afterward, I was offered the part of Googie Gomez in an off-Broadway production of *The Ritz*, which starred another porn star by the name of Cal Culver. The show ran out of money in its first week and closed before it formally opened. I was one destitute diva until one day Mark Shaiman and his partner Scott Whitman offered me a cameo appearance in their satire musical *Trojan Women*.

Trojan Women was a pandemonic romp starring Chickie Boom Boom, Donna Destri, Marge Gross, Arlene Solkin, and Karen Bahari. I played the high priestess of a temple and danced a ferocious tarantella in a shredded hot-pink number designed by Frank Piazza, wearing my hair entwined into a long, bejeweled braid. Then I was thrown into a volcano and sacrificed to the gods.

One night during my big solo dance routine, Scott decided to speed up the record in the middle of my dance! I danced as fast as I could, trying to keep up with the pace, then he'd slow it back down and then all the way up again. I was a tortured woman on that stage, so no one can say I didn't suffer for art. When it was time to be sacrificed, I fled to the volcano—anything to get me off my feet.

With all this madness going on, the show became a big hit with the subculture, and *Details* magazine (which was only a rag back then) raved about it! When the show eventually closed, the Shaiman/Whitman team decided to produce yet another satirical romp called *The Sound of Muzak*. It was being staged in the basement of Club 57, which, ironically, had at one time been a church.

I had the starring role of Maria, Alexis Del Lago played the Countess, and all the nuns were played by various women and men. Michael Musto played Sister Sledge and Lenny Dean played Sister Boogie Woman. Two lesbians played nuns, coming onstage in leather, nipple clamps, and harnesses. They also doubled as the children! It was insane madness to the hilt, and one night Sister Boogie Woman, in a drunken stupor, set the abbey on fire with a candle! Fortunately, someone doused the flames with beer and saved the show.

Due to our small confined space, there was no room for scene changes. Scott solved the problem by painting THE ABBEY at one end of the room and THE ALPS at the other. During scene changes he could scream, "Scene change!" (sometimes we'd yell, "Sex Change!") and the audience would turn their folding chairs around to face the opposite direction while the cast ran down the aisle for the following scene. It was pandemonium, but the audience loved it.

"My heels are alive with the sound of Muzak," I'd sing, as a mad Puerto Rican, against the background of the Alps painted on the wall.

John Sex sang, "I am sixteen going on seventeen," to Wendy Wild while they did a torrid sex dance. John had silver hair that shot straight up in the air, which looked like he was wearing an ice skate on top of his head.

One day I was telling Scott about how Estelle and I used to scream "Free pussy!" at men from my window at the Chelsea Hotel. He thought it was brilliant and told me that whenever I forgot a line (which was quite often) I should scream out the same. So whenever I was stumped onstage, I just lifted my dress and let 'em have it.

Shortly after *The Sound of Muzak*, I began rehearsals for another Off-Broadway show, *Tinseltown Tirade*, which starred a friend of mine named Hibiscus. During the last week of rehearsal, Hibiscus caught a cold. We thought nothing of it, assuming he would shake it by opening night. A week later, however, he still had the cold, and when the play opened his condition had worsened. He had gone to a doctor and was taking antibiotics, but they didn't seem to help.

Hibiscus kept getting weaker and weaker, but he refused to miss a show. This was his baby and he wasn't about to desert it. Determined to perform, he was at the theater every night, but whenever he finished a scene, he walked offstage into the wings and covered himself with a blanket because he had the chills. We were all very concerned, but he still refused to check into a hospital. Finally, he had no choice, as he had developed pneumonia.

A stand-in replaced him and the show went on. Two days later I went to visit him in the hospital and I was horrified. He was plugged into all of these strange machines, one that fed him oxygen and another that monitored his heart and yet another that fed him antibiotics. It was like walking into a space ship. Two days later he died and the play closed. He was only twenty-nine.

All of a sudden, I started hearing stories about all these gay boys who were dying of pneumonia. It seemed to happen overnight. No one really knew what to think. We had no idea what was causing this to happen. It was as if a strange plague had struck.

A year later, in the summer of 1982, Vincent Nasso suddenly fell very ill. He just got weaker and weaker, but no one could define what it was that was killing him. He died that September.

Vincent's death hit me the hardest because we were so close. I felt so much guilt, because I was alive leading this debauched life and here was this young, innocent man who had been killed by what was now being termed a gay cancer. I became so depressed that one night in a drunken stupor, I downed a handful of pills and said, "See ya, suckers!"

And then I thought, "Oh, shit, now I've really gone off the deep end!" I didn't want to die. I wanted to live! I immediately called up a friend of mine named Joyce whom I had met in the play with Hibiscus, and I told her what I had done. She understood my feelings because she had been in the same depression herself. She came over and we taxied to St. Vincent's Hospital, where they pumped my stomach. It was the most abhorrent, unglamourous, tasteless event I have ever endured. God forbid I ever have to go through it sober.

Joyce checked me in to the alkie tank, and Blue Cross footed the bill. I made a holiday out of it and stayed a week. I dried out, went into therapy, and pulled myself together.

By this time in New York there was a new wave of underground. Joey Arias, Wendy O. Williams, and John Sex had stolen the show and at the age of thirty six, I was beginning to feel like a relic. I had stopped using drugs on a regular basis, and I lost interest in staying out all night and partying till dawn. Also, I was making cameo appearances—at the most twice a year—usually at a club called the Limelight. The most it ever paid was fifty bucks, which I considered cab fare. Meanwhile, it cost me five hundred dollars just to get myself together because I had to buy a dress, my hair had to be set, and vocal coaches ain't cheap, honey!

Then one morning in the summer of 1985 the phone rang. Lenny answered. He suddenly became very serious and handed me the receiver. By the look on his face, I knew that something was wrong. Kevin Bradigan was on the line, and before I even had the chance to ask how he was, he blurted out the disturbing news.

"Jackie's dead, Holly," he said, catching me off guard. I felt myself weaken and sat on the sofa. "She died of a heroin overdose," he continued.

Heroin? Jackie was always shooting speed—when did she start

shooting heroin? My ears seemed to grow numb to what I was hearing. I knew Jackie was a serious drug user but I never thought it would result in death. I just didn't want to believe that Jackie was gone.

Jackie's death was the turning point in my life. I felt a great sense of loss. It was as if I had lost a sister. Sure, we weren't close in later years, but I had always entertained the idea that one day Jackie would put on a dress and we'd get together on the stage again. It was something to look forward to—something to fall back on. If nothing else ever happened to me again, I could always call up Curtis, throw together an act, and have a night of fun. But now Curtis was dead and I was more alone than ever.

I felt alone not because I didn't have friends. I had plenty of good friends, but Jackie was the only person left from my Warhol days with whom I could relive those times. Now those days seemed to drift further and further away until I finally realized that that time was dead as well. It was over. The notorious fame. The unabashed glamour. Max's Kansas City. The Factory. Andy. None of it seemed to make a difference anymore.

I attended the funeral in a man's blue suit, a suit I was to wear many times in later years.

When Lenny and I arrived at the church, I was floored. Jackie never looked better. Unlike Miss Darling, Jackie was laid out as a man, tastefully attired in a dark suit with his hair slicked back and a big white flower on his lapel. The casket, surrounded by funeral arrangements of white roses, mums, carnations, and gladiolus, was silver and had long-stemmed red roses lying across the top. Photographs of Jackie as a woman were arranged on a table, and inside the casket were various show-biz momentos as well as a plaque which read: "John Holden, a.k.a. Jackie Curtis."

The funeral was held at a small church on First Avenue and Nineteenth Street, where I ran into John Heyes, Ruby Lynn Reyner, Penny Arcade, and other cast members from our jaunts with the Theater of the Ridiculous. I didn't see anyone from the Factory, although there were flowers from Andy and Paul Morrissey. I felt awkward because people were coming up to me and complimenting me on how I had managed to survive. "Holly, you're such a survivor," they said, and I felt I was being credited with an attribute I didn't deserve. Even though Jackie was killed by a lethal dose of heroin, that didn't mean she wasn't a survivor. Curtis was more than a survivor; Curtis was a fighter. A real go-getter. She wanted what she wanted and she bulldozed through whoever was in the way to get to it. A survivor is one who hangs on and waits for a better tomorrow. A fighter is one who sets out to make it better today.

As I sat in the pew and listened to the sermon, I couldn't help but remember the very first time Curtis ever got into drag. It was on a cold Halloween night not long after we first met. Jackie had gotten bit by the bug of womanhood and decided "he" wanted to become a "she" for Halloween. So Candy and I joined forces, grabbed Curtis by the hair, shook out the gnats, pancaked his face, colored his eyes, painted his lips, pinched his cheeks, and threw him into a pair of high heels. Curtis went out that Halloween night and had such a blast, he stayed in costume for the next ten years! And that, my darlings, is how Jackie Curtis—the legend, the myth, and the tramp—was really born.

After the ceremony, when the pallbearers were taking the casket out of the church, I heard this loud boo-hoo-hooing coming from the back of the pews. I turned around to see who this wailing hyena was and saw a hysterical woman about to throw herself on the coffin, bawling uncontrollably. As it turned out, she was the woman who was shooting heroin with Jackie at the time of his death. She shrieked at the top of her lungs, "Oh, God, please forgive me! Oh, God, Jackie! Please! I didn't mean it. I'm so sorry. I'm so sorry." Finally, she broke down, blubbered herself into a stupor, and was hauled away. And they thought Pola Negri created a fuss over Valentino!

Lenny, who was sitting at my side, turned to me and said, "Leave it to Jackie. Wherever she goes, she causes a commotion."

This funeral could not have been more of a Jackie Curtis production. It was loud, there were photographers, and every weirdo and junkie off Avenue D showed up! It was a show-biz bonanza right up to the burial. I wanted to sing "Anything Goes," bust a cheap bottle of booze across the casket's bow, and really give her a splashy send-off, but I drank it on our way to the church. Nonetheless, when the queen of "Glamour, Glory, and Gold" finally descended into the grave, the mourners didn't throw flowers onto the casket. Instead, they threw glitter.

After the funeral, I went home, poured a glass of wine, and considered the life I had chosen. I pictured myself years later being stopped on the street in dark glasses and a fedora by some Andy Warhol fanatic.

"Weren't you one of those Superstars? Didn't you make movies with Andy Warhol?"

And I would smile over the recognition. I was a Superstar. I was a sensation. And now it's over. What else is there for me? So what if I was a survivor. Anyone can tread water; I needed to swim! My heyday was over, and I needed to go on with my life. I didn't have a direction, nor did I have a plan. And goddamnit, I didn't even have a manager! All I had was the intelligence to know that if I was ever to survive this day and face tomorrow, there had to be something better waiting for me on the horizon. And it couldn't be a cocktail.

After Jackie's death, I kept a fairly low profile. I would see Andy occasionally, but we weren't that close any longer. Then on February 23, 1987, as I was en route to Puerto Rico, Andy died. When I landed at the San Juan International Airport, I had no idea about Andy's death, and took a taxi to the seaside villa in the Condado I had rented with Lenny. Lenny had arrived at the villa days before and he *had* heard of Andy's death that morning.

When I arrived, Lenny was acting very strangely, and so was his friend Jose, who was staying with us during the holiday. I couldn't understand what I had done to warrant such behavior, and finally I said, "What's the matter with you two?"

"You haven't heard?" asked Lenny.

"Heard what?"

"You better have a drink," he said and crossed to the bar to find a glass.

"Why—what happened?"

"Andy Warhol died this morning."

I was shocked. While I was in the air, Andy was dying. It was strange, because I was thinking of the last time I saw him—only months before, at Chrissy Berlin's Thanksgiving dinner. Andy had arrived with Steven Sprouse and was handing out autographed copies of *Interview* magazine just before dinner.

"Holly, you should make a comeback," he suggested.

"And do what?"

"Do your act as a man! Gee, that would be something. If you want, I'll be your manager."

"Pass the turkey," I said, thinking that he was the real turkey even to suggest such a thing. I had tried my act out of drag and vowed never to do that again.

By now I held a glass firmly as I stared out onto the clear blue ocean. The memory of Andy's voice had faded away. On the plane, I was thinking of calling him once I returned to New York to say, "Okay, manage me." But now it was all over. Andy was gone and for a moment I almost felt the same way I had when Jackie died. Lost.

Later that day, after I had changed clothes, we went to the local bar outside on the ocean. Helicopters started flying over us, and we smelled smoke. One of the tourist hotels on the beach was on fire, and eighty-five people died in the casino. When we got home, we turned on the news to find out what had caused the disaster, and they were showing a clip of Andy at one of his openings as the anchorwoman spoke of his death.

For the next two weeks, all I ever heard about was Andy. People were telling me how sorry they felt for me and my loss. People were treating me like I had lost a mother. Well, to tell you the truth, I didn't feel that bad. But I kept thinking about the other people—all those hangers-on. Now the club owners couldn't brag, "Andy comes here." No more Superstars, no more soup cans. No more Warhol. It was the final bow that ended an era. The crown jewel of pop culture was dead.

When I got back to New York, I found an invitation from the Factory in my mailbox, inviting me to the memorial service at St.

Patrick's Cathedral on April Fool's Day. It was an appropriate date, considering all the thousands of people Andy had fooled throughout his life.

The memorial was by invitation only, with a separate invitation for a luncheon that followed. The cathedral was a circus. Everyone was abuzz, and as my cab neared Fiftieth Street and Fifth Avenue, it looked as if there was a movie premiere nearby. Limousines were backed up for blocks, cameras were popping, and smiles were flashing, taking me back to the days of Studio 54. I told the cabbie to pass the chaos and drop me off a few blocks away, since I was nervous and I wanted to avoid the fashionable hysteria.

It was a media blitz, a press agent's dream. So many faces dazzled the press with their designer smiles, dressed in their Halstons and Armanis and looking picture-perfect. Plastic mannequins, that's what they were. Out on the town to get their mugs in the paper or on the six o'clock news. True, their souls had been hollowed, but their heads were held high, strikingly posed for whatever camera snapped. And that's all that mattered, wasn't it? How pretty, handsome, or fabulous one looked. God forbid should anyone shed a tear and smudge their mascara.

This was an elite affair—the social gathering of the year, so it seemed. All of my friends told me to arrive in full regalia, just as in my old party days. But as always with funerals, out of respect I chose to wear my blue suit. Not so much for Andy; this time, for myself. It was the last time I ever wore that suit, because I never wore it anywhere but funerals. So many of my friends had died. Who was next? And as I approached the massive cathedral, I thanked God that I was all right. I had been tested for AIDS continuously, as I had been seeing a doctor regularly for the past seven years.

Paparazzi were everywhere. People were posing and blowing kisses as if they were going to the Oscars. The whole world was there, it seemed, each trying to outshine the other in his or her own tasteful (or should I say tasteless?) way. Andy would have loved it—his own premiere! He was probably looking down at us all, saying in his timid little voice, "Gosh, how glamourous."

And glamourous it was, to say the least. There were more shades of black than there were colors in the spectrum. And in the midst of this carnival, all I could see was Grace Jones. Well, I was in no mood for her, so I avoided the crowd entirely and entered the cathedral through its side entrance.

There were white flowers everywhere. A section was cordoned off by garlands of the white flowers. It was the V.I.P. section. I looked around the room and saw Fred Hughes and Vincent Fremont approaching. Fred thanked me for sending the flowers (what flowers? I thought), and I said, "You're welcome." He told me to sit in the V.I.P. section, but I was not in the mood to walk all the way down that long aisle, as people were straining their necks to see anyone who came in. I'm surprised there weren't paramedics on hand for the whiplash victims.

For some reason, I would have thought this to have been a smaller affair.

The service got underway with Yoko Ono reading the eulogy. Why Yoko I'll never know, because Andy never liked her in the first place. Well, maybe her publicist arranged it. Anyhow, as she read on, I heard sniffles coming from a woman beside me. I thought the poor dear had been touched by Yoko's words, but as I turned to offer my hankie, I noticed this broad wasn't crying at all. She was snorting cocaine out of her powder compact! It was Warholesque right to the very end.

After the service, I decided to skip the luncheon. These people made no difference to me anymore. Besides, I wasn't hungry. They were relics out of my past, and they could junk up somebody else's life as far as I was concerned. I had no time for their social bullshit. I ducked out of the cathedral's side exit and darted across the street to Saks Fifth Avenue. There but for the grace of God go I . . . and I was going shopping!

Shocking, but true. It was my calling all along, and to think I went through hell and high water before I accepted it. The populuxe puta who emblazed the stage, scorched the screen, and rocked the underground had regressed to her former shopaholic self.

I took one last glimpse of the pandemonium outside the cathedral, and a haunting truth lingered in my mind. The voice is blurred by my fading memory, but the words, spoken to me shortly after Jackie's death, made an indelible impression: "You made one mistake. You lived." Although said in jest, the words weighed heavily on me, ringing over and over in my head.

Yes, I lived. And I was going to keep on living! I'll crawl out of any hole to see the light! After all, I was Miss Donut of Amsterdam, a near-nominee for an Oscar, and the heiress to the Woodlawn Cemetery, darling. It's difficult to keep that kind of person down.

I shook my can and jiggled my jugs all the way to the cosmetic counter, where I loaded up with enough makeup to paint the Statue of Liberty . . . which wasn't a bad idea. After all the money that had been spent to renovate her, she was still green as ever. And a dull green at that. What she needed was some color! Well, tra la, la, bustier! My panties began to twitter over the possibilities, and I immediately pictured myself hanging off her nose, dressed in a cute artist's smock with a matching beret while painting her lips a divine ruby red. It was fabulous!

Epilogue

Well, poopsies, there you have it, my haughty, gaudy, sometimes bawdy little life. It's been four years since Andy's memorial and Miss Liberty is still green as ever while I sit poolside in a ruffled bikini of my own design trying to figure a way to tag L-A-W-N onto the Hollywood sign. Of course, I'd have to do something about spacing the "Holly" and the "wood," but anything's possible if you want it bad enough. When there's a will, there's a way.

My life has gone full circle, as if I've picked up where I left off in Miami when I was fifteen years old. Thirty years ago, I ran away from home to find an identity that eluded me, and I recently left New York to do the same. My life had become stagnant and I was suffocating. There was nothing left to sustain me. So much had changed as far as my career was concerned, and so many of my friends had perished from AIDS: Peter Dallas, Bill Corley, Frank Kolleogy, just to name a few. I heard that even my dear friend Estelle took one last swig, kicked up his heels, and waved good-bye. Well, to all of you at the Pearly Gates Beauty Salon, I thank you, I love you, and I miss you. I am the product of all our doings and we didn't do too bad after all.

Yes, I have yet another ticket on this carousel "La Vida Fabulosa," and this time I'm not jumping off before it stops! That's right, I'm hanging on for the brass ring and a couple of festive gowns on the side.

And speaking of gowns, I am now enrolled in the prestigious, highly respected (and extremely expensive!) Fashion Institute of Design and Merchandising in Los Angeles, where I roam the hallowed halls with a bolt of chiffon in one arm and a pin cushion on the other. Move over, Chanel, here comes Holly of Hollywood! Like my inspirations, Balenciaga, Givenchy, and Delores of Santurce, I too will make a dart in the fashion world.

I lived to tell and I told all (well, all that was fit to print, that is), changing only a handful of names to avoid dragging the innocent ones to the sacrificial slab. Writing this book was exhausting; a cat would have thrown in the towel four lives ago. But not *moi*—Onward and upward, and hi-ho Silver! And as I close, and I must, I want to say that this book never would have happened without the love, support, help, and encouragement of so many friends who took the time to help me recall my sordid yet illustrious past. And boy, are they sorry! After all, for the last twenty years I've been somewhere between a coma and a lobotomy; I could have never remembered it all without their support. Many of the memories were good and there were the ones that were downright horrendous, but a sense of humor eases the pain and makes them fun.

Also, this worthless rag would've never even begun without the efforts, push, drive, belief, love, and kick in the can of both my cohort, Jeffery Copeland, and my agent, Robert Drake. Jeffery, this is about the toughest letter I've had to write since I told my parents I was coming home in 1976. Without you these last two years (you beast!), this pile of rubble would've never been sorted out. You caught me when my ever-precious self-esteem was not letting out much gas and reminded me of who I was—even though you didn't know what I was! Holly Woodlawn, star of stage, screen, and Max's Kansas City! After all our insanity together, including the times you had to be me (on many occasions), I love you and thank you for helping me reach up from the gutter to the front door. The one to my apartment!

And Robert Drake, you sleazy pimp! You spent endless hours peddling this hogwash to anybody who bought your song and dance. I know there were times when you probably hoped this marathon would be over so they could shoot you, but you believed in me and kept dancing. Your legs have never looked lovelier!

To Michael Denneny and Keith Kahla at St. Martin's Press, you suckers bought this fandango. Now, let's all rumba to the bank! And for once, I'd like to meet you for dinner, not a deadline. Thank you both for making this possible.

If there's any moral at all to be found in this tawdry tale of mine, it is to believe in yourself and, most importantly, believe in your dreams. It's crazy to think that once upon a time, a fifteen-year-old boy ran away to New York and lived life as a woman. Some would have deemed it impossible. Others would have damned me to hell. But regardless, I did it and I was fulfilled. Honey, after pulling a stunt like that, there's nothing I can't do! The way I see it, the dreams of today are the realities of tomorrow. And of course, I always dream in Technicolor!

Love you madly,
Holly Woodlawn

P.S. To those of you, and you know who you are, whose names I have left out, forgive me but there was only room for one book.

Jeff Copeland

Jeff Copeland was born in the lush cornfields of O'Fallon, Missouri, to a country-western-singing barber named Denny and a theatrical, feather-clad commotion named Dottie. He has worked on several films and is the recipient of the Houston International Film Festival's Gold Award. He currently lives in Hollywood, California.